# GETTING YOUR HEAD AROUND THE BRAIN

**Amanda Ellison**
Durham University, UK

palgrave
macmillan

First published 2012 by
PALGRAVE MACMILLAN

Palgrave Macmillan in the UK is an imprint of Macmillan Publishers Limited, registered in England, company number 785998, of Houndmills, Basingstoke, Hampshire RG21 6XS.

Palgrave Macmillan in the US is a division of St Martin's Press LLC, 175 Fifth Avenue, New York, NY 10010.

Palgrave Macmillan is the global academic imprint of the above companies and has companies and representatives throughout the world.

Palgrave® and Macmillan® are registered trademarks in the United States, the United Kingdom, Europe and other countries

ISBN: 978–0–230–29855–2

This book is printed on paper suitable for recycling and made from fully managed and sustained forest sources. Logging, pulping and manufacturing processes are expected to conform to the environmental regulations of the country of origin.

A catalogue record for this book is available from the British Library.

A catalog record for this book is available from the Library of Congress.

10  9  8  7  6  5  4  3  2  1
21  20  19  18  17  16  15  14  13  12

Printed in China

Getting your head around the brain

*For my Mum and Dad: Mary & Aidan Ellison*
*Without whom, nothing*

# Contents

# Figures

# Preface

Let your curiosity guide you. Not only is this a great motto for life but also applies quite nicely to this book. If there is something that twists your biscuit, jump right in there. Be mindful however that the background to what happens in the later chapters has often been covered in the earlier ones if you don't fancy reading from the very beginning. But don't let your curiosity end there. At the end of each chapter, you will find pointers for further reading and within chapters you will be able to use the information relating to the different experiments mentioned and the scientists who did them to search for more details on the internet. Curiosity is always hungry; don't forget to feed it.

# Acknowledgements

Fun and all as it is to write a book like this, it's sometimes not so much fun for those around you. That being said, their backing is invaluable and now it is time to say thanks. Thanks to my editors at Palgrave Macmillan for their brilliant assistance at all stages. Thanks to my spouse and igneous rock Rachel for, well, everything and knowing exactly what beverage to put in front of me merely by the look on my face. Thanks to our pup Pip for doing without me on weekend walks. He didn't go by himself; Rachel took him. Pip can't drive, so getting to his favourite hills would clearly be a bit of a problem without her. Thanks to my friends for their encouragement and for allowing me to use them to gauge how interesting things that I find fascinating *actually* are. Thanks to my sister Aideen Ellison for her captivating cartoons dotted throughout this book and to the rest of my family, Irish and English, for their unending support.

The publisher and author would like to thank the organization listed below for permission to reproduce material from their publication:

Worth Publishers for permission to reproduce figures from *An Introduction to Brain and Behavior*, Third Edition by Bryan Kolb and Ian Q. Whishaw © 2011 by Worth Publishers.

# CHAPTER 1 Engage your brain

We all have a brain, and most of us use it to great effect. In fact, it no longer comes as any surprise to people that it is their brain which governs all that we do throughout our lives. Not only does it determine everything that we consciously want and think but it also keeps our insides ticking over through many mechanisms we are not even aware of. There are two main ways to examine our behaviour, one being through psychological enquiry which doesn't even need to acknowledge the workings of the brain, e.g. "if this happens, how do we react?" The other direction of attack is through neuroscience, e.g. "how does the brain generate our behaviours?" Nowadays these fields interchange at will; however, every behaviour will have an underlying basis in the brain. It is the most enigmatic organ of the body as, to look at it, there is no indication about how it works and so for long periods in history, it was not given the praise it deserves for being the most important part of our existence.

In times long past, neuroscience and psychology were preceded by philosophy, which in literal terms translates from its original Greek into "the love of knowledge". This is why the highest qualification in the land is a Ph.D (or Doctor of Philosophy) regardless of the field of study. The ancient Greek philosophers were in disagreement over the role of the 1.5 kg gelatinous bag of mostly water. Hippocrates (460–379 BCE) purported that the brain was the seat of intelligence and that it was involved in sensation. The father of modern medicine's view did not come out of the blue; he was one of the first proponents of reasoning and observation in medical practice. Hippocrates had a more "humoral" (related to the body fluids) theory of health by which he meant the recognized body fluids of the time, i.e. the blood, phlegm, yellow bile and black bile, needed to be kept in balance for good health. Illness was thought to be caused when these fluids were out of balance and treatment of this would include bloodletting or purging of the body fluids. Three millennia previous to this, the ancient Egyptians also used a form of purging for diseases of the head. Called trepanation, it involved boring holes in the skull while the patient was still alive. We know this because in the skulls found in archaeological digs in whom trepanation has been carried out, there is evidence of healing.

This procedure may have been carried out to relieve headaches or mental illness, often attributed at that time to the presence of trapped spirits in the head. A hole would be the obvious way to let them out. On the other hand, the ancient Egyptians didn't rate the brain highly enough to bury it with the body, instead sucking it out through the nostrils prior to burial. They believed the seat of the soul (or the very essence of our existence) was in the heart and this view prevailed until the time of Hippocrates who, as we know, believed in the opposite.

So it would seem that we have all been agreed about the brain's role in our behaviour since around 400 BCE, right? Wrong. Not everybody agreed with Hippocrates, the most influential of which was Aristotle, born around five years before Hippocrates died. Aristotle (384–322 BCE) favoured the heart as being the place where our mind "lives" and like any good philosopher, he had arguments he thought proved it. Among these was the view that the brain was on the periphery, sitting as it does on a stalk on the top of the body, and so its function must be to cool the blood whereas the heart was placed at the centre of bodily function thereby heating up the blood. Aristotle also thought that the heart was essential to life, the brain not so much. Of course, now we know this is completely untrue as you can live for a finite period of time (albeit short) with a stopped heart but once your brain stops, you are legally dead. He also thought that the heart is affected by emotion and the brain is emotionless, unlike the current view that the brain is central to emotional processing and production. Further to this he thought that the heart is connected to the sense organs via the blood vessels but that the brain is not connected to the sense organs. Well, we now know we can't sense anything without our brain and that the sensory connections are neural, not vascular. There is no doubt that Aristotle, student of Plato, teacher of Alexander the Great, was a fine thinker and indeed was the founder of one of the pillars of logic that still stands today, but the scientific grounding of these influential thoughts still left a bit to be desired. Sometimes knowledge is led down the garden path by supposition or personal belief; this was one such time.

Philosophy and early medicine, including investigations of the function of the brain, was a truly international affair. The Roman Empire had Aelius Galenous (130–200 CE), known as Galen, a Greek physician, writer and philosopher, who clearly followed the clinical observation tradition founded by Hippocrates. Galen was employed to treat gladiators after arena battles and as such witnessed some horrific injuries including those to the brain and spine. His impression of the effects of the damage he saw was no doubt influenced by his "hobby" of dissections of sheep, pig and monkey brains (Roman law prohibited dissection of human bodies.). Galen could have produced some "garden path" science of his own as his deductions were reportedly based on poking a freshly dissected brain with his finger; however, he came to the right conclusions, amazingly. The two main visible parts of the brain are the soft cerebrum, and the hard cerebellum, which is at the back of the brain and underneath the cerebrum. Galen deduced that the cerebral cortex is involved in sensation and perception as well as memory whilst the cerebellum is primarily involved in movement control. These views are restricted, but not essentially wrong, but I think they must have been based on Galen's experience with gladiator injury and not just poking brains with his finger. If only he had stopped there, but he went on to establish a different garden path entirely. In his dissected brains, he found hollow areas called ventricles, which to him, fitted the humoral theory of Hippocrates to a T and so he purported that the fluid of the four humours flows from ventricle to ventricle via the nerves which he thought were hollow tubes, initiating movement and registering sensation.

This view was to last for nearly a millennium and a half. René Descartes (1596–1650) in fact was a great proponent of the ventricular view as he tried to explain the brain in terms of machines.

This was around the time that inventors were coming up with ideas for hydraulically controlled machines. If fluid is forced out of the ventricles through the nerves then this could bring about movement as the muscles are "pumped up" so to speak. Think about that next time you are on a fairground ride. However, Descartes was more specific than Galen in that he placed the seat of the mind in the brain and linked the mind to the body. The interaction between the non-material mind and the physical body was still unclear at this time though with Descartes believing that the mind controls the brain through the pineal body, the structure of the brain through which the mind flows (although now we know that pineal damage doesn't lead to a "loss of mind" but a rather more minor disturbance to your biological rhythms like your body not knowing the difference between night and day). And so, the mind–body problem was born leading quite naturally to the field of dualism, the philosophical position that behaviour is controlled by two entities. The test for the presence of a mind was twofold: the presence of language and reasoned action. Unfortunately, this pretty much discounted animals as being in possession of a mind (although Descartes himself by all accounts was devoted to his dog, Monsieur Grat) and also led to the gross mistreatment of patients in mental institutions, as if they were "out of their mind", they could feel no pain etc. Nowadays it is accepted that our mind, or consciousness as it is now called, is brought about by the activity of our brain and is not a separate entity, a movement termed materialism, but its ethereal nature still causes neuroscientists problems in trying to define how it comes about.

Within 200 years, scientists were less concerned by the ventricular humoral view of Hippocrates, Galen and Descartes and had dissected the brain to observe bumps or gyri on the brain's surface as well as sulci or fissures, grey matter and white matter as well as the definition of lobes within which certain functions must lie (now called the frontal, parietal, temporal and occipital lobes). However, there was one more garden path yet to walk and discount. Just at the time scientists were beginning to attribute different functions to different areas of the brain, Franz Joseph Gall (1758–1828) started his pioneering work into the localization of function in the brain. Gall had a stepwise argument that went something like this. The brain is the organ of the mind. The mind is composed of multiple distinct, innate faculties. Because they are distinct, each faculty must have a separate seat or "organ" in the brain. The size of an organ, other things being equal, is a measure of its power. The shape of the brain is determined by the development of the various organs. And now, the pièce de résistance – are you ready? Here it comes, brace yourself. As the skull takes its shape from the brain, the surface of the skull can be read as an accurate index of psychological aptitudes and tendencies. Well, Gall was doing fine purporting the view that is the cornerstone of materialism, that all behaviour can be fully accounted for by brain function, the view that guides contemporary research, even without recourse to philosophy of the mind. But in his last point, Gall was proposing that we could tell what somebody was good at based on the lumps and bumps on their head. Originally called cranioscopy, it was later renamed as phrenology. Due to the lack of scientific proof, phenology was marginalized by the scientific community although it was popular amongst the talking classes with the presence of one of Lavery's Electric Phrenonmeter in the country shows of the early 1900s being

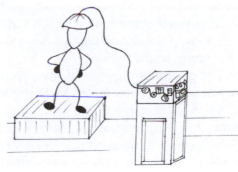

a real draw at least 75 years after the theory was put forward. You had to stand on a box and have a helmet type apparatus "read" your skull features and then it would tell you your strengths and weaknesses. A map was devised, through correlating numerous people's skills with their skullscapes, showing what the different regions were for. Some of these skulls are still on show in the Rolletmuseam in Baden, Austria, Gall's birthplace. According to this, I should be good at the accordion, duelling and imitation, all at the same time I should imagine. Suffice it to say, I am not good at any of these things, even in isolation. My skull is shaped the way it is simply because I was always bumping into things as a kid and it has no bearing on the function of the brain housed inside. Thankfully, in my case.

It was around this time of the late 1800s that Camillo Golgi (1843–1926) and Santiago Ramon y Cajal (1852–1934) used similar staining techniques to discover what the brain was made of. Neurons are translucent under the microscope and so the application of a stain shows up the different components of neurons and shows their structure. Golgi used a silver stain to show that it was composed of a large network of interconnected "tubes" but Cajal showed that in addition to this, nerve cells were in fact discrete entities and also that they became more complex in their structure with age. Golgi and Cajal were awarded a joint Nobel Prize for Medicine in 1906. But the two had fallen out over their differing views, Golgi believing that the nerve cells that he could see through the microscope acted like the blood vessels of the body whereas Cajal correctly saw them as separate entities with their own functions and not just "transit stations" in a network. The argument even bubbled over into their acceptance speeches for the Nobel Prize with one attacking the other's views in their respective speeches. Well, it wasn't the Peace Prize they won…. In truth however, there would be no Cajal without Golgi's methods and Cajal knew and acknowledged this saying that Golgi's theories of the nervous system were based on his education and the prevailing views at the time whereas Cajal looked beyond this to see what was possible and not just what should be based on what was thought to be the present case.

The grouping together of these nerve cells or neurons as they are now known was shown by Korbinian Brodmann (1868–1918) in 1908 to be a clue to the localization of different functions. In fact, this classification of regions still survives use to this day. Simultaneous to these cellular discoveries, physicians and scientists were documenting patients with different forms of brain damage more rigorously. In this field called neuropsychology, inferences could be made about the function of the damaged regions based on what function was lost. If a patient was impaired in some way, say he couldn't see, and he had damage to the back of his brain, then a neuropsychologist puts two and two together to determine that information from the eyes must be processed at the back of the brain. In 1861, Pierre Paul Broca (1824–1880) had a patient called Tan, so called because the only thing he could say was "TAN". When Tan died, a post-mortem revealed that syphilis had damaged a specific part of his frontal lobe, forever to be attributed to speech production and indeed named Broca's area. Later, Karl

Kleist (1879–1960) compiled a comprehensive functional mapping of the cerebral cortex from the case notes of some 1600 head-wound casualties from the First World War which advanced our knowledge about the brain regions involved in certain functions. However, the problem with neuropsychology is twofold; you usually had to wait for a patient to die before you could attribute their behavioural change to a particular brain region and the brain regions damaged were often very large so it was hard to define small regions as having particular functions.

Although neuropsychology is still a valuable tool in our quest to understand the brain, we now have other methods at our disposal to understand how the normal, healthy human brain works. We can eavesdrop on brain waves using electroencephalography (EEG). Since Luigi Galvini (1737–1798) and his experiments on frog muscles, we have known that electricity is very important to muscle contraction whether or not the muscle is attached to a living body. In fact, this point got Galvini's nephew, Giovanni Aldini, into trouble. He travelled all over Europe reanimating dead bodies with electricity and is reported to have inspired Mary Shelley to write Frankenstein two decades later. The most famous of his "performances" involved a rectal probe and the attempt to bring the recently hanged body of murderer (although the evidence was allegedly thin) George Forster back to life shocking the Royal College of Surgeons in London in 1802 with the spasmodic movements like kicking out and punching the air that the dead body produced. The London Times was worried and wrote, "It appeared to the uniformed part of the bystanders as if the wretched man was on the eve of being restored to life". Unsurprisingly, such public displays were soon after outlawed. Undeterred, Aldini continued his experiments with live animals and found that he could excite the brains of oxen and went further to report electrical cures for a number of mental illnesses, his methods being a direct precursor to electroconvulsive therapy used as a last resort in mental illnesses which do not respond to other treatments today.

His work was also the forbearer of cardiac shock treatment. Of course, we now know that the nervous system including the brain and all the peripheral nerves and the transfer of signals between neurons and between neurons and muscles for example, works by the transference of an electrical signal via chemicals (more of that later). The electrical activity in a particular part of the brain tells us that that bit is active and even better, we can listen out to see how different bits talk to each other. This is very useful when investigating epilepsy – when the neural activity is very erratic, but it is also very handy when exploring what happens in our brain when we are asleep or doing tasks requiring attention for example. It is one of the gooier techniques as it involves placing a cap, with varying numbers of listening posts, or electrodes, generally from 64 to 128 embedded into it, on the head and injecting electrode gel into each electrode so that there is good contact between the electrode and the scalp through which the brain waves can pass so that the computer software can represent them as squiggles on a screen. Therefore, one of the most important components in an EEG lab is a nice big sink in which to wash your participants' hair!

Imaging techniques, on the other hand, are not messy at all and let us see structural components within the head. These range from X-ray through to its more advanced counterpart CT (computerized tomography) scanning which differs from X-ray in that it produces cross-sectional pictures of the brain without having to put the patient into awkward positions. The scanning technique most commonly used in neuroscience today however is MRI or magnetic resonance imaging, which uses a strong magnetic field to align all the water molecules in your brain in one direction and then applies a radio wave to see how the water molecules respond. The response is different across areas and depends on damage etc. and it produces very detailed (and beautiful) pictures of the brain by taking images at 1mm intervals called slices. The computer software then reconstitutes these into the entire brain so that we can look at structures from any angle. We can also track the blood flow in the brain using functional MRI (fMRI) which is particularly useful when trying to work out what part of the brain is involved if the person lying in

the scanner is doing a visual task, or thinking about the Queen, as blood will flow to the area involved. The software translates this blood flow into areas of activity with different colours denoting how much the area is involved in the processing of the task. These are then located on the picture of that person's brain, my so-called splodges of activation (see Figure 1.1).

However, one disadvantage of fMRI is that areas not really necessary for the processing of the task can "light-up"; also you can only correlate activations with behaviour; you don't know that that area caused the behaviour. So, we need a way of examining the absolute involvement of a brain region in the production of a function in the non-damaged brain.

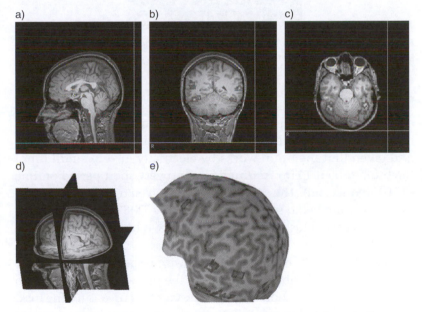

**Figure 1.1** fMRI activations in my brain when I am looking at faces. In the upper pictures (sagittal, coronal and transverse views respectively) the scans are flipped so that the right of my brain is on the left and the left is on the right according to radiological convention. This is my excuse for not knowing my left from my right. The bottom pictures represent a multiplanar reconstruction and a curvilinear representation. Images acquired using BrainSight™ software (Rough Research, Canada).

Neurostimulation, the most common of which is Transcranial Magnetic Stimulation (TMS for short), allows us a window on this issue. A brief magnetic pulse is sent through the skull (see Figure 1.2), and via Michael Faraday's groundbreaking principles of

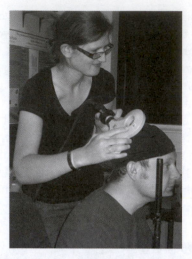

**Figure 1.2** My colleague Dr Alison Lane applying magnetic pulses to Dave Knight. We get our subjects to wear a swimming cap as it means we can mark the place we want to send our magnetic pulse into easily. We used to mark the scalp but this saves us fishing about in people's hair.

electromagnetic induction (a magnetic field outside a tissue can induce an electrical field inside the tissue) first put forth in 1831, and given that the brain works by electricity, a very small bit of the brain (about 1 cm) is turned on for a very short period of time (0.001 of a second). The subject is usually given a task to do, and if the bit of brain being safely switched on by TMS is involved in the processing of that task, then subjects will be a little bit slower doing the task.

This is because if the brain is active with respect to the magnetic pulse, it will not be able to respond to the processing of the task so this gives us an indication of how necessary that area is for the task. TMS has been used to ask questions about normal human brains that were previously asked using neuropsychological patients or animal experimentation. It has big advantages over these methods however in that in patients for example, the lesion tends to be large and so localizing a function to a particular area is difficult, and the effects of TMS are completely reversed within seconds.

The techniques mentioned so far have not just been used to discover what individual neurons look like, and how they are grouped but also how they work together to bring about functions such as reading, writing, talking, seeing and all of the other things you will find out about in later pages. The structure of the brain has been examined such that we have names for all the different parts. Sometimes these names relate to what the area does so we'll talk about that later but most of the time our names are based on where the area is in the brain. So, here's a brief overview of all the different parts you will come across later when we are talking about how the brain does what it does. The cerebrum (Latin for "brain") comprises the outer layer, which is called the cerebral cortex, and also the sub-cortical (under the cortex) structures. The cerebral cortex has a right hemisphere and a left hemisphere and the subcortical structures are also paired including the basal ganglia (ganglion means a biological tissue mass, in this case a bunch of neurons) which are important in the control of movement amongst other things, and the hippocampus (Latin for "sea horse" which is what the structure looks like) and entorhinal cortex and fornix (Latin for "arch", which is what it looks like), the cingulate cortex and amygdala (Greek for "almond", which is what each amygdala resembles) which are all important in memory formation and emotion.

The two hemispheres of the cerebrum are connected by a tract of nerve fibres that allow the two sides of the brain to communicate with each other and is called the corpus callosum. Each hemisphere can also be divided up into lobes, so called because of the bones of the skull they lie underneath; frontal, important in movement, thinking and planning; parietal (parietal bone relates to the Latin for wall), important in touch, balance and spatial awareness; temporal (the temporal bone supports the part of the face known as the temple), important in hearing, speech comprehension, memory and visual recognition; and the occipital (occipital bone relates to the Latin for back of the head), which is devoted to visual processing. The frontal lobe is separated from the parietal by the central sulcus and the bottom of the parietal lobe is separated from the top of the temporal lobe by the lateral fissure and the two hemispheres are separated by the longitudinal fissure (see Figure 1.3).

The sub cortical structures fall under this lobe system too; for example, the hippocampus is in the medial (or middle of) temporal lobe. Underneath the cerebrum we have the brainstem made up of the cerebellum (Latin for little brain because that's what it

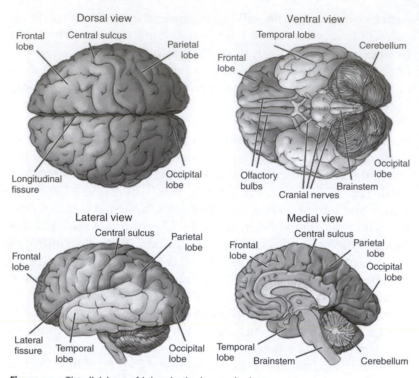

**Figure 1.3** The divisions of lobes in the human brain.

*Source:* From *An Introduction to Brain and Behavior*, 3rd edn, by Bryan Kolb and Ian Q. Whishaw © 2011 by Worth Publishers. Used with permission.

looks like, the hard part Galen liked to poke at) at the back of the brain, a region very important in the timing and accuracy of movements; the midbrain and diencephalon (Latin for inter-brain), which includes the thalamus, hypothalamus and pituitary. This is my favourite part of the brain. It controls all of the mechanisms that keep us ticking over without our knowledge (known as homeostatic or control mechanisms) that are mind blowing in their sheer vastness of effect and the simplicity of their control. Various clumps of cells in the midbrain and diencephalon control the brain's general level of alertness and regulate processes such as breathing, heartbeat and blood pressure. Utterly marvellous system. I'll convince you later. The brainstem evolved more than 500 million years ago and is rather like the entire brain of a present day reptile. As you move down from the midbrain through the brainstem to exit the cranium or skull you pass through the pons (bridge) and medulla, and beyond the cranium this tract of nerve fibres becomes the spinal cord. The cerebrum is what gives us voluntary behaviour and thinking skills, better visual and movement abilities whilst the brainstem takes care of the unconscious part of our existence.

There are also a few ways to think about the nervous system as a whole (see Figure 1.4). The central nervous system (CNS) refers to the brain and spinal cord whilst the peripheral nervous system (PNS) consists of all of the nerves outside of the brain and spinal cord. Within the PNS we have the somatic nervous system, all the nerves involved in voluntary control of our skeletons, as well as the autonomic nervous system (ANS), which helps to carry out all of our homeostatic mechanisms by sending neurons to the heart, kidneys and all the other visceral organs. The ANS has two aspects, the sympathetic nervous system, which is the excitatory one, and the parasympathethic system, which calms us down. It is the ANS that is involved in the "fight or flight response" you will no doubt have heard of.

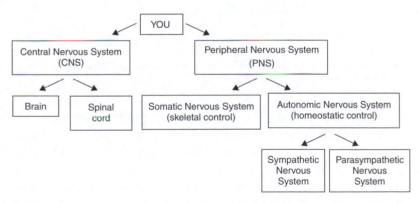

**Figure 1.4** How your nervous system is split up according to whether your neurons live in the central (CNS) or peripheral nervous system (PNS). The PNS has responsibility for all of your internal processes that you are not aware of.

As neuroscientists, we have many technical terms to make us sound very clever indeed but really, there's no need to be freaked out. We could use simpler terms like forward, back, to the side, but instead we like to use anterior, posterior and lateral (see Figure 1.5). Medial means to the middle, inferior means below

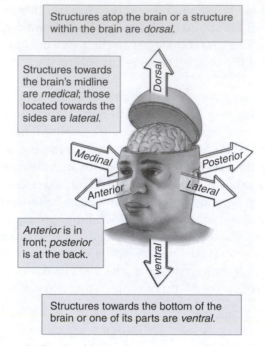

Structures atop the brain or a structure within the brain are *dorsal*.

Structures towards the brain's midline are *medical*; those located towards the sides are *lateral*.

*Anterior* is in front; *posterior* is at the back.

Structures towards the bottom of the brain or one of its parts are *ventral*.

**Figure 1.5** The main directional jargon that we use to talk about places in the brain. In addition to which lobe you are in, you can signpost to any part of the brain using these words.

*Source:* From *An Introduction to Brain and Behavior*, 3rd edn by Bryan Kolb and Ian Q. Whishaw © 2011 by Worth Publishers. Used with permission.

and superior means above. Dorsal means towards the top of the brain, ventral means towards the bottom. Rostral, rhymes with nostril, and means to the front, where your nostrils live funnily enough. Caudal comes from the Latin "Caudum" meaning tail and indeed means towards the tail. In animal, caudal can be interchanged with posterior but in non-tailed humans it is more accurately interchanged with inferior. Pre- means before, and so the prefrontal cortex is the part of the frontal cortex that lies before the frontal pole, the bit at the very front of the brain which is called the orbitofrontal cortex as it is near the eye socket (orbit) region.

And so if I ask you where the dorsolateral prefrontal cortex is, you will be able to confidently tell me that this is a region that lies towards the top and to the side of the prefrontal cerebral cortex.

You can really work out where any region is using these short cuts. Easy right? Ok, maybe not. But once you start finding out what these different regions do, it gets much easier. But first of all, we must find out what the brain is made of and how these bits make it work.

## Feeling curious?

*Brain, Vision, Memory: Tales in the History of Neuroscience* by Charles C. Gross. 2009; MIT Press and *A Hole in the Head: More Tales in the History of Neuroscience* by Charles G. Gross. 2012; MIT Press. *Entertaining stories from the history of neuroscience. A great way in to the topic.*

*Philosophical Foundations of Neuroscience* by M. R. Bennett, P. M. S. Hacker. 2003; Wiley-Blackwell. *A provoking read that challenges assumptions.*

*Milestones in Neuroscience Research* compiled by Eric Chudler, a director of education and outreach at the University of Washington. http://faculty.washington.edu/chudler/hist.html *A handy timeline of important events in the history of neuroscience.*

Kenneth S. Kosik (2003) Opinion: "Beyond Phrenology, at Last". *Nature Reviews Neuroscience* 4, 234–239 (March) | doi:10.1038/nrn1053. *An account of the history of the integrated nature of neuroscience research.*

Vincent Walsh and Alan Cowey "Transcranial Magnetic Stimulation and Cognitive Neuroscience" *Nature Reviews Neuroscience* 1, 73–80, doi:10.1038/35036239 *A great introduction to the technique even if we all now agree that the term virtual lesion is very misleading! If you liked this, Vincent Walsh (with Alvaro Pascual-Leone) also wrote a book on the subject called Transcranial Magnetic Stimulation: A Neurochronometrics of mind published by MIT press in 2005.*

*Neuroanatomy: An Illustrated Colour Text* by Alan R. Crossman & David Neary. 2010; Churchill Livingstone. *A good guide to the anatomy of the brain.*

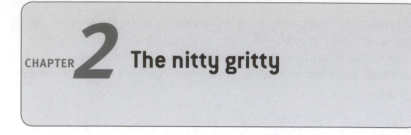

CHAPTER 2 **The nitty gritty**

Even though different parts of the brain have different specializations, it has become increasingly clear that in order for us accomplish all of our everyday tasks, lots of these regions have to talk to each other. The currency of this "talk" is electricity. Since the advent of the electron microscope in the 1930s, it has been easy to see that there is a distinct gap, called a synapse, between the neurons. The electrical pulses don't jump over the gaps like you do on stepping stones. Instead, the electrical signal causes chemicals to be released into the gap that then set up the electrical signal again in the next neuron. Electrical impulses are therefore chemically passed between neurons, activating regions involved in things like walking, thinking, hearing, seeing, etc. and bringing about and mediating these functions.

First of all, let's visualize a neuron. Neurons involved in sensation, those that bring information to the brain, look a bit different from those involved in movement, or those going from the brain to the body, with the main difference being that the cell body (where all the organs that keep the cell alive are) is located along the length (or axon) of a sensory neuron whilst the cell body of a motor neuron is at the beginning of the axon. It is the presence of many cell bodies that makes grey matter, and an area containing many axons makes white matter in the brain. There are also interneurons in the brain that associate sensory and motor activity that take three forms: stellate cells found mainly in the thalamus, pyramidal cells that are found in the cortex and purkinje cells found in the cerebellum. All neurons have common structures; they all have a cell body and axon but they also have dendrites which collect information from other neurons and the axon splits up into axon terminals called terminal buttons (or the posher "bouton") to link with other neurons.

Inside the neuronal cell body are the organelles responsible for keeping the cell alive, and these are no different from the organelles found in other cells of the body. There is the nucleus, or the brain of the cell, which contains the DNA, and there is the mitochondria, which is the engine of the cell using glucose to give the cell energy. There is also the endoplasmic reticulum, which makes proteins, and the Golgi bodies, which package up the proteins so that they can be transported to their correct destination. The Golgi bodies are so called because they were discovered by Camillo Golgi in 1897, not because they look like his body. Golgi bodies are not the most attractive organelles so this would not be a complement for old Camillo. There is also the requisite lysosome present which can cause the cell to self destruct if something goes horribly wrong.

So how does a neuron become active? What are these nuts and bolts involved in causing the electrical activity in neurons? Well the beauty of this system lies in its simplicity, honestly! The main characters in our story are called ions. A technical definition of what an ion is this: "an atom or molecule whose total number of electrons is not equal to the number of protons, giving the ion a net positive or negative charge". Lost? Well, look at it with respect to salt. Salt is made up of sodium ($Na^+$) and chloride ($Cl^-$). As we all know, opposites attract and this is why sodium (positive) ions bond so happily with chloride (negative) ions to

make salt. It turns out that these two characters ($Na^+$ and $Cl^-$) are very important in our story along with potassium ($K^+$), which is also a positive ion.

Two other aspects which play a role in our story relate to how ions move. They are both based on the idea of diffusion. When you pour cordial into a glass of water, you might have to wait a while but even without stirring it, the colour will eventually distribute itself equally to all parts of the glass. This means that every ml of the water will have an equal concentration of cordial in it. This is a key point to how ions move – they will always try to distribute themselves equally and will move from an area of high concentration to an area of low concentration to achieve this; this is called the concentration gradient. The second player works just like this but relates to electrical gradient; ions will always try to distribute the electrical charge so that there is balance between positive and negative ions so that the charge is neutral. Positive ions will move to an area dominated by negative ions and vice versa.

So let us now set the stage. The neuron is encased by a phospholipid membrane which has a fatty layer on the inside and the outside (see Figure 2.1). This does a great job of keeping all of the fluids inside the cell and stops fluids from the outside from getting in as this would result in burst cells all over the place. The membrane also tightly controls how ions pass through via ion channels embedded in the membrane, which can be open or shut according to the conditions. In every neuron, there are large proteins inside the cell that can't move; these have a negative charge and are collectively called large anions (or negatively charged particles A-). These make the inside of the cell more electrically negative with respect to the outside of the cell. At rest, the only ion that is allowed to move freely across open ion channels is potassium ($K^+$). Lots of potassium moves into the cell to try to neutralize the big negative charge inside the cell. But this means that there is more $K^+$ inside the cell than outside and so $K^+$ will move out of the cell, down its concentration gradient. $K^+$ can't have it all however, and will never neutralize the A- as well as achieve a concentration balance between the inside and the outside. But it reaches a compromise where the electrical force

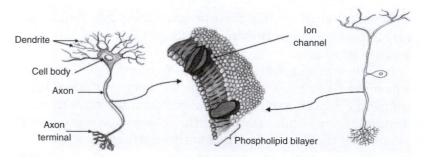

Dendrite

Cell body

Axon

Axon
terminal

Ion
channel

Phospholipid bilayer

**Figure 2.1** The neuron (both motor neuron, left and sensory neuron, right) The phospolipid bi-layer (centre) has proteins embedded in it which act as gates for different ions to pass through.

drawing $K^+$ into the cell to neutralize the $A^-$ is equal and opposite to the concentration force pulling $K^+$ out of the cell to where it is less concentrated. At this stage we have an equilibrium and with all of the ions considered, we have a resting membrane potential voltage of –65 to –70 mv (The mv or millivolt is a measure of electrical potential named after Alessandro Volta, whose pioneering work in the early 1800s led to the development of the first chemical battery capable of producing a steady current. His work was actually based on Galvini's ideas about electricity in frogs' legs but Volta, in contrast to Galvini, thought that electricity could exist outside of biology, as he went on to prove). This means that the inside of the cell is more negative with respect to the outside of the cell. We now know that it is this very imbalance that allows the flow of these ions to create a current (a change in the electrical potential) which underlies a nerve impulse called an action potential.

We can study the electrical activity of a single neuron by sticking a listening electrode into it to detect what the charge is inside the cell relative to the outside. This is easiest with big neurons with large axons such as can be found in the giant squid; you can actually see their neurons with the naked eye. It is also possible to suck up a bit of the axon into an electrode so that we can control what ions and other chemicals the ion channels are exposed to (this is imaginatively called the "patch clamp" technique). When a neuron is stimulated by injecting some positive ions into the cell, the inside of the cell gets a bit more positive with respect to the outside of the cell. If the potential reaches –50 mv (remember, the resting membrane potential was –65 mv, so we have made it less negative and more positive) the cell reaches a threshold at which sodium channels responsive to this voltage (voltage gated $Na^+$ channels) open. There is much more sodium outside the cell than inside as it is not normally allowed to move freely and so $Na^+$ will rush into the cell down its concentration gradient. There is also the added impetus to rush in to neutralize the negative inside of the cell with sodium's positive ions. As a result of all of these positive ions rushing in, the inside of the cell becomes much more positive with respect to the outside of the cell, to the tune of +40 mv. The cell is now depolarized. At this point, $K^+$ channels that only respond at this voltage (voltage gated) open and potassium rushes out of the cell down its concentration gradient and down the electrical gradient to repolarize the cell. Because positive ions are leaving the cell, the inside becomes more negative with respect to the outside again back to a level even more negative than before, and is now hyperpolarized. So, all voltage gates shut and the sodium–potassium pump (an enzyme sitting in the membrane) swings into action to make sure that there is more sodium on the outside and more potassium on the inside of the cell. It kicks three Na⁺ ions out for every two K⁺ it allows in, thus redressing the balance (see Figure 2.2).

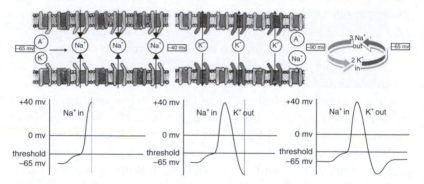

**Figure 2.2** Ion movement during the action potential and the resulting potential diagram. The influx of positive sodium (Na⁺) causes the inside of the cell to become less negative and more positive with respect to the outside of the cell. The efflux of positive potassium (K⁺) makes the inside of the cell more negative with respect to the outside again. The sodium–potassium pump restores the resting membrane potential to –65 mv again.

So how is this electrical impulse or action potential passed on to the next neuron? The action potential travels on down the length of the neuron (the axon) by two possible methods. One is via a domino effect, where an action potential in one bit of neuron depolarizes the next bit of neuron by opening the next bit's volt-age-gated sodium channels and so on down the neuron. Neurons that need fast action however are covered in a fatty myelin sheath, which is made up of glial cells. There are five types of glial cells all involved somehow in the nourishment of neurons but two types serve this myelinating purpose depending on where the neuron is. In the brain and spinal cord it is oligodendroglia that wrap them-selves around axons whereas in the peripheral nervous system,

Schwann cells do the same thing, wrapping themselves around the axon many times to create the myelin sheath. There are gaps in the myelin sheath in between the glial cells called nodes of Ranvier. The action potential jumps between nodes and this is called saltatory conduction (see Figure 2.3). This is a much faster way of getting the action potential from one end of the neuron to the other as action potentials have to happen only at the nodes as opposed to all along the neuron. It's almost like Schwann cells and oligodendroglia provide insulation to the neuron like you see on electrical wires. If you didn't have this insulation (as happens in multiple sclerosis for example) nerve conduction would be very slow and may even break down completely.

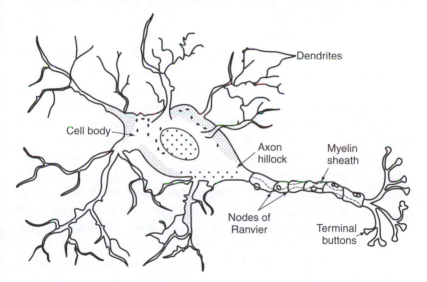

**Figure 2.3** The myelin sheath allows action potentials to "hop" down the neuron between the glial cells that make up the sheath.

Neurons are not connected to each other; there is a miniscule gap called a synaptic cleft between them which was discovered only after the onset of electron microscopy in the 1930s. So the electrical signal from the pre-synaptic neuron has to be turned into a chemical signal to cross the synaptic cleft to then set up an electrical stimulus in the post-synaptic neuron (see Figure 2.4).

When the action potential reaches the end of the neuron at the pre-synaptic terminal, the depolarization opens up the

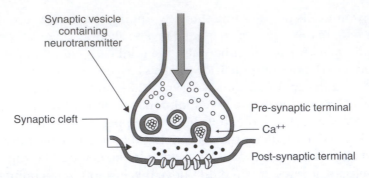

**Figure 2.4** The Synapse. The arriving action potential at the pre-synaptic terminal results in an influx of calcium which causes the synaptic vesicles to fuse with the terminal membrane and dump their contents into the synaptic gap. The neurotransmitter then binds with post-synaptic binding sites which open ion channels specific to excitatory ($Na^+$) or inhibitory ($Cl^-$) ions.

voltage-gated calcium channels ($Ca^{++}$). The calcium comes into the cell and binds with vesicles, little sacs filled with chemicals called neurotransmitters, causing them to move to the pre-synaptic membrane and release their contents into the synaptic cleft. These neurotransmitter molecules float across the cleft and bind with receptors sitting on ion channels on the post-synaptic membrane to give them the signal to open. Because the neurotransmitters are the key to the ion channel's lock, these are called ligand- (or substance-) gated ion channels. Different neurotransmitters bind with different ion channels that will allow only a certain ion through and this determines whether neurotransmitters will have an excitatory effect on the next neuron or an inhibitory effect. These are called ionotropic channels. If the ion channel lets in a positive ion, like $Na^+$, then it will have an excitatory effect, called an excitatory post-synaptic potential (EPSP). If the ion channel lets in a negative ion, like $Cl^-$, then it will have an inhibitory effect, called an inhibitory post-synaptic potential (IPSP). Another form of neurotransmitter receptor is called a metabotropic receptor; it isn't as simple as the ionotropic one as it involves a few steps before the ions are let in, but their activation results in longer-term effects and is useful in functions such as smell. An area of the cell body (the business end of the neuron where the nucleus lives) at the beginning of the axon called the axon hillock adds up all the EPSPs and IPSPs (which are graded potentials) to decide whether there is enough net positive charge to reach the threshold of −50 mv in order to send an action potential down the axon and the whole process starts again. If the IPSPs outweigh the EPSPs then no action potential is sent and the activity of the neuron is inhibited.

Action potentials are "all or nothing events" in that, while one is happening, another can't happen in the same bit of neuron. They can't be added together to get a stronger signal. The way we know whether the signal is stronger is by the rate at which a neuron fires, i.e. generates action potentials. It takes less than one millisecond (1/1000 of a second) for an action potential beginning to end. Neurons are generally active at a tonic firing rate when the system is resting, meaning they fire every now and again anyway. So a higher firing rate means the neuron has been stimulated and a lower firing rate means it has been inhibited. Once it has done its job, the neurotransmitter has to be removed from the synaptic cleft as if it were left there; it would keep trying to open ion channels on the post-synaptic membrane. So, most of the neurotransmitter is taken back up into the pre-synaptic cell and packaged up into synaptic vesicles to be recycled the next time an action potential comes along.

Given that there are so many steps in getting one neuron to talk to another or for a signal to be sent to a muscle, we can see that there are many things that could go wrong. In fact, many poisonous animals rely on being able to interfere with this system to capture their prey. Scorpions interfere with Na$^+$ channels allowing sodium to move more freely. Because the strict differential of "sodium outside, potassium inside" is lost, the neuron becomes confused and action potentials are less likely to happen. Puffer fish tetrodoxin blocks the voltage-gated Na$^+$ channels, meaning action potentials can't happen. So if you have fugu sashimi, you have to trust your chef has not left any tetrodoxin in your meal, or you will leave the restaurant paralysed. α-latrotoxin is the black widow spider's weapon of choice. It causes a massive release of neurotransmitter at the nerve – muscular junction resulting in paralysis.

The tetanus toxin on the other hand works by preventing inhibitory neurotransmitters to be released in the spinal cord. This causes hyperactivity of the muscles and so, paralysis (are you sensing a theme yet?). α-Bungarotoxin, which is found in the venom of the branded krait snake, blocks neurotransmitter receptors on the nerve–muscle junction effectively paralyzing the prey so that they can't run away. These venoms and poisons all act with the ultimate aim of stopping movement, but can eventually lead to the death of the prey as they act on the nerve–muscle junction of the heart and lungs also.

Bacteria that make us sick can also affect the electrochemical balance by which our nervous system functions. Botulism, from the clostridium bacteria, works by stopping the release of excitatory neurotransmitters at the nerve–muscle junction and is a major culprit in causing the symptoms of food poisoning. It prevents the contraction of the affected muscles and so the muscles relax. In our digestive system this can have disastrous effects. However, purified botox (as it is fashionably called) can be injected locally and is mainly used as a cosmetic procedure to relax muscles in the face. This has the fortuitous effect of smoothing out wrinkles as they can form only via contraction of the facial muscles but it can reduce your control over your facial features leading to that "rabbit caught in headlights" look if the dosage is not quite right. Botox has also been used to good effect when the musculature of organs in the body such as the bladder contract uncontrollably (as happens in incontinence).

However, many everyday medicines act at this level also to improve our health. These include many cardiac drugs and also anti-depressants such as Prozac, which blocks the re-uptake of one of the neurotransmitters involved in emotion called serotonin (serotonin selective re-uptake inhibitors or SSRIs), which gives rise to a feeling of well being. Other drugs such as cocaine act to block the re-uptake of another neurotransmitter involved in feeling reward, called dopamine. In fact most drugs (e.g. heroin, nicotine etc.) act on this pathway but as the user gets used to the drug, they need more and more to get the same sense of reward and so become addicted (another factor of which is the difficultly to withdraw from the drug as it has widespread effects on the body). People with Parkinson's disease have a lack of neurons which use dopamine as their neurotransmitter in the basal ganglia, and so this chemical is important in movement also.

Another neurotransmitter that is important to our story is acetylcholine (ACh), which is the only neurotransmitter used at the nerve–muscle junction but is also important in alertness in the brain as it is excitatory. ACh also has a role in memory with a decrease in ACh in the cortex linked to Alzheimer's disease. Noradrenalin and adrenalin are important excitatory neurotransmitters in arousal too. Glutamate, the most abundant excitatory transmitter in the brain, is important in learning and memory amongst other things. GABA (or gamma aminobutyric acid) is the main inhibitory transmitter in the brain and were it not for the control that GABA gives the brain, neurons all over the place would be firing like mad. Transmitter gases like nitric oxide are not stored and released as regular neurotransmitters are. Rather they are synthesized as needed and act to dilate blood vessels in the brain and also activate metabolic processes in the brain leading to the synthesis of other neurotransmitters.

The action potential and synaptic transmission of action potentials is the cornerstone of neural activity in the entire body, be they sensory systems or movement related or other aspects of behaviour such as eating, or sleeping. Each of these aspects has their own story to tell but ultimately, it is the brain that writes the script.

## Feeling curious?

*An Introduction to Molecular Neurobiology* by Zach W. Hall. 2003; Sinauer. *This is a great book which will guide you into the depths of neural transmission.*

*Patch Clamping: An Introductory Guide to Patch Clamp Electrophysiology* by Areles Molleman. 2003; Wiley-Blackwell. *An introduction to this important technique in electrophysiology.*

Edmund D. Brodie III (2009) "Toxins and Venoms". *Current Biology* Vol 19 No 20 R934. *A thorough examination of the difference between toxins and venoms and their action.*

*The Deadly Dinner Party: And Other Medical Detective Stories* by Jonathan A Edlow. 2009; Yale University Press. *Entertaining account of loads of nasties that can hurt us. You'll never eat again.*

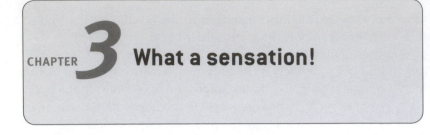

CHAPTER **3** **What a sensation!**

Let me ask you a question. If a tree falls over in a forest, does it make a sound? The obvious answer is, "of course it does". But the philosophical answer is, "no, stupid, it doesn't". Not intuitive admittedly, but true nonetheless. When a tree falls over, air molecules are moved about but this is categorized as a sound only if there is an ear there to sense it. So, if a sensory receptor is not around to experience a stimulus, it cannot be categorized as a sensory experience like light for vision or sound for hearing for example. You might need to think about this and make your brain hurt a bit before you believe me. I can live with that.

The five senses, vision, audition (hearing), somatosensation (pain and touch), taste and olfaction (smell) all have sensory organs and similar pathways to the brain where the sensory experience is interpreted. Thus, what most people lump together as "sensation" is actually a two-step process. There is the translation of a sensory stimulus into an electrical signal (action potentials) via a sensory organ of which we have – the eyes, ears, skin (and other tissues), tongue and nose – but there is also the brain's processing of these signals which is called perception. As individuals, our perception of the same sensory stimulus can vary widely from somebody else's. Take touch for example. A grasp of one person's arm may be felt as merely a firm touch to them but another person may scream in pain. So, touch and consequently pain thresholds vary across humans as do our visual, auditory, somatosensory, taste and olfactory thresholds. Scientists who investigate this absolute performance are called psychophysicists. Again, sensation is the registration of a physical stimulus from the environment by the sensory organs whereas perception is the interpretation of the sensations by the brain. Our version of reality is, in effect, our perception of the sensory world, but without the activity of either the sensory organ or the brain, our senses are useless. We will be discussing vision and hearing in later chapters, but for now let us first discuss somatosensation and then the chemical senses of taste and smell.

Somatosensation comprises three sensory systems in the body: hapsis or touch, noiciception, which is pain and temperature, and proprioception, which is body awareness. The main sensory organ for hapsis and nociception is the skin with the muscles containing the sensory organs for proprioception (see Figure 3.1). There are five types of sensory receptors contained in the skin that respond to haptic or fine touch and pressure stimuli. These are the Meissner's corpuscle for touch, the Pacinian corpuscle for fluttering sensations, the Ruffini corpuscle for vibration, Merkel's receptor for steady skin indentation and the hair receptors, which are also for steady skin vibrations as well as fluttering sensations. Pressure on any of these receptors causes mechanical opening of ion channels and generation of action potentials in the dendrites of the sensory neurons that are attached to them.

These receptors can be either fast adapting or slow adapting. Fast adaptation is important for the detection of on/off signals

| Nocioception (pain and temperature) | Adaptation | Damage to the dendrite or to surrounding cells releases chemicals that stimulate the dendrite to produce action potentials. |
|---|---|---|
| Free nerve endings for pain (sharp pain and dull pain) | Slow | |
| Free nerve endings for temperature (heat or coldness) | Slow | |

| Hapsis (fine touch and pressure) | Adaptation | Pressure on the various types of tissue capsules mechanically stimulates the dendrites within them to produce action potentials. |
|---|---|---|
| Meissner's corpuscle (touch) | Rapid | |
| Pacinian corpuscle (flutter) | Rapid | |
| Ruffini corpuscle (vibration) | Rapid | |
| Merkel's receptor (steady skin indentation) | Slow | |
| Hair receptors (flutter or steady skin indentation) | Slow | |

| Proprioception (body awareness) | Adaptation | Movements stretch the receptors to mechanically stimulate the dendrites within them to produce action potentials. |
|---|---|---|
| Muscle spindles (muscle stretch) | Rapid | |
| Golgi tendon organs (tendon stretch) | Rapid | |
| Joint receptors (joint movement) | Rapid | |

**Figure 3.1** A cross-section of a piece of skin and the sensory receptors it contains in addition to the sensory receptors contained in the muscles. From *An Introduction to Brain and Behavior*, Third Edition by Bryan Kolb and Ian Q. Whishaw © 2011 by Worth Publishers. Used with permission.

and doesn't give you much information during the stimulus particularly if it is there for a long time. A really good example of this is when you wear glasses or shades. When you pop them on, you feel their presence on your nose and over your ears, but after that, you don't really notice them. How many times have you walked in to find your granny looking for her specs when they were on her face all along? The Meissner, Pacinian and Ruffini corpuscles are all fast adapting. In contrast, the hair cells and the Merkel receptor are slow adapting and so it takes longer for these receptors to become immune to the stimulus, although given the glasses example, it does happen. Because they are slow adapting, they also take some time to catch up to the fact that the stimulus has been removed and so you may actually feel the indentation when the stimulus is gone. Try this: press the cap of your pen into your arm, not so that the stimulus is painful, just so that you can feel it. The Meissner, Pacinian and Ruffini corpuscles feel the onset of the cap but rapidly adapt; they don't constantly produce action potentials. The hair cells and Merkel receptors continue to produce action potentials and this is how you know the stimulus is still there. Indeed, when you remove the cap after 20 seconds or so, it takes a second or two for the sensation of the cap to go away as these receptors are slow adapting, but the other fast-adapting corpuscles have already told you the cap has been lifted. This works even without visual input, so get one of your mates to press the pen into your arm while your eyes are closed. My advice? Pick a gentle one, friend that is…when did you know the pen was lifted and when did the sensation go away?

Proprioception or body awareness is brought about by three fast-adapting receptors in the muscles. These consist of the muscle spindles, which detect the amount of stretch in a muscle, golgi tendon organs, which do the same job but in our tendons which are the tissues that tie the muscle to the bone, and joint receptors, which monitor the status of the ligaments that hold the bones of the joint together. Movement of the muscle and therefore the joints stretches these receptors to mechanically open ion channels in the dendrites attached to them to produce action potentials.

Nociception, or pain and temperature detectors, are all slow adapting and in the skin consist of free nerve endings either for sharp pain or dull pain, or for heat or coldness. Polymodal nociceptors respond to mechanical, thermal and chemical stimuli, but many nociceptors are selective to one stimulus type. In essence, nociceptors are activated by stimuli that have the potential to damage tissue such as from strong mechanical stimulation, extremes in temperature, oxygen deprivation or chemical exposure. The stimulus causes damage to the dendrite or surrounding cells which release chemicals that stimulate the dendrite to produce action potentials. These chemicals include Bradykinin, Substance P and prostaglandins. These increase the sensitivity of nociceptors and cause vasodilation resulting in increased blood flow (inflammation) and the release of histamine, which increases the permeability of the blood vessels so that the big white blood cells of the immune response can get to the scene of the crime. However, this can set up a vicious circle called hyperalgesia, which is most commonly seen in children who have little or no top–down control of their perception of pain. A soothing caress can add to their pain so much, due to the increased sensitivity of nociceptors, that their world comes crashing down around their ears, and yours if you happen to be close to the screams. Nociceptors are present in most body tissue including skin, bone, muscle, visceral organs, blood vessels, heart but none are to be found in the brain explaining how and why many brain surgeries are done while patients are awake. It doesn't hurt them and it is then possible to electrically stimulate regions to help surgeons spare "important" regions for speech or movement for example.

Not only do they have separate sensory receptors but pain and temperature signals are carried differently to touch and pressure information to the brain. Let's take the example of the index finger on your right hand (see Figure 3.2). Some enemy of yours pricks your index finger on your right hand with a pin. Nasty person, you must make sure to keep away from them in the future. Your sensory neurons' cell bodies are grouped together in the dorsal root ganglion (or clump) which lie in a vertical row next to the spine. Remember, in sensory neurons the cell body lies along the length of the neuron and not at the beginning. The neurons that detect the touch and pressure of the pin are large and are well myelinated mediating quick detection. You feel the touch before

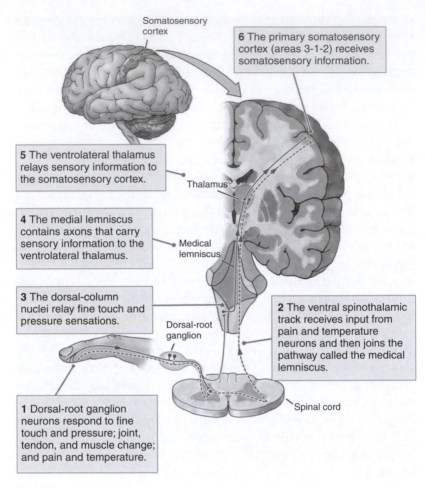

**6** The primary somatosensory cortex (areas 3-1-2) receives somatosensory information.

Somatosensory cortex

**5** The ventrolateral thalamus relays sensory information to the somatosensory cortex.

Thalamus

**4** The medial lemniscus contains axons that carry sensory information to the ventrolateral thalamus.

Medical lemniscus

**3** The dorsal-column nuclei relay fine touch and pressure sensations.

Dorsal-root ganglion

**2** The ventral spinothalamic track receives input from pain and temperature neurons and then joins the pathway called the medical lemniscus.

**1** Dorsal-root ganglion neurons respond to fine touch and pressure; joint, tendon, and muscle change; and pain and temperature.

Spinal cord

**Figure 3.2** Pain and temperature pathways from the finger all the way up to the brain. From *An Introduction to Brain and Behavior*, Third Edition by Bryan Kolb and Ian Q. Whishaw © 2011 by Worth Publishers. Used with permission.

the pain because the pain signal is carried by smaller axons that have little or no myelin. Our dorsal root ganglion neurons also respond to the proprioceptive information from the finger in addition to the haptic (touch) and nociceptive (pain) information. The neurons of the dorsal root track up the right arm and enter the spinal cord at the level of the shoulder in the cervical segment of your vertebrae. The touch and pressure information travels up through the dorsal neurons on the right, or ipsilateral, side of the spinal cord whereas the pain and temperature pathway crosses over the spinal cord to be carried in the ventral pathway which is contralateral to the pin-prick, i.e. on the left side of the spinal cord. This difference in transit of signals to the brain leads to a curious effect on sensation following unilateral damage of the spinal cord. It means that a partial severance of the cord will lead to a loss to fine touch and pressure sensation from the same side as the damage but the loss of pain and temperature sensation on the opposite side of the body.

The dorsal and ventral pathways meet up in the medial lemnisus, a pathway in the brainstem that carries information up to the thalamus. The term lemniscus is a lovely quick way of saying "band of nerve fibres". Since sensory pathways from the body eventually go to the thalamus, their initial stop on the way to the cerebral cortex, the pathway from the spine up to the brain is called the spinothalamic tract of which we have dorsal and ventral pathways. The dorsal pathway crosses over in the medial lemniscus so that all information from the right index finger is processed in the left side of the brain. Its first stop is the ventrolateral thalamus which then relays the information up to the somatosensory cortex in the post-central gyrus (the bump behind the central sulcus, in the parietal cortex) of the cerebral cortex. Up till now, we have talked about information below the neck area of the spinal cord, but the pathways from the face and head follow a similar pathway. The sensory neurons form part of the trigeminal nerve (5th Cranial Nerve) which synapse in the spinal trigeminal nucleus of the brain stem. The axons of these nerves cross to the contralateral side and ascend to the thalamus in the trigeminal lemniscus. The most common head pain is dental pain and (unsurprisingly) headache of which there are many forms; not all headaches are migraines you know. One of the most common headaches is caused by dehydration. As at least 75% of the brain is made of water, it really suffers when we haven't drunk enough. Not only does it cause pain as the shrinking brain pulls on the meninges (the covering membrane of the brain), thus causing pain (remember, the brain itself has no pain receptors) and signalling something is wrong. It's not just headache that dehydration can cause; it can also cause cognitive deficits like muddy thoughts, jumbled speech and even hallucinations.

However, not all signals from the somatosensory system go to the brain. Some of them can mediate behaviours that our brain knows nothing about via synapses in the spinal cord with motor neurons. The simplest of these is the mono-synaptic reflex which comes about via the synapse of one sensory neuron on one motor neuron. You will all recognize this as the knee-jerk reaction which we all had fun with as kids. It is brought about by tapping (in a leg that is hanging free) the patellar tendon (the one just below your knee cap) that holds the quadriceps muscle of the thigh to the leg bone. By tapping this tendon, the quad is stretched and the golgi tendon organs and muscle spindles in the muscles detect this stretch sending the information up the sensory neuron to the spinal cord. These synapse on the motor neuron that projects to the same muscle causing the muscle to contract to get the muscle back to normal tension. This results in a spectacular (if you are lucky) extension of the leg. I have seen this done where the tendon tapper was standing too close to his subject resulting in him being kicked in a most inopportune place. He didn't find this at all funny but it did demonstrate the lack of control his subject had over the reflex. Unless, of course, there was no love lost there. I digress. There are more complex, multi-synaptic, reflexes that control muscles on both sides of the body but in general they are an important way for our bodies to monitor their positions second to second and reduce the stress on our tendons and ligaments, thus lessening the risk of injury to our muscles or joints. This is my way of detecting whether football players are really injured or faking it. If you see a player jerk in an unnatural way before falling to the ground screaming it is likely you have just witnessed a reflex trying to lessen the stress on the joint that has been damaged in some way. It's excruciating to watch. They're not faking it. Call the stretcher and book the scan. That's an 8–10 week layoff, minimum. Pain also serves the purpose of keeping us from injury or from aggravating an injury. We'd all love to live our lives pain free, but unfortunately, we wouldn't last very long. Miss C was a Canadian patient who suffered from Congenital

Universal Insensitivity to Pain (CUIP) the cause of which was never determined but the effects of which were profound. Miss C did not cough, sneeze, gag or protect her eyes in a reflexive way. She developed problems in her joints due to lack of discomfort and the rearrangement of her body posture that would have resulted, and died aged 29 from infections she would have avoided had she been able to perceive pain signals. Therefore, we can see that pain serves a very real purpose in keeping us healthy. How many times do we hear of people going to their doctor saying "Doctor, it hurts when I do this" and the doctor says "well, don't do it then". Helpful? Not so much, but generally speaking if something hurts, you should take it as a sign to stop whatever it was that caused the pain. Pain is also special with respect to how signals are transmitted to the brain. In addition to the spinothalamic and trigeminal pathways, other pain pathways send axons into the central brainstem before they reach the thalamus. These are involved in slow burning and chronic pain; others are involved in arousal. The ganglion neurons from the internal organs such as the heart, kidneys and blood vessels synapse with spinal cord neurons that receive pain information from the body's surface. Therefore the pain relay neurons receive two sets of signals it cannot distinguish – so neither can we. So, pain from the heart is often felt in the left shoulder and arm, pain in the midline of the trunk can indicate pain signals from the stomach whilst problems with the kidneys present as pain in the lower back. From the thalamus, pain signals are projected not just to the somatosensory cortex but also to other areas where the haptic and proprioceptive signals are not sent such as the frontal cortex for the rationalization and top down control of pain.

One of the most misunderstood cases of referred pain is that of ice-cream headache or "brain freeze". You know that dull throbbing ache that you get in your temple or forehead when you bite into a lump of ice cream? This is not because of sensitivity in your teeth as is commonly thought. It is actually referred pain from the roof of your mouth that you feel coming from the temple area of your forehead. If you think about it, it is most commonly seen when people drink cold beverages through a straw, sucking the offending liquid directly onto the palate; the drink doesn't have a chance to warm up before it hits the roof of the mouth. Loiter around your local smoothie shop, and you will see an astonishing array of people hitting their heads with their hands in the universal "D'oh" motion. Great fun! The ice-cream headache passes very quickly with a lovely rush of natural pain-killing endorphins cancelling out the pain. But are there ways of avoiding it? The simple way, if we are talking about drinking through a straw, is to not angle your straw in the direction of your palate, but you can hardly avoid the roof of your mouth if you are eating ice-cream. Well, Maya Kaczorowski and Janusz Kaczorowski, a father-and-daughter team from Hamilton in Canada, investigated this with the help of Maya's pallywags in her 8th Grade class. At age 12 (as she was in 2002), Maya has to be the youngest first author in the *British Medical Journal*. Anyway, what Maya and Janusz did was split the class up into two; half of the class had to eat their tub of ice cream at their leisure and the other half had to gobble it as fast as they could. Gobbling doubled the likelihood of ice-cream headache. So, listen to your mother and eat your ice-cream in a ladylike manner, boy or girl. Others have suggested that ice-cream headache can occur only in hot weather due to the temperature differential between the palate and the cold stimulus, but according to Mark Harries from the British Olympic Medical Centre in Harrow in the UK, getting brain freeze whilst surfing is a common occurrence and that can be a cold way to pass the time. I have no personal evidence for this; I look like a plonker surfing and broke my nose boogy-boarding once. I don't think I'm suited to it. But it's clear that ice-cream headache happens whatever the weather and the causes are varied.

The control of pain is the cornerstone on which the pharmaceutical industry sits. However, sometimes, no drugs are required and all we need to do is employ a little bit of "afferent regulation therapy". It sounds like something you would pay money for, right? But actually, what I'm talking about is free, and we are all qualified to do it and in fact, do it on a regular basis. We do it when we "rub it better" and it works on a very simple principle. An interneuron in the spinal cord receives excitatory input from touch receptors and inhibitory input from pain receptors. Therefore, when we stimulate a touch neuron from the same region that the pain signal came from, the interneuron will inhibit the pain neuron meaning that its information never gets to the brain. It's called the gate theory of pain and was first put forward by Ronald Melzak and

Patrick Wall from MIT in 1965; it's the principle on which TENS (transcutaneous electrical nerve stimulation) machines work. In their following investigations, Melzak and Wall believed it is also possible that there are gates in the brainstem and cortex which may explain why diverted attention lessens pain. Based on this, dentists have begun to make television available to patients in the chair as watching telly seems to be able to delay the administration of pain relief to the patient. When you are next vetting a dentist, include this on your list of things they must have. Sterilizing autoclave? Check. X-ray facilities? Check. TV? Hmmm...so long as your dentist doesn't get distracted...In fact, we have much to thank Ronald Melzak for as it is he who devised the scale of pain descriptions (called the McGill Pain Questionnaire as it was at McGill University in Montreal that much of the groundwork was done) that doctors use to determine what our pain means and how severe it is. The next time your doctor asks you whether it is a searing or a piercing pain, don't be facetious and say "it's a painful pain". Instead, help him or her out; your description of your pain means a lot thanks to Professor Melzak.

Regulation of pain by the brain is called descending regulation and can occur due to behavioural mechanisms such as anticipation, religious belief, prior experience, watching others respond or excitement for example. These mechanisms seem to involve regions known to be involved in emotion such as the cingulate cortex and the midbrain, which project to the brainstem to inhibit the pain signals coming from the body, thus decreasing the perception of pain. As we will find out in Chapter 11, neurotransmitters involved in the emotional system are dopamine and serotonin, and higher levels of these chemicals, caused for example when we fall in love, can decrease the rating of pain through the reward pathway. Therefore, falling in love, or re-awakening passion in an existing relationship can even mediate pain perception in chronic pain sufferers, presumably through this mechanism. It was Sean Mackey and colleagues in Stanford University who found this out, in the same fMRI experiment that showed distraction mechanisms such as TV interact with pain via cognitive pathways. Another chemical that explains the variability in pain perception between people is the endogenous opiod, more commonly known as endorphins. Endorphin receptors are widely distributed throughout the central nervous system but are particularly concentrated around the areas that process or moderate pain. The more endorphins we have, the less likely we are to feel pain due to their inhibitory action at the level of the brainstem and spinal cord, blocking the signals from getting to the brain. This is the body's own form of analgesia or the damping down of pain signals without loss of consciousness. Our endogenous endorphins also mediate the placebo (latin for "I will please") effect and we know this because if we administer naloxone, a drug which blocks the action of the endorphins, the placebo effect goes away and the patient feels pain again. It is a curious phenomenon which results in a decrease in the perception of pain when an ineffective treatment (such as a glucose pill instead of a painkiller) is administered. The mere idea of treatment is sometimes enough to boost the levels of the endogenous endorphins thus producing the natural painkilling effect. The placebo effect can also be seen in the treatment of problems other than pain such as depression and even cancer.

Of course, the way most of us treat mild to moderate pain is by popping a painkiller. These take a few different forms the most common of which are paracetamol (acetaminophen in the USA) and the family of non-steroidal anti-inflammatory drugs (NSAIDs) such as ibuprofen and aspirin. Each of these works- by blocking the release of prostaglandins, which act on pain receptors at the site of the pain signals to indicate pain to the brain. Some NSAIDs have added advantages, for example, all are antipyretics and work to reduce temperature but ibuprofen and aspirin also disrupt the white blood cells, this has a direct effect on the responsiveness of the immune system to tissue injury lessening the inflammation (and resultant pain) normally seen following harm. However, you can probably see an inherent problem with this. If we decrease the inflammatory and immune response at the level of the injury, we can decrease the symptom of pain for sure, but we are also disrupting the body's mechanism to heal itself. Therefore, for certain conditions such as back injury for example, physiotherapists will advise waiting for 24 hours before taking NSAIDs to give the body a chance to heal. Of course, in the case of arthritis pain for example, where the inflammation serves no curative function, this point is irrelevant. Long-term use of NSAIDs is not recommended however as they are badly tolerated by the gastrointestinal system as they decrease the ability of the stomach wall to protect itself from the stomach acid resulting in ulcers and other gastric problems. Paracetamol is more selective in how it blocks prostaglandin release and so is better tolerated by the stomach.

There are other forms of medication that work on the central pain pathways of the brain, dulling perception but not interfering with the healing process. Codeine is one such drug. It is actually a precursor to morphine, named after Morpheus the Greek God of dreams, which is a powerful analgesic similar in structure to endorphins. It needs to be administered intra-venously as it is metabolized and not absorbed well by the gastrointestinal system. Codeine has the advantage of oral administration as it is broken down in the liver by an enzyme called CY2PD6 into morphine. However, up to 10% of people do not have this enzyme and so they may as well be taking sweets as the codeine will have no effect whatsoever. Might I recommend chocolate sweets as chocolate contains a precursor to serotonin which makes us happy? This will not be the last time you hear this from me... In contrast, up to 2% of the population are extra good metabolizers of codeine due to higher-than-normal levels of CY2PD6. However, certain other drugs such as certain anti-depressants and anti-histamines can inhibit the action of CY2PD6, thus reducing the efficacy of codeine in people taking these drugs.

Each sensory receptor, be it for touch or pressure related or pain and temperature, is sensitive to physical stimuli that impinge on a circumscribed area of the body. This area is known as the receptive field. For example, the receptive field of a touch neuron is the portion of skin that stimulates the dendritic processes of one receptor neuron. The size of the receptive field is an important factor in determining the sensitivity of a sensory system as receptor neurons with smaller receptive fields allow greater sensitivity. You can test this out yourself by using part of a mathematical set, the compass with two prongs on the end. If you have the prongs close together and get somebody to gently prod your arm, if you feel it as two touches, then you are activating two receptive fields. If you only feel one touch, then both

prongs fall within the same receptive field. You can map how far the prongs have to be to feel two touches and therefore roughly know how big the receptive field is. Now see whether this is the same for other parts of your body. The hairy side of your arm should be less sensitive than the underside as glabrous (non-hairy) skin is much more sensitive to touch. Sensory receptors indicate how strong a stimulus is by the number of action potentials that they fire as action potentials are all or nothing events. Stronger stimuli therefore produce more action potentials per unit time than weaker stimuli.

Except for the chemical senses of smell and taste, sensory pathways from the body to the cerebral cortex are organized to preserve the spatial relations of adjacent receptors in the body. An example of these brain maps is shown in the somatosensory cortex, which lies in the post-central gyrus, for touch and pain (see Figure 3.3).

Here we can see that more space is devoted to regions that require good sensory experience; therefore there is a big representation for the fingers, lips and the tongue, for example, relative to their actual size in the body. In contrast, there is a relatively small

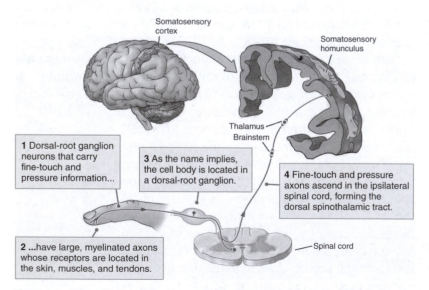

Somatosensory cortex

Somatosensory homunculus

Thalamus
Brainstem

**1** Dorsal-root ganglion neurons that carry fine-touch and pressure information...

**3** As the name implies, the cell body is located in a dorsal-root ganglion.

**4** Fine-touch and pressure axons ascend in the ipsilateral spinal cord, forming the dorsal spinothalamic tract.

**2** ...have large, myelinated axons whose receptors are located in the skin, muscles, and tendons.

Spinal cord

**Figure 3.3** The somatosensory homunculus, or body form, in the somatorsensory cortex. From *An Introduction to Brain and Behavior*, Third Edition by Bryan Kolb and Ian Q. Whishaw © 2011 by Worth Publishers. Used with permission.

representation for the leg for example given how big it is. In this case, size doesn't matter at all. Try the compass test on your thigh; are the receptive fields bigger there, denoting fewer receptors? You get a similar map in the motor cortex which governs movement of the body. Those areas that require a lot of dexterity have large representations as opposed to relatively static areas that have smaller representation.

It is possible to have "cross-talk" between regions in the somatosensory cortex. For example, if a limb is lost through accident or amputation, 60% of these patients experience phantom limb sensation. It occurs when patients feel the presence of their lost limb despite the fact that it is not there. These feelings arise because neurons in the somatosensory cortex that once took their input from the sensory receptors of the amputated limb, now receive input from the neighbouring regions of the body giving the patient the feeling that the limb is still there. Neuroscientist Vilayanur Ramachandran, who loves a good mystery, has investigated this phenomenon with many patients and has found that you can find a map of the amputated limb on the part of the body that took over the part of the somatosensory strip that used to serve the amputation. One such patient, when touched on the face with a cotton bud, will report that Ramachnadran is touching one of his fingers; an entire representation of his hand can be mapped onto his face in this way. Phantom limb sensations are interesting and fascinating for sure, but amputees often have something more sinister to deal with, and that is phantom limb pain. It is well accepted that it is mediated by the changes in the somatosensory cortex following amputation and that there may be disruption to the pain processing regions responsible for the amputated limb, meaning that patients feel pain although it is not there. However, Ramachandran has a much more firm view as to what is going on. He sees it thus: if you want to pick up a glass, your brain sends signals down your arm to move towards the glass and pick it up with your hand. However, if your arm is not there, no movement results. You know this because you can't see or have the sensory experience of any movement. So the brain keeps sending "move" signals. This results in the phantom becoming cramped, and indeed this is the most common description of phantom limb pain. So, Ramachandran came up with an elegant solution. What if we

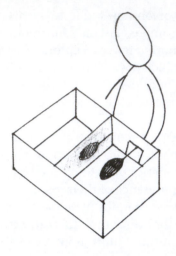

gave the brain some visual feedback of the missing phantom by using a reflection of our intact arm/hand in a mirror? Could we fool the brain into stopping the "move" signal from being sent? Amazingly yes! Patients place their intact limb into one side of a box which is bisected by a mirror with the inference that the phantom is behind the mirror on the other side of the box. The patient looks in the mirror and can see a reflection of their good limb moving about (looking suspiciously like their lost limb). They immediately report release from the cramping and relief from the pain using words such as intriguing and exquisite and so phantom pain may be mediated by a mismatch between expected feeling and visual reality. The effects seem to last some time, but given the economical treatment, repeated use seems to be a great hope for phantom limb pain sufferers without recourse to long-term drug analgesia.

Less is known about our sense of smell but olfaction is different from somatosensation in a few ways. For one thing, the sensory receptors are less varied and it is a chemical rather than a physical sense. The stimuli for the sense of smell are scents which dissolve in the olfactory mucosa in the nose and interact with the cilia of which there are 10 to 20 on the end of each receptor cell which lives in the nasal epithelium (or lining of the nose). In contrast to the other senses, these receptor cells are replaced about every 60 days, as our noses put up with a lot of damaging input. If the receptors are affected by the particular scent then opening of the metabotropic ion channels is initiated. The use of metabotropic as opposed to ionotropic receptors is more useful in the sense of smell as it is a slower process and lasts for longer. This explains why we can still sometimes smell an odour even though the stimulus has been removed; it is still "in our nose" so to speak.

Our ability to detect smells is directly related to the surface area on which we have receptor cells in our nose. The human receptor area is 2–4 cm², about the size of a postage stamp, with dogs having up to 18 cm² and cats even more at 21 cm². Olfactory neurons respond to a range of odours, and summed activity over a range of neurons allows perception of a particular smell. This is controlled by a 350-strong gene family that allows discrimination of 10,000 different smells. Different receptor types synapse on odour-specific glomeruli or tufts of cells in the olfactory bulb, which can be found underneath the frontal cortex. The activity of the neurons in the glomeruli are summed into an output carried by the mitral cells and on to various areas of the cerebral cortex. Odours entering one nostril are processed by the same side of the brain. Unlike other senses, smell signals bypass the thalamus and go directly to the amygdala (an area important in emotional processing and hence the emotional impact of smell) and pyriform areas for smell identification. From here the projection goes to other areas of the limbic system for the emotional response to odours and another projection goes to the orbitofrontal region, via the thalamus, for the integration of smell signals into social situations including eating.

Olfactory receptors are also used to detect pheromones, chemicals that are not perceived consciously as smells but do nevertheless influence behaviour. These are processed by the vomeronasal organ in the nose, which passes information on to the accessory olfactory bulb, which lies adjacent to the main olfactory bulb. Pheromones have a role in sexual behaviour which we will see in Chapter 10 but it would also seem that pheromones can affect glucose metabolism in the brain also even though we are not aware of the signal, which is a bit fascinating. The actual reason for this and its mechanism is still unknown although it could be due to group arousal mechanisms back in our earlier evolution when we were all chasing woolly mammoths to survive.

What about those of us who can't smell? Well, there are different ways to lose your sense of smell, and hence display anosmia. You can expose your nose to toxic fumes or a virus like a bad cold thus killing off all of the cilia and receptor cells in your olfactory epithelium. Although they do grow back, constant replacement means that they are less likely to form the correct connections. Alternatively, you could sever the pathway from your olfactory bulb to your brain or damage the olfactory bulb itself and this can happen by a blow to the head. Another way of impairing your sense of smell would be to damage the brain regions involved in the conscious perception of smell. Loss of olfaction is a curious debilitating disorder not just because you could get yourself blown up because you forgot to turn off the gas and you can't smell it, but also because smell has an important role to play in your perception of flavour. As you know, your sensation of flavour is decimated when you have a cold that stuffs up your nose or even if you hold your nose while you eat. You do need your sense of taste to detect flavour too though.

Taste stimuli, or tastants, are chemicals that are detected by taste receptors in the mouth. Different taste receptors detect 6 basic tastes: salty, sour, sweet, bitter, fatty and unami, which is a protein or meaty like taste. The taste receptors are contained in our taste buds which live on the tongue, under the tongue and on the roof, sides and back of the mouth. Kids tend to have many more taste receptors than adults hence their aversion to strong tasting foods like spicy curries, although it is a source of enormous fun watching their faces while they try them. Seriously though, there is an experiential aspect to what taste receptors are developed and lost through development, and so it is important to expose children to different tastes in order to inform their preference to a wider range of healthy foods in later life. Taste buds contain all kinds of receptor types which have microvilli (tiny hair like structures) at their tips that open ion channels following interaction with tastants. There is no such thing as the taste map on your tongue (another urban legend I'm afraid); you can find receptors for every tastant all over the mouth. Poke around your mouth with a salty stick and see whether you believe me or not. Of course you might vomit in the process but the paramount issue here is that I'm right.

Each taste bud is connected to the brain via one of three cranial nerves, the facial (#7), the glossopharangeal (#9) or the vagus (#10) nerve together forming a tract called the gustatory nerve or the solitary tract. It proceeds to the brainstem where it splits in two. One pathway goes to the ventroposterior medial nucleus of the thalamus (catchy huh?) which then goes to the somatosensory cortex for texture information and the primary gustatory cortex in the insula (which is where the frontal, parietal and temporal lobes intersect sub-cortically underneath the lateral sulcus) for the processing of taste. This region sends a pathway to the orbitofrontal cortex near the olfactory cortex which gives rise to our perception of flavour and as we've already seen, without input from olfaction the perception of flavour is not possible. Damage here in the right hemisphere turns people with previously normal feeding behaviour into fanatical seekers of fine food, which is appropriately named Gourmand syndrome. The other pathway from the brainstem goes to the hypothalamus and amygdala and are probably involved in the emotional impact of food as well as feeding behaviour.

It is very hard not to use all of our senses in our perception; in fact, it is easy to prove that the senses don't usually work in isolation. Charles Spence and his colleagues from Oxford University have repeatedly proved that it is impossible for even experienced tasters like chefs to keep their senses separate. You might expect your taste to be influenced by colour (for example if an orange juice is made to look older than it is, it will be tasted as stale), or even smell, an important component of flavour. But in one cool experiment, Charles piped low and high frequency sounds into the headphones of chefs who where testing the crispiness of crisps. It turned out that when low frequency crunch sounds were heard, the chefs rated the crisps as being less crispy than when no sounds were piped in! Chefs who heard high frequency sounds rated the crisps as being crispier. So even sounds can influence how you taste things; if your crisp gives off a low frequency crunch when you bite into it, you will find it very hard to rate it as crunchy, even if it actually is. This could actually explain why airline food tastes uniformly bad. When you are travelling on a plane, the prevalence of low frequency sound is huge thus dulling your perception of the tastiness of the food. Catering companies try to compensate for this by adding extra flavourings such as salt, but based on Chuck Spence's work, perhaps a change in the texture is the way forward.

Aside from this cross modal perception we are all susceptible to, some people experience the mixing up of the senses, or synesthesia. We have all experienced fleeting examples of this in our lives such as the sharp taste of a lemon or the sound of an oboe that may raise the taste or smell of soup. In fact, only one in every 25,000 people consistently experience two or more senses together. One such synesthete was Michal Watson, who for all his life experienced the feeling of shape when he tastes food. On the other hand, Vladimir Nabokov sees the sound of a letter in a different colour or texture. The long "aaa" of the English language has the texture of weathered wood where as the shorter French "a" evokes polished ebony. One explanation for synesthesia is that signals from receptors in one sensory system have diverted to the wrong part of the brain that is important in the processing of another. Some recent work by Devin Terhune, Alan Cowey and colleagues from Oxford University has shown that people who associate colours with numbers (so-called grapheme-colour synesthesia) have overactive occipital cortices meaning that co-activations we wouldn't normally be aware of actually reach consciousness in these synesthetes. It is also possible to have mirror-touch synesthesia which means that it is possible to feel touch that occurs on another's body simply by watching them. This effect is thought to be mediated by the mirror neuron system. When you are watching somebody else being touched, mirror neurons in your somatosensory system fire to give you an empathic understanding of how that touch would feel for that person. This is usually never raised to a conscious perception of a touch on your skin however, but in synesthetic touch, it is. More alarmingly however, this kind of synesthesia also extends to synesthetic pain which clearly serves no purpose (as we have previously discussed) for the synesthete. It is not known how many suffer from this condition, but it gives us a clear understanding of how correct wiring in the brain is vital for the functioning of our sensory systems.

## Feeling curious?

*Pain: The Science of Suffering (Maps of the Mind)* by Patrick Wall. 2002; Columbia University Press. *A philosophical, physiological and sociological examination of pain from the inventor of the TENS machine.*

Maya Kaczorowski & Janusz Kaczorowski (2002) "Ice Cream Evoked Headaches (ICE-H) Study: Randomised Trial of Accelerated versus Cautious Ice Cream Eating Regimen". *British Medical Journal.* 325: 1445. *The original ice-cream gobbling experiments.*

Ronald Melzack (2005) The McGill Pain Questionnaire: From Description to Measurement. Anesthesiology. 103(1): 199–202. *This is the classification of how we describe pain and what it actually means.*

*Phantoms in the Brain: Human Nature and the Architecture of the Mind* by V.S. Ramachandran & Sandra Blakeslee 1999; *Fourth Estate and The Tell-Tale Brain: Unlocking the Mystery of Human Nature* by V. S. Ramachandran 2011; William Heinemann. *Extraordinary cases concerning phantom limb and synesthesia (amongst others) and what they tell us about the brain.*

# CHAPTER 4 See what I mean?

Vision seems like a relatively simple thing to do; we open our eyes and we can see. Marvellous. But it is deceptively simple. Our visual system has to keep up with an ever-changing landscape, work out where we are in relation to it and also decide how best we might want to interact with it. Meanwhile, we are scooting around, thinking about a gazillion other things, moving our eyes, scanning the scene and deciding what's next whilst being open to getting attracted by something else that catches our interest. Does it seem amazing that we do all this effortlessly and without many mistakes? It does to me. But when you think that nearly 50% of our brain is devoted to various aspects of vision alone, we can pretty much understand why we don't go around bumping into things. The visual system still has a huge job to do as it has to translate light, the sensory input for vision, into electrical signals that our brain can understand and so allowing us to pick up information from the world. It is this complexity that has drawn thousands of neuroscientists into its clutches, but happily, this means that we now know a lot about how vision actually happens.

Vision can be split up into two phases. There is the sensory end of things and this involves vision's sensory organ (the eye) in which light is converted at the retina at the back of the eye into an electrical signal. There is also the perceptual end of things where the brain has to decide what this electrical signal means making us see what we do. Without either of these aspects we would be functionally blind. Light is pretty important too; light is just the electromagnetic radiation that we can see but other forms are actually all around us even though we can't see it. The microwaves that reheat your dinner are electromagnetic waves with long wavelengths (10 mm between peaks) and low energy; radio waves from your mobile phone and uh, your radio, are even longer waves (up to 300 m which is why they travel so far through the air). In contrast, gamma waves and x-rays are high energy waves with small wavelengths less than 1 nm ($10^{-9}$ m). Bang in the middle of these two ends is the range of wavelengths we see as light and from 400 nm to 700 nm every colour from blue through green to red is represented by a particular wavelength. So the visual world that we see is completely determined by our sensitivity to electromagnetic radiation and the structure of our visual system. We are set up to see only between 400 and 700 nm, but that doesn't mean the other wavelengths are not there; we just can't see them.

In the immediate vicinity of the visible spectrum of light is ultraviolet light (less than 380 nm) and infrared light (greater than 750 nm) that we can't see unless we wear special lenses. What if we had receptors that could see outside of our normal range? What would the world look like then? Well, stickleback fish normally look a tad boring to us; they are mainly grey looking sometimes with vertical striations along their length. During the breeding season however the male sticklebacks up their act by developing red and yellow markings. There is also an ultraviolet component to their colouration to which humans are not sensitive but the stickleback can detect it, meaning that sticklebacks have a more sensitive means of telling potential mates apart and can use this information to find the perfect mate for them. Therefore, what the stickleback sees is entirely different from what we do; our vision is the product of an interaction between the world and our visual system. You could almost say that our vision is quite limited!

It is the structure of the eye and the receptors it contains that constrains our visual experience to light. There actually is more to the world than meets the eye. Light has to go through an awful lot of treatment before it can even get to the sensory receptors which are located at the back of the eyeball in the retina (see Figure 4.1). First of all, the light has to pass through the cornea or the hard outer layer of the eye ... the bit you touch when you accidentally poke yourself there. In the outer eye, beyond the centre where the light enters the eyeball, this becomes the sclera or the white of your eye which is just as tough and actually covers the entire eyeball including the bits you can't see. The cornea doesn't have a blood supply but is nourished by the watery fluid behind it called the

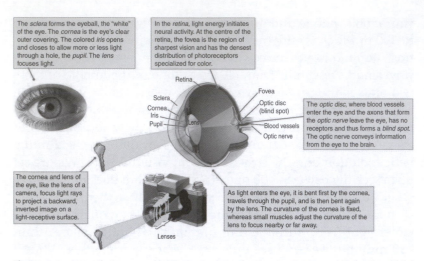

The *sclera* forms the eyeball, the "white" of the eye. The *cornea* is the eye's clear outer covering. The colored *iris* opens and closes to allow more or less light through a hole, the *pupil*. The *lens* focuses light.

In the *retina*, light energy initiates neural activity. At the centre of the retina, the fovea is the region of sharpest vision and has the densest distribution of photoreceptors specialized for color.

The *optic disc*, where blood vessels enter the eye and the axons that form the *optic nerve* leave the eye, has no receptors and thus forms a *blind spot*. The optic nerve conveys information from the eye to the brain.

The cornea and lens of the eye, like the lens of a camera, focus light rays to project a backward, inverted image on a light-receptive surface.

As light enters the eye, it is bent first by the cornea, travels through the pupil, and is then bent again by the lens. The curvature of the cornea is fixed, whereas small muscles adjust the curvature of the lens to focus nearby or far away.

Retina · Fovea · Sclera · Optic disc (blind spot) · Cornea · Iris · Pupil · Lens · Blood vessels · Optic nerve · Lenses

**Figure 4.1** How the eye works. From *An Introduction to Brain and Behavior*, Third Edition by Bryan Kolb and Ian Q. Whishaw © 2011 by Worth Publishers. Used with permission.

aqueous humour. The next structure the light comes across is the iris, the smooth muscle whose pigmentation gives you your distinctive eye colour. As it is a muscle, the iris can contract or relax to make the pupil (the opening in the iris) bigger or smaller thereby controlling the amount of light that can enter the eye. Your pupil is smaller in bright light so as not to overwhelm your retina while in dim light your pupil is really big to let as much light in as possible. You can play with this in front of the mirror.

Look at the size of your pupils in dim light then flash a light near your eye. You should be able to see your iris relaxing to make your pupil smaller. Unless of course you have blinded yourself with your torch...I digress. The pupil is black because of the light absorbing vitreous humour you can see behind it. But between the pupil and the vitreous chamber is the lens which focuses the light on the part of the retina which has maximal sensitivity to light, the fovea. The lens can change its shape depending on what it is trying to focus on. If you are looking at something close to you, your lens has to get fatter in order to focus the light properly on the fovea. The ciliary muscles, attached to the lens by suspensory ligaments, contract and swell inside thus decreasing their hold on the lens via the ligaments, so the lens gets rounder and thicker due to its natural elasticity. In contrast, if you are looking at something further away, the ciliary muscles relax, pulling on the suspensory ligaments to make the lens longer and flatter. The lens projects an inverted image in to the retina just as looking at your reflection in a spoon turns you upside down.

The lens can therefore accommodate the light and focus it on the retina no matter where it comes from. However, the action of these ciliary muscles are susceptible to the ravages of age leading to a decreased ability of the lens to accommodate leading to that curious effect of older people holding their menu at arm's length in a restaurant in order to get good focus of the light on their eyes so they can read the words contained therein. This is because the lens, which is normally quite elastic, gets a bit stiff and can't contract so well as you get older. People are therefore left with a lens which prefers to be flat so instead of the lens accommodating, the reader has to do the accommodation by bringing the menu to the distance that the lens is comfortable with, i.e. further away. However, instead of propping their menu up against the cruets and taking five steps backwards and knocking over who knows how many bustling wait-staff in the process, they could always wear corrective lenses. These will work in conjunction with their own lens to focus the light on the retina. Called glasses (or contact lenses if they don't mind sticking their finger in their eye every day), even young people wear them.

The two main reasons people have to wear corrective lenses are if they have myopia or hyperopia (see Figure 4.2). Myopia, or short-sightedness, occurs when light entering the eye is erroneously focused shy of the retina because the eyeball is too long. Vision in this case is better up close because the lens can't flatten enough to get the things in the distance in focus. Artificial concave lenses can correct this to move the image point back to the retina. Hyperopia or long-sightedness is the opposite. The eyeball in this case is too short and so the image is focussed behind the retina. In this case, the lens can't contract enough to see the near things in good focus and so you need to correct this with a convex lens. In the case of presbyopia ("old eye" in Greek) that our restaurant patron above had, bifocals are in order. These lenses are concave on the top to help far vision with convex lenses on the bottom to help near vision, so not only are they wearing glasses in their old age (about 40), but they have a new "head bob" mannerism like

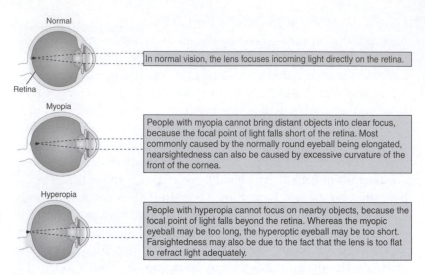

Normal

In normal vision, the lens focuses incoming light directly on the retina.

Retina

Myopia

People with myopia cannot bring distant objects into clear focus, because the focal point of light falls short of the retina. Most commonly caused by the normally round eyeball being elongated, nearsightedness can also be caused by excessive curvature of the front of the cornea.

Hyperopia

People with hyperopia cannot focus on nearby objects, because the focal point of light falls beyond the retina. Whereas the myopic eyeball may be too long, the hyperoptic eyeball may be too short. Farsightedness may also be due to the fact that the lens is too flat to refract light adequately.

**Figure 4.2** Where the light falls in abnormal vision; unless it is focused on the retina, our vision will be compromised. From *An Introduction to Brain and Behavior*, Third Edition by Bryan Kolb and Ian Q. Whishaw © 2011 by Worth Publishers. Used with permission.

all the other old people they used to laugh at as they get used to looking out the top or bottom of their new specs. These are things we all have to look forward to … and it's certainly not the worst thing. For example, a cataract is the clouding that forms in the lens severely decreasing the amount of light that can pass through. They account for 48% of the world's blindness and usually form in the elderly (senile cataracts); however they can be congenital or caused by a trauma to the eye or can be induced by various drugs or by diabetes. Senile cataracts are caused by long-term exposure to ultraviolet and other electromagnetic radiation and it is thought that the depletion of the ozone layer will increase the prevalence of cataracts in the old age of the current population. Indeed, a study by Vilhjalmur Rafnsson and colleagues at the University of Iceland in Reykjavik determined that Icelandair pilots were more likely to develop cataracts than people with non-flying jobs. By adjusting for age, smoking and sunbathing habits they showed that it was the amount of cosmic radiation the pilots were exposed to that was the causative factor in their development of cataracts. Happily, there is now a treatment for cataracts which involves removal of the lens and its replacement with a plastic one. This is generally done under local anaesthetic and the patient is allowed home the same day. It is also now possible to have a multifocal lens which decreases the need for the patient to even wear glasses after the surgery.

This was all a bit different in Claude Monet's day. He battled with cataracts for years and it severely impaired his visual world with Monet complaining to friends that the world seemed dull and it was getting harder to tell colours apart. We can see the effects of this in his painting as he (very helpfully) painted many scenes again and again over the course of his life. Monet eventually had surgery to remove the cataract in his right eye in 1923, just three years before his death from lung cancer at the age of 86. He refused to have the cataract in his left eye removed meaning he still couldn't use both eyes together due to their differences in colour perception and acuity. As the father of the impressionist movement, Monet himself attributed his late change in style to his declining eyesight. The differences in clarity and colour between the painting of the Japanese Bridge finished in 1899 and that finished in 1926 are stark; the delicate and fine blues and greens are gone, replaced by muddy browns, reds and yellows. Even though the painting was started after the surgery, we can see that Monet's visual system couldn't adapt to the restoration of vision after so long an impairment; he thought his vision was too yellow and blue post-op. The second Japanese Bridge shows how he tried to compensate, resulting in a darker and more murky view. Monet had probably had his cataracts since 1905 and so the moral of this story would seem pretty clear: in order to cause minimal harm to your long-term vision, you should not wait 18 years to get them sorted out. Admittedly, the operation is much less of an ordeal now.

Behind the lens is the vitreous humour, a black jelly-like substance, the pressure of which keeps the eye roughly spherical. The vitreous is stagnant and not replenished and if debris or anything else gets into this chamber, they will be perceived as floaters. We all generally see one or two of these when looking at a cloudless sky for example, and something that looks like a transparent worm floats downwards through the visual field. This is because the debris in the vitreous humour is floating down. The perception of floaters is called myodesopsia and some people born with debris in their humour (vitreous, this has nothing to do with how funny they are) will have seen the same floaters all their lives. Generally they don't cause a problem but the only treatment is removal of debris from the vitreous fluid. Sudden onset of floaters can be indicative of eye damage however and so are a good diagnostic indication.

Finally, the light can hit the retina, which is a layer of photoreceptors on the back wall of the eyeball (see Figure 4.3). In fact, the light has to pass through four layers of other cells before it hits the photoreceptors but since these cells are translucent this doesn't cause much of a problem. We'll come back to these cell layers a bit later. There are more than 125 million photoreceptors arranged across the retina that convert light to electrical signals. Humans have two types of receptor sensitive to light, the rod and the cone. Rods and cones are so called for their shape: the outer segment of the rod looks like a rod and the outer segment of a cone looks like, well, a cone. Very imaginative stuff this.

The outer segments are the bits that contain the photopigment making the rod or the cone specialized to a particular wavelength of light. Rods are 1000 times more sensitive to light than cones because they contain much more photopigment and are mainly used for night vision. Cones are therefore only responsive to bright light and are used for colour vision and fine detail. The inner segment of the rods and cones contains the cell body and the synaptic terminals on the end are the bits that transmit the electrical signal on to the next layer of cells in the retina. The rods and cones are

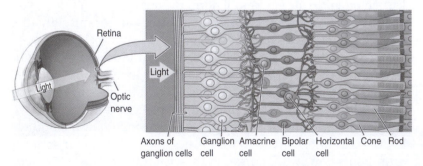

Retina

Light

Light

Optic nerve

Axons of ganglion cells    Ganglion cell    Amacrine cell    Bipolar cell    Horizontal cell    Cone    Rod

**Figure 4.3** These are the layers of the retina from the rods and cones at the back to the retinal ganglion cells to the anterior. From *An Introduction to Brain and Behavior*, Third Edition by Bryan Kolb and Ian Q. Whishaw © 2011 by Worth Publishers. Used with permission.

distributed differently on the retina with rods being spaced across the entire retina but cones are mainly grouped at the fovea, which is Latin for "pit". That's because the four layers of cells diverge at this point so that light can hit the cones directly and it looks like a dent in the cell layers. This is why the lens does all it can to focus light here as there is the highest density of cones responsible for fine detail and colour vision. The peripheral retina is very sensitive to light, but is no good for colour as only the rods live there. You can demonstrate the difference in acuity across the retina to yourself by looking at a page full of text. Oh, like this one. You can clearly see the word that you are foveating, but the words next to it are less clear, and then ones next to them are less clear again. Indeed, in order for the words in the periphery to be viewed with the same clarity as the foveated words they would need to be in a much bigger font. Look at the line below and focus on the middle word.

# consider     this     example

The peripheral words are just as clear as the middle one only because I've made them bigger to compensate for the lack of acuity there.

We have three types of cones in which the photopigment is responsive to three different wavelengths, short 430nm, medium 530 nm and long 560 nm, which roughly correspond to the blue, green and red parts of the visible spectrum respectively. The colour that we perceive is determined by the relative activity of these three cone types. For example white light (made up of all the colours of the spectrum) will activate all cone types and yellow light will activate green and red cones (as it falls in between green and red on the spectrum of wavelengths). Because our colour perception is based on the relative activity of three cones (sensitive to three different wavelengths) humans are sometimes called trichromats. However, some people are born without one of these cone types; the most common are people who are missing the red or green pigments and this makes them red-green colour blind and so they are termed dichromats as they have to work from just two types of cone. The lack of red cones leads to a condition called protanopia, the lack of green cones leads to deuteranopia whilst the lack of blue cones (which is much rarer) is tritanopia. "Colour-blindness" is a misleading term as it doesn't mean that dichromats can't see colour at all; it's just that they are less sensitive to the colour for which they have the missing pigment and will confuse certain red and green colours that would seem distinct to a trichromat. It is very rare, but not impossible to have no cones at all; people who cannot perceive colour usually have some form of brain damage. It is mostly men who experience colour blindness as the gene that encodes the red and green pigments are on the X chromosome; a defective gene therefore has an effect in males but not in females as females have another X chromosome to compensate (see Chapter 10). For a woman to experience red-green colour blindness, they would have to have inherited a defective gene from both the mother and the father. The gene for the blue pigment isn't sex linked and so has a theoretically equal chance of occurring in men and women but for dichromacy in general, the relative incidence in men is 1% but only 0.01% in women. It is also possible to have only a partial lack of one of the cones and the incidence for this is much higher: 5% for men and 0.4% for women.

But what actually happens in rods and cones when light coming into the eye hits them? This is the process of phototransduction or the generation of an electrical signal from a light stimulus. The light is absorbed by the photopigment in the outer segment of the receptor. In the case of rods this pigment is called rhodopsin, which is made up of a protein called opsin, a molecule which is a derivative of Vitamin A called retinal (and THIS is why carrots are good for your eyes as they are packed with the stuff). The retinal changes its shape in response to light; the fancy term for this is isomerization. The retinal changes from being in the form of 11-cis-retinal in the dark to all-trans retinal in the light; the molecule does a bit of a flip which changes its shape. This activates the opsin eventually causing the $Na^+$ channels to close leading to hyperpolarization of the membrane. In contrast to regular nerve cells, the resting membrane potential of the rod outer segment membrane is $-30$ mv, caused by a steady influx of $Na^+$ ions through special ion channels in the dark and so is called "the dark current". More light causes this dark current to stop, the $Na^+$ influx is stopped by closing the channels and so the membrane potential becomes more negative. So, photoreceptors hyperpolarize in response to light.

Continued stimulation by light makes the retinal break down into Vitamin A and opsin and it is only after a period of regeneration in the dark that it can become rhodopsin and be sensitive to light again. Hence when you first walk into a dark room, you can't see anything, but after about 20 minutes you become fully dark adapted, all of your rhosopsin has reformed and your rods are again maximally sensitive to light. In cones, the process is similar but with three different opsins sensitive to different wavelengths. However, these opsins require more energy to become active, which is important, as on a bright sunny day rhodopsin saturates quite quickly; more light will not cause greater hyperpolarization and so it is no good at detecting fine changes in bright light. In fact, the way our eyes detect changes in the brightness of light leads to my favourite law on the whole planet. Ok, I like the law that says you shouldn't murder people, but this law is much more fun. What amount of extra light do you need to perceive a change in its brightness? Or to put it another way, how bright does your flashlight need to be in order for you to see it against the background illumination? It turns out that the amount of light required to see a change in the overall brightness is directly proportional to the background illumination. This was first demonstrated by a German physiologist called Ernst Heinrich Weber with respect to the perception of relative weights in 1834 but his student Gustav Theodor Fechner later applied it to the measurement of sensation. It applies to all sensory experience and a day doesn't go by that I don't think about it in some way, shape or form. Let me give you an example. The light that comes from your flashlight won't seem very bright on a nice sunny day, will it? But if you have the same flashlight with the same intensity of light in the beam in a dark room, it will seem a lot brighter. It's the same with hearing. It's much easier to hear a whisper in a quiet room than in a nightclub. It turns out that we can perceive a 2% difference in sensory intensity but of course, if your starting intensity is very low, 2% of this is hardly anything. But if your starting intensity is very high then you will need a large change to notice a difference. It's called Weber's Law. Tell your friends; mine love it.

The changes in membrane potential in the photoreceptors are graded potentials; remember these from Chapter 2? The signals are passed on through three layers of cells before they become action potentials in the retinal ganglion cells, which then carry the signal to the brain via the optic nerve. These layers are made up of horizontal cells, bipolar cells and amacrine cells. There is much collation of signal and summing of responses from the rods by the horizontal and amacrine cells and this further explains why your visual acuity isn't great in the dark; in order to be maximally sensitive to light, the visual system adds up input from many cells but detail is sacrificed. The passing of information from the cones is much more faithful with a one-to-one mapping between cone and bipolar cell; thus much finer detail is possible. Hyperpolarization of the photoreceptor causes depolarization of the bipolar cell and this leads to depolarization of the ganglion cell. If the ganglion cell detects enough depolarization via all of these graded potential inputs, an action potential will fire.

Even at this stage, the visual system knows where a light came from as different locations in the visual scene project to different parts of the retina. As mentioned previously, the image is inverted in the two eyes because of the lens but the brain can determine where the light is coming from depending on what part of the retina is stimulated. Every retinal ganglion cell is responsive to part of the visual field. We came across receptive fields in somatosensation in the previous chapter but I like to think of visual receptive fields with the aid of chicken wire. Hold a piece of chicken wire with its roughly circular holes up at arm's length in front of your face. Now, what you can see through one hole could represent the part of the world that one ganglion cell is responsible for. The smaller the hole in the chicken wire (i.e. the smaller the receptive field) the more sensitive to fine detail that ganglion cell is, and so it's probably hooked up to a cone. Receptive fields for ganglion cells that take their input from rods are much bigger as the responses of many rods are added together for greater sensitivity to light, and it means that they are sensitive to movement across that bigger receptive field. You can check this out yourself. Wiggle a coloured pencil in the peripheral vision of a mate (remember, this is the area for which rods are the predominant processing force). I bet they will be able to detect the movement, but won't be able to tell you the colour of the pencil, for which they would need the cones.

The optic nerve, which contains axons from retinal ganglion cells fed by both rods and cones, then exits the retina at the optic disk and enters the brain. There are no photoreceptors at the optic disk and so in effect we have a blind spot here which you can demonstrate for yourself by staring at a point on a table with only your right eye and moving a pencil horizontally to the right away from the point you are looking at. At about 15 cm to the side, you won't be able to see the tip of the pencil anymore as its image is falling on your blind spot. We don't notice this in everyday life as the blind spot is to the left of the fovea in the left eye and to the right of it in the right eye and so the left eye can see what is in the blind spot of the right eye and vice versa. Even people with only one functional eye, when this compensation cannot happen, don't notice their blind spot due to perceptual fill-in carried out by the brain. Damage to the optic disk can have profound effects on vision with optic neuritis or inflammation of the optic nerve, caused by infection or diabetes leading to a complete loss of vision in that eye. This is the most common neurological visual disorder and treatment is usually very effective. However, a birth defect of the optic nerve leading to a cleft, or coloboma, in the optic disk can lead to moderate to total blindness in that eye as the information from the retina is not transmitted to the brain due to the structural deformity of the disk. Due to its similarity to the flower when viewed through an ophthalmoscope, this rare eye disorder is called Morning Glory Syndrome.

There are actually three roads that the visual information can now travel. The main pathway for visual perception (which is the second stage of vision) is called the Geniculostriate System. The second is the Tectopulvinar System, which takes information only from rods (and so knows where something happened but not necessarily what happened) and is important in the orientation of eye movements and involves a pathway to the visual cortex via the superior colliculus and the pulvinar. We'll talk more about the third pathway later on in Chapter 9 because it is important in establishing your circadian rhythms. Called the retino – hypothalamic pathway it is pretty self explanatory and is fed by input from the cones via the retinal ganglion cells to the suprachiasmatic nucleus and on to the hypothalamus.

As you already know, the first stop for all sensory systems (except smell) in the brain is the thalamus and for the main pathway of vision, the Geniculostriate Pathway; this means an area of the thalamus called the lateral geniculate nucleus or LGN. But the input from the eye goes through a bit of jiggery pokery before that. The information from the two eyes partially crosses over at the optic chiasm, which is just before the optic nerves enter the brain (see Figure 4.4). It does this in order to make sure that all of the information from the right side of the visual space goes to the left side of the brain and the information from the left side of space goes to the right side of the brain. Let's think about it from your left eye's point of view (sorry). The left side of your left eye (the bit closest to your temple so called the temporal retina) looks at what is happening in the right side of your visual field whereas the right side of your left eye (the bit closest to your nose and so called the nasal retina) looks at

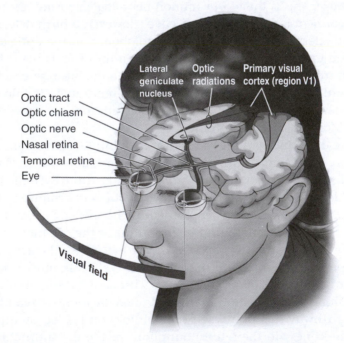

**Figure 4.4** The geniculostriate system. The right side of each eye picks up visual information from the left side of space. The partial decussation means that all of this information from the left side of space ends up in the right hemisphere. From *An Introduction to Brain and Behavior*, Third Edition by Bryan Kolb and Ian Q. Whishaw © 2011 by Worth Publishers. Used with permission.

what is happening on the left side of visual space. It's the same in the other eye, but the temporal and nasal retinas are now on the right and left respectively. So, each optic nerve carries information from the left and right of space. In order for the brain to have a clear "left hemisphere does the right side of visual field and right hemisphere does the left side of the visual field", an exchange of information has to happen. It is the information from the nasal side of each retina that crosses over at the optic chiasm. The information from the temporal retinas doesn't cross and so it is only a partial crossover, or partial decussation in fancier terms.

So now we have all of the information from the right side of space entering the LGN in the left hemisphere and that from the left side of space entering the right LGN. The LGN is organized in 6 layers (remember, 6 is the magic number in the brain as the cortex has six layers too!). The input from the two eyes is kept separate, again helping the visual system determine where a light came from. The axons of the retinal ganglion cells that are fed by rods synapse on Layer 1 and 2 (one for each eye) in the LGN which are made up of magnocellular cells and so are called the M layers. These cells have large cell bodies and large receptive fields and so they are not very good for fine detail but are good for the processing of movement. The axons of the retinal ganglion cells that are fed by the cones synapse in the other four layers of the LGN made up of parvocellular cells (Layers 3 to 6) and so are called the P layers. These cells are very small and have small receptive fields i.e. they can see only a little bit of the visual field, and so are good for fine detail and colour since they take their input initially from cones. In between the layers are the recently discovered koniocellular cells which take their input from retinal ganglion cells fed by cones and have a role in colour vision.

A neuron's receptive field is the region of the retina (and so the visual field) that activates the neuron but we can also describe a receptive field according to the type of stimulus it responds to. Retinal ganglion cells and LGN cells respond to spots of light from different parts of the retina and so there was method in my madness choosing chicken wire with its circular holes to help you understand receptive fields. These receptive fields have centres and surrounds and some cells respond to bright spots of light falling in the centre of the receptive field (on centre, off surround) and some respond to light falling in the surround (off centre, on surround). The responsivity of the cell depends on whether the light falls in "on" area, which will cause excitation, or the "off" area, which will inhibit activity. If the entire receptive field is stimulated, the "on" area's activity will be cancelled by the "off" area's inactivity and no change will be detected. Physiologically, this is mediated by the input of the cones and the horizontal cells to the bipolar cells in the retina in the first instance and by summation of inputs later on and is a really neat way for the visual system to determine the shape of a light. We know what LGN cells respond to by the experiments done by David Hubel and Torston Weisel from Harvard University in the 1960s. They stuck a listening electrode in the LGN of a cat and shone lights on a wall in a darkened room in order to see what the cell they were listening to responded to. They could tell that a cell was responding as an active cell producing action potentials sounds like a bunch of crackling. By drawing on the wall wherever the light was when the cell crackled, they found out where that cell responded to on the wall (its receptive field) and could map its on centre and off surround. Other cells they listened to had off centres and on surrounds.

Information leaves the LGN via a tract of neurons called the optic striatum and projects to the primary visual cortex (or V1) in the occipital lobe at the back of the brain. Inputs from each eye are kept separate here too as are the M and P pathways. The M layers project to layer IVα and the P layers project to layer IVβ. V1 contains a map of the visual world because neurons in different parts of the primary visual cortex (V1) receive input from spatially distinct parts of the LGN. Thus, neurons in V1 also form a retino-topic map. Lesions to different regions of V1 causes blindness in specific locations of the visual field. If we imagine that the calcer-ine sulcus denotes the horizontal midline of the visual field, then damage above the calcerine sulcus will mean that there will be a visual deficit below the centre of the contralateral visual field and vice versa. The extent of the damage in V1 determines how big the deficit will be and it can range from a small spot (a scotoma) to a quarter of the field (quadrantanopia) right up to half of the visual field (hemianopia).

Hubel and Weisel repeated their experiment listening to cat neurons but in this case listened to V1 neurons. They found that instead of responding to spots of light, these cells responded to bars of light. In fact, they have rectangular receptive fields still with on centre and off surrounds (and off centres and on surrounds). But how did we get from seeing spots in the LGN to bars of light in V1? Well, V1 cells receive input (via the LGN) from a row of retinal ganglion cells in a particular orientation. If we look at Figure 4.5,

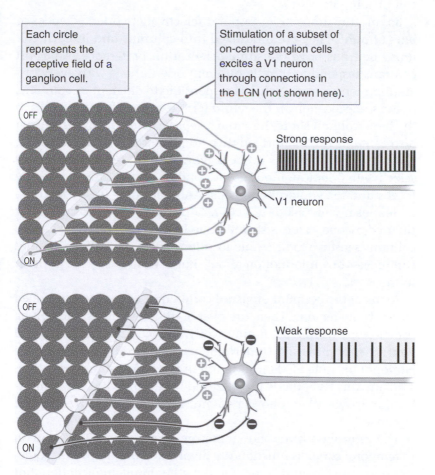

**Figure 4.5** One V1 neuron selective for a particular orientation takes its input from LGN cells whose receptive fields represent that line in the visual field. If light of a different orientation is presented, the cell will only weakly respond as less LGN cells that feed this V1 neuron will be active. From *An Introduction to Brain and Behavior*, Third Edition by Bryan Kolb and Ian Q. Whishaw © 2011 by Worth Publishers. Used with permission.

we can see that each circle represents the receptive field of a retinal ganglion cell, some of which input into our V1 cell. If a bar of light falls on the retina in such as way as to activate all of the receptive fields our V1 cell is listening to, then our V1 cell will be maximally activated. If the bar of light is the wrong orientation however, only some of our receptive fields will be stimulated, leading to less firing of our V1 cell. This shows how inputs over the course of the visual system are added together to allow us to perceive ever more complex inputs.

So, most neurons in V1 respond selectively to oriented edges or bars of light. They are organized into columns and in each column, neurons have the same orientation preference. Adjacent columns respond to slightly different orientations with every orientation represented. Neurons responding to different orientations at the same location on the retina form a hypercolumn; all cells in the hypercolumn share the same receptive field. The hypercolumn also contains two blobs (I kid thee not, this is the technical term!). Blobs are groups of cells in the primary visual cortex that are not selective to orientation but do respond to colour. They are fed by P cells and the koniocellular cells. Another name for V1 is striate cortex; as if you look at a section of primary visual cortex under the microscope, it looks striated due to the grouping of cells into columns sensitive to the same location. These processing modules can process any information about shape within a specific location in the world.

Areas of the occipital or visual cortex that are not V1 are called extra-striate regions. There are over 30 different areas and can be functionally as well as anatomically divided into the dorsal and ventral stream. Leslie Ungerleider and Mort Mishkin from the National Institute of Mental Health in the USA first proposed their Two Streams Hypothesis in 1982 and it purports that when information leaves V1 it follows two main pathways, or streams (see Figure 4.6).

The ventral pathway that goes from V1 through V2, V3 and on to temporal cortex is functionally involved in deciding what something is: object identification. On the other hand, information that exits V1 and is further processed in V5 and V3 and goes on to the parietal cortex constitutes the dorsal stream and will eventually tell you where something is. These pathways were therefore dubbed

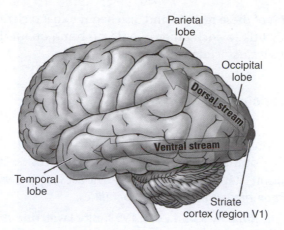

Parietal
lobe

Occipital
lobe

Dorsal stream

Ventral stream

Temporal
lobe

Striate
cortex (region V1)

**Figure 4.6**  The dorsal and ventral streams in the brain in which visual information goes to the parietal cortex to process spatial information relating to how we will interact with our environment and the temporal cortex in order to identify objects. From *An Introduction to Brain and Behavior*, Third Edition by Bryan Kolb and Ian Q. Whishaw © 2011 by Worth Publishers. Used with permission.

the "What and Where" pathways. Based on findings from patients however, David Milner and Mel Goodale, then at the University of St. Andrews, refined the theory. They found that patients with damage to the ventral stream had real trouble recognizing objects (called visual agnosia), but they could interact with them whilst patients who could name objects but could not interact with them (called optic ataxia) had damage to their dorsal stream. This dissociation of function led to Milner and Goodale proposing the "What and How" functional streams.

Neuropsychology has taught us much else about the gross function of many visual areas. For example, patients with damage to V5 cannot process movement and see the world in strobe, particularly dangerous when trying to cross the road. This deficit is called akinetopsia. Meanwhile, prosopagnosia is a recognition deficit selective for faces and is caused by damage to an area called fusifom face area. Area V4 is involved in processing colour and using colour to identify shapes with lesions here resulting in achromatopsia or complete colour blindness. People with parietal lobe damage have problems orienting their attention (and their bodies) in space. However, with the advent of more precise experimental methods such as fMRI and TMS, we can ask more particular questions about the function of these regions and also begin to get a clearer picture of how they talk to each other in order to bring about the variety of functions we associate with the visual system.

## Feeling curious?

Michael F. Marmor, (2006) "Ophthalmology and Art: Simulation of Monet's Cataracts and Degas' Retinal Disease". *Archives of Ophthalmology*;124: 1764–1769. *This article uses computer simulation to comment on these artists' visual capabilities.*

*A Vision of the Brain* by Semir Zeki. 1993; Blackwell and *Inner Vision: An Exploration of Art and the Brain* by Semir Zeki. 1999; Oxford University Press. *A journey from sensation to perception and how our understanding of art relates to what we know about visual processing in the brain.*

*Brain and Visual Perception: The Story of a 25-year Collaboration* by David H. Hubel & Torsten N. Wiesel. 2004; Oxford University Press. *A delightful romp through the ground-breaking experiments of these eminent neuroscientists.*

L.G. Ungerleider, & M. Mishkin. (1982) "Two Cortical Visual Systems". In Ingle DJ, Goodale MA, Mansfield RJW (eds) *Analysis of Visual Behavior*. The MIT Press. *The seminal and first hypothesis purporting two functional streams of vision in the brain.*

*The Visual Brain in Action* by David Milner & Mel Goodale. 2006; Oxford University Press. *This book proposes another two streams theory; vision for perception and vision for action.*

So, we've talked about the chemical senses, smell and taste, and also our photosensation, which is vision, as well as our physical sensation, which is somatosensation. The last sense that we have is again mechanical in nature and is audition (and not the X-factor kind). In humans particularly, hearing is integral not just to the perception of sound, but also its specialized knock on effects such as language comprehension and production. The sensory organ as we all know is the ear, but this is a multi-tasking organ as it is also central to our balance via the vestibular system, a very important component of which is contained in the ear also. We'll talk about that more when we hit movement in the next chapter.

I think of hearing as being a mechanical sense as it involves a bunch of things banging against each other. Sound is actually created by air molecules knocking off each other and vibrating. The most used example of this is a tuning fork (any fork will do really, but use one of those carving forks, it's clearer). If you wallop it off a hard surface like a table, it creates sound waves that you can hear quite clearly if you bring the fork up to your ear very quickly. Be careful here, I almost impaled myself a minute ago doing this. I'm not talking about the clatter the fork makes when you hit the table; when you bring it up to your ear you should hear something that sounds like a hummed note. Sound waves are therefore caused by the changes in pressure caused by vibrating air molecules. When air molecules are compressed by the prongs on the fork moving closer to each other it causes a higher density of sound waves and less dense sound waves occur when the air is more rarefied (or with sparser molecules when the prongs go back to normal).

Sound waves have two basic features: frequency and amplitude (see Figure 5.1). Amplitude is the size of the wave and is related to

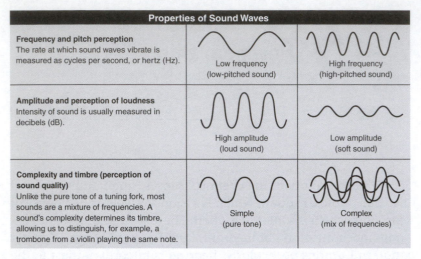

| Properties of Sound Waves | | |
|---|---|---|
| **Frequency and pitch perception**<br>The rate at which sound waves vibrate is measured as cycles per second, or hertz (Hz). | Low frequency<br>(low-pitched sound) | High frequency<br>(high-pitched sound) |
| **Amplitude and perception of loudness**<br>Intensity of sound is usually measured in decibels (dB). | High amplitude<br>(loud sound) | Low amplitude<br>(soft sound) |
| **Complexity and timbre (perception of sound quality)**<br>Unlike the pure tone of a tuning fork, most sounds are a mixture of frequencies. A sound's complexity determines its timbre, allowing us to distinguish, for example, a trombone from a violin playing the same note. | Simple<br>(pure tone) | Complex<br>(mix of frequencies) |

**Figure 5.1** The frequency and amplitude of sound waves determine what kind of sound we hear. From *An Introduction to Brain and Behavior*, Third Edition by Bryan Kolb and Ian Q. Whishaw © 2011 by Worth Publishers. Used with permission.

the number of air molecules that are vibrating in a sound wave. It is measured in decibels (dB), a measure of relative loudness, named by Bell Telephone Systems in America in 1928 in honour of Alexander Graham Bell, inventor of the telephone. Needless to say, it became important to quantify these things around this time. Just like the Richter scale used for earthquakes, loudness is measured using a logarithmic scale in that 10dB is ten times louder than 1dB and 20dB is 100 times louder, 30 dB is 1000 times louder. So, an increased number of air molecules increases the amount of energy in a sound wave which makes the sound seem louder.

If you just tap your fork off the table, it will be hard to hear anything from the fork, but if you whack it, you will hear a louder note as you have displaced more air molecules. The energy of sound waves decreases with the distance from the source, so the hum from the fork gets fainter as you move it away from your ear. The rate at which air molecules vibrate is known as the frequency and is measured in Hertz (Hz, not to be confused with the car rental company), which is the number of peaks (of sound waves) per second. Heinrich Hertz studied for his Ph.D under Herman von Helmholtz, who was very important in determining how we perceive the world in vision (amongst many other things). Hertz went on to discover electromagnetic radiation in the late 1800s; thus the unit of frequency is named in his honour. Slow vibrations generate low frequency sound waves and are perceived as having a low pitch whereas high frequency sound waves are caused by fast vibrations and have a high pitch. If you bang a couple of different forks off the table you'll find that the pitch is different from each fork because the different shapes will vibrate air molecules at different rates.

Both the frequency and amplitude of sound can change for the listener if the object emitting the sound is moving. We have all heard how a siren in an emergency vehicle changes as it gets closer to us and then passes us by. This is called the Doppler effect, named after Christian Doppler, an Austrian physicist based in Prague in 1842. The basic principle is that when a siren is coming towards you, you hear a higher pitch as the frequency is higher than usual because the vehicle is catching up with the sound waves it is emitting to you, the listener. You hear the true pitch only when the vehicle is right beside you; once it has passed the vehicle is moving away from the sound waves it is emitting towards you and so the frequency is lower than usual, making the siren lower in pitch. The amplitude (and therefore loudness) increases as the siren comes towards you as the energy of the sound wave increases as it gets closer to the listener and decreases as it moves away.

You can also think about sound waves in terms of wavelength just as we do with light as this is simply the distance between peaks of sound waves. As the frequency and therefore pitch gets lower, the wavelength increases; as the frequency gets higher, the wavelength decreases. However, sound is always conventionally talked about with respect to frequency, unlike light which is always related to wavelength. Now you know how they are related but remember, this works only for waves which travel at constant speeds. In normal conditions such as air, sound travels at a constant 343 m/s (or 767 mph; that's how fast the Concorde had to fly to break the sound barrier) whereas light travels through the air at a much faster 299,792,458 m/s thus explaining why we perceive lightning before thunder although they happen at exactly the same time in the atmosphere. The time difference between the lightning and the thunder clap can be taken as an indicator as to how far the storm is away from the observer with 5 seconds roughly equalling one mile or 1.6 km.

As with vision, humans can't hear the full range of auditory frequencies out there. We can hear between 20 and 20,000 Hz but frogs and birds have the smallest range. Dogs have a wide range which is why you can use whistles that we can't hear to call your dog back. These whistles are in the ultrasound range, which is above the 20,000 Hz frequency we can typically hear. Ultrasound is also important in medical diagnostics as we can bounce high frequency sound safely off the organs of the body and we can reconstruct the reflected waves into a picture of what the organs look like. It is most spectacular when it is used to look at human foetuses in utero but it has lots of other applications too. The technology was first developed in the 1950s by Ian Donald and his team in Glasgow's Western Infirmary and nowadays across the city in the Royal Infirmary, Angus MacLean and his colleagues are pioneering the use of ultrasound to speed up healing in fractures. Elsewhere in the animal kingdom, ultrasound explains how bats can fly around so safely at night. Called echolocation, bats emit high frequency sounds of up to 200,000 Hz up to 30 times a second in all directions and the way the sound waves bounce off the environment give the bat a "view" of what is around it. Indeed, certain people (only some of whom are blind) are just as skilled as bats at using echolocation to identify the layout of their surroundings; however they merely emit sounds in our normal frequency range. Anopthalmics or people who were born without eyes, some of whom are incredibly adept at echolocation, may be helped by the fact that much of their visual cortex is taken up by hearing functions. Holly Bridge and Alan Cowey at Oxford University used a specialized form of MRI called fractional anisotropy to show that sub-cortical and cortical re-organization takes place in such subjects. Another band of sound is infrasound which categorizes frequencies below 20Hz. It can travel long distances and even get around obstacles and is particularly useful for monitoring earthquakes but it also has a role in examining heart function in humans.

Most sounds are a mixture of different frequencies – the particular mixture determines the sound's complexity. Language and music differ from other auditory inputs, because they convey meaning and as a result, our auditory system is better at processing speech and music when compared to other sounds in our brain. Our auditory attention also allows our auditory system to "tune in" to certain frequencies. We all have experienced this; if you are in a busy place and you hear your name, your attention is immediately diverted to the direction that conversation came from. This is called "the cocktail party effect" but it is not restricted to cocktail parties (nice as they are); it can happen anywhere with background noise. So how does our auditory system pick up sound waves and translate them into neural signals our brain can understand?

The ear structure itself comes in many shapes and sizes but the key components are generally the same (see Figure 5.2). The pinna collects and amplifies the sound waves and funnels them down the external ear canal; both the pinna and external ear canal comprise the outer ear. Theoretically, the bigger your pinna, the better your hearing but the effect of this is miniscule really in the normal variations that we see amongst people, unless of course you have ears like a hare and you have lovely furry sticky up ears that can move in different directions. As a human, you'd look a bit funny, people may even stare, but what would you care? Your hearing would be so much better. I digress. Even at this stage, sound waves that have a frequency of about 3000 Hz, which is the general frequency of human speech, are selectively amplified. Within the external ear canal are cerumen glands whose function is to produce ear wax.

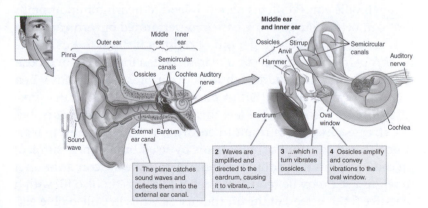

**Figure 5.2** The structure of the ear and the pathway of sound waves from the movement of air molecules captured by the pinna all the way to the cochlea. From *An Introduction to Brain and Behavior*, Third Edition by Bryan Kolb and Ian Q. Whishaw © 2011 by Worth Publishers. Used with permission.

This sticky substance protects the ear canal lining, repels water and traps any dust or dirt before it gets to the business end of the ear and it also has anti-bacterial properties. The production of too much ear wax following recurrent ear infections for example will lead to hearing loss as the sound waves cannot pass through the wax. Trapped wax often occurs because of people sticking cotton buds in their ear to clean them thus pushing the wax further down the canal from which it cannot escape. Needless to say, this is not medically advised. Ordinarily the ear wax dries up and falls out as waxy flakes we don't even notice. Our pillows are probably full of the stuff. Nice.

Having passed through the ear canal, the sound waves now hit the tympanic membrane and as this name suggests, it is also known as the eardrum. I don't use the term "hit" lightly; this membrane acts just like a drum and just as a drumstick hits the skin of a drum, the sound waves hit the tympanic membrane which vibrates and the rate of vibration depends on the frequency of the sound wave. The eardrum vibration sets up a vibration in the ossicles which are three tiny bones called the hammer, which is attached to the eardrum, the anvil and the stirrup (also known as the stapes). These names may lead you to think that some horse obsessed anatomist named these bones but actually their monikers are much more phlegmatic. They simply look like a hammer, anvil and stirrup. The eardrum and ossicles make up the structures of the middle ear. Problems here can lead to hearing impairments that can be profound in the case of a perforated or torn eardrum; how much sound do you get out of a drum if the skin has a hole in it? A perforation can occur due to a sudden loud noise or a bash to the ear or even a sudden change in air pressure such as when you a landing or taking off in an aeroplane. Usually, the pressure stabilizes itself and we feel this as a popping in our ears, but in extreme cases it can result in eardrum tension leading to tear. A perforated eardrum usually heals by itself but a small surgical procedure to insert a scaffold so that the membrane can grow on it to repair itself may be required. The middle ear can also fill with a glue-like fluid instead of the air that usually fills it. Called glue ear, imaginatively enough, it means that the ossicles can't move as well thus not transmitting the sound well from the eardrum to the next step. This results in dulled hearing and its treatment varies from doing nothing as the fluid often drains away by itself to having an operation to insert a drain from the middle ear through the eardrum so that the fluid can exit the ear and the middle ear can fill with air again. The insertion of these drains, or grommets, is a common procedure in children as the drain falls out as the eardrum grows. Glue ear happens most in children but it can occur in adults following a cold or ear infection.

The banging of the hammer on the anvil, and the anvil on the stirrup amplify the wave and the banging of the stirrup on the oval window, a membranous porthole to the cochlea, transmits it to the inner structures of the cochlea in the inner ear. This is where the mechanical sound waves get transduced into action potentials. The cochlea itself looks like a snail shell and has a bony casing but inside the cochlea is hollow and is filled with lymphatic fluid. The banging of the stirrup on the oval window moves the cochlear fluid but the pressure of the fluid doesn't change as another membranous window in the cochlea called the round window bulges outwards to compensate. This way, the cochlea doesn't burst with excess pressure. Floating in the lymphatic fluid is the thin basilar membrane, and the flowing of the fluid over this membrane is the business end of sound transduction.

The basilar membrane has hair cells attached to it on the inside and the outside surface (see Figure 5.3). Above the basilar membrane is another membrane called the tectorial membrane. The tips of the hair cells have little filaments called cilia and those on the outer hair cells are embedded in the tectorial membrane. This is important as a further tuning in mechanism of the ear as the outer hair cells contract and relax on instructions from the brainstem thus changing the stiffness of the tectorial membrane. The cilia on the inner hair cells are only loosely connected to the tectorial membrane and it is these inner hair cells that transduce the sound waves into nerve impulses. Waves travel through the lymphatic fluid in the cochlea in response to the banging of the stirrup on the oval window and this causes the basilar and tectorial membranes to bend. The bending stimulates the cilia at the tips of the inner hair cells, which opens mechanically gated ion channels allowing an influx of positive ions. The resultant change in membrane potential brings about changes in the amount of neurotransmitter released to the next step, which is the auditory

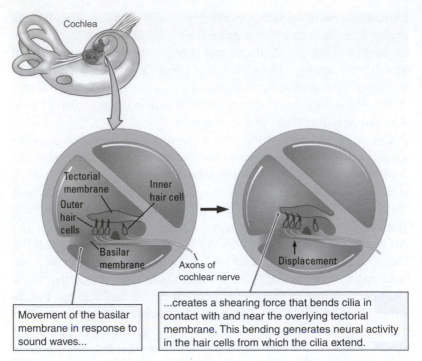

**Figure 5.3** A cross-section of the cochlea. Movement of the basilar membrane according to a particular frequency of sound waves results in bending of the cilia and the release of neurotransmitter from the inner hair cells leading to action potentials. From *An Introduction to Brain and Behavior*, Third Edition by Bryan Kolb and Ian Q. Whishaw © 2011 by Worth Publishers. Used with permission.

nerve, which carries the signal to the brain. If the hair cells are bent in one direction, depolarization results whereas bending in the opposite direction results in hyperpolarization.

Loss of either the outer or the inner hair cells leads to profound hearing loss, but here is one of the really cool things about the auditory system. Different places along the length of the basilar membrane are important for different frequencies. If you uncoil the cochlea until it is flat out, you will be left with a basilar membrane which is narrow and thick up at the base or the start of the membrane, near the oval window and is wide and thin at the apex. Sound waves of high frequencies (up to 20,000 Hz) lead to a peak bending of the basilar membrane at the base, medium frequencies bend the membrane along the middle of the membrane, with low frequencies (around 100 Hz) causing maximal bending at the apex. So, it is possible to damage hair cells at some point along the length of the basilar membrane leading to hearing loss for that particular frequency, a permanent happenstance as these cells do not re-grow. Overuse of one particular part of the basilar membrane due to the input of noise of a particular frequency can lead to damage to those hair cells and hearing loss. This happens a lot in people who work with machines and so ear plugs and defenders are very important to preserve full hearing function. Damage to outer hair cells means that listeners find it hard to filter out background noise and so may find it hard to hear conversation in a busy restaurant for example. Damage to inner hair cells leads to the inability to hear anything at that frequency as the signal cannot be sent to the auditory nerve and on to the brain. If you are unlucky enough to lose the ability to decode the frequency of your partner's voice for example, you will find them harder to hear but you could hear others who speak with other frequencies perfectly well. This is a constant source of consternation in some relationships with the hearing loss sufferers being accused of selective hearing. Whilst the hearing loss is selective to a particular frequency, it is often not of the listener's choice ... of course, sometimes it is!

So, what can we do to help people with hearing loss? Well, the obvious way is to fit them with a hearing aid of which there are many different types, some worn behind the ear with a component in the ear and some are worn entirely in the ear. These aids selectively amplify the frequencies of sound relating to speech. Other hearing aids combat conductive hearing loss which is when the ossicles do not work properly. In this case a bone-anchored hearing aid is surgically implanted and works on the principle that the skull is used to transmit the sound to the inner ear. The skull bone is actually very good at transmitting sound. Even if you stick your fingers in your ears, you will still be able to hear certain sounds through the skull bone behind your ear. Press the ear plug of your MP3 player to that bone and stick your finger in that ear ... you'll be able to hear the music (maybe not as clearly but good enough). Now try it with the ear plug in your teeth, or on your cheekbone or any other place that takes your fancy ... is it just as good? Best do this in private methinks. Some hearing aids contain a telecoil, or a T function, that allows the pickup of electromagnetic signals straight from a telephone or a PA system and so the sound appears less distorted with less background noise. The hearing of profoundly deaf people, i.e. people for example who were born without hair cells or malformed inner or middle ear structures, can be vastly improved by cochlear implants which directly stimulate areas of the basilar membrane based on the sound waves that are picked up by a microphone linked to a speech-processing computer worn behind the ear. However, as we will see in Chapter 7, children who are diagnosed with deafness early in life would have to be fitted with one of these "bionic ears" early in life in order to ensure correct development of the auditory and language systems.

Amplitude or loudness is denoted by the frequency of action potentials (remember, action potentials are all or nothing events so the only way of signifying strength of stimulus is by upping or decreasing the number of action potentials). The inner hair cells in the cochlea first connect to bipolar cells which send their axons via the auditory nerve to regions of the brainstem. These signals are then relayed to the midbrain structure of the inferior colliculus (remember the role of the superior colliculus in vision?) and on to the medial geniculate nucleus (MGN) in the thalamus (visual input goes to the lateral geniculate nucleus) and onto the cerebral cortex. Although signals from one ear are processed in both hemispheres, the opposite hemisphere receives preferential input; however input from both ears must be mixed in order to form the perception of one sound. In fact, this integration of sound is the central tenet of how we localize where a sound comes from. Sounds that originate in the left side of the body reach the left ear before the right ear. These differences are not interpreted as being two different sounds but are perceived as a single sound coming from one location. These differences are detected by neurons in the brainstem and the inferior colliculus. Detecting the location of sound is not just important for humans but also animals that hunt at night such as owls.

The MGN divides the auditory input into two pathways, a ventral pathway and a dorsal pathway. Just as in vision, the ventral stream seems to be involved in the identification of sound whereas the dorsal stream is involved in determining how we react to that sound. There is a similar dissociation in where these streams go in the cerebral cortex with the ventral regions of the MGN projecting to the primary auditory cortex (A1) in the temporal lobe and the dorsal regions projecting to a region adjacent to A1 and onto posterior parietal regions important for coordinating your reaction to the sound, be it turning your head or throwing an arm out to whack your alarm clock. We determine what a sound is via the input to A1 in Heschl's gyrus, which is gyrus inside the lateral fissure in between the temporal and frontal lobes. You can only see Heschl's gyrus, so named after the Austrian anatomist who lived in the 1800s, by using a retractor to pull back the lateral fissure. The neurons here are arranged in a tonotopic map so that neurons that respond to high frequency tones are grouped together and neurons that respond to low frequencies are grouped together. The anterior end of A1 corresponds to the low frequencies that the apex of the cochlea responds to whereas the input from the high frequencies that activate the base of the cochlea go to the posterior end of A1.

Most sounds that we hear in real life are complex mixtures of frequencies and so it makes sense that we have more sophisticated and specialized neural circuitry for processing speech and music. In fact, we have known since the late nineteenth century that an area of the left posterior superior temporal gyrus was particularly important for understanding speech (see Figure 5.4). Carl Wernicke was a German neurologist and psychiatrist who worked with patients with different forms of speech difficulties. He found

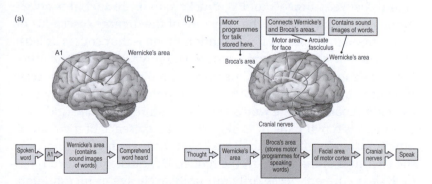

**Figure 5.4** The communication between Broca's and Wernicke's area brings about good comprehension and speech production. From *An Introduction to Brain and Behavior*, Third Edition by Bryan Kolb and Ian Q. Whishaw © 2011 by Worth Publishers. Used with permission.

that damage to this region of the cortex led to a distinct lack of understanding of language and so sufferer's speech production was impaired. The speech rhythm seemed fluid enough but was made up of jumbled up words; the patients could not hear that they were not making any sense as they didn't understand what they were saying. This disorder has since been called Wernicke's aphasia and this area of the superior temporal gyrus in the left hemisphere is called Wernicke's area. Another node in the brain important for language is the area that is important for language production. Also in the left hemisphere, this area is located in the frontal lobe in an area just anterior to the central sulcus down near the lateral fissure.

It was discovered by Paul Broca, a French physician, who had a patient nicknamed "Tan" as this was all he could say even though he seemed to have accurate comprehension. When Broca examined his brain post-mortem, he found damage to the inferior frontal gyrus and attributed the production of fluid speech to this area which is called Broca's area, damage to which causes Broca's aphasia (see Figure 5.4). It wasn't long before Wernicke, Broca and other neuroscientists of the day were putting 2 and 2 together and coming up with four. We need these two areas to talk to each other in order to bring about proper language function (both spoken and written); thus hearing and speaking are inexorably linked. It turns out that these areas are anatomically and functionally linked via the arcuate fasciculus, a tract of nerve fibres that carry signals between Broca's and Wernicke's areas. In fact, it is developmental problems with the structure of the arcuate fasciculus or problems with the flow of information along it that causes at least one form of dyslexia, the one dubbed cognitive dyslexia. The other form is visual dyslexia and has to do with a deficit in the processing of the magnocellular pathway in vision. Sufferers from visual dyslexia report that the words "dance around" the page and clarity of text is a real issue. It is helped by the presence of a yellow or blue transparent film being placed over the text and this improves the clearness of the words to the reader. Of course, these two types of dyslexia are not necessarily mutually exclusive as investigators in the field such as John Stein from Oxford University point out. If a child is born with a visual system which results in visual dyslexia, the development of the connections between Broca's and

Wernicke's area may be deficient leading to cognitive dyslexia. Understanding the mechanism of the relationship between these two phenomena could explain why seemingly strange solutions such as different colour filters, closing one eye or taking Omega 3 fish oils may help ameliorate symptoms in some dyslexic children allowing for normal development of the links between the visual and auditory systems.

The actual production of language is carried out via an area adjacent to Broca's area where the motor plans for words are stored. We can test this in various ways but it was first examined by the American neurosurgeon Wilder Penfield and his colleague Herbert Jasper in the 1950s. Penfield and Jasper used electrical stimulation of the brain to localize the area of the brain responsible for their patient's epilepsy so that the area could be destroyed or removed. It also allowed them to check what functions would be lost by the area's removal, meaning they could be more precise and achieve a better functional outcome for the patient. Whilst they were there with a brain wide open on the operating table, they took the opportunity to electrically stimulate regions of the motor and sensory cortex along with other areas thought to be involved in language in order to localize functions in the brain. Stimulation of three different regions of the inferior frontal cortex relating to speech production (including vocalization movement regions) can disrupt fluent speech from causing slurring or confusion of words through having difficulty finding the right word all the way up to disrupting speech entirely, a happenstance they called speech arrest. Stimulation of the auditory cortex led to patients hearing sounds such as a buzzing noise or a doorbell. Nowadays we don't have to crack a skull open to localize these functions. We can see regional involvement using imaging techniques and we can investigate the necessity of these regions for language using TMS. Great fun in the lab on a Friday afternoon.

As you will have noticed, I have just talked about areas of the left hemisphere and their importance to language. In fact, in most people, hearing and language function is localized to the left. It is a myth that left-handers are the opposite in their asymmetry with their hearing and language function localized to the right hemisphere. About 70% of lefties' brains are organized the same as the righties. Fifteen per cent have bilateral representation of

speech and only the remaining 15% have the opposite organization to righties. So, the urban myth is only 15% correct. In fact,
language initially develops in both hemispheres as we have seen;
in most people it shifts by the age of five to the left hemisphere.
A disturbance to this lateralization of function may underlie the
problems faced by people with stutters. When reading aloud, people with a stutter show different patterns of activity in imaging
experiments to non-stutterers. These experiments suggest that stuttering may be due to competition for dominance between the left
and right hemispheres. It seems that neither side can decide which
is in control and so both try to produce words with generally poor
effect. However, it has also been shown that there are less functional connections between Broca's area and the motor planning
and execution areas for speech in the left frontal lobe in stutter-
ers. This latter point explains why many people whose speech is
profoundly impaired by stuttering can sing fluently and also why
people undergoing speech arrest with TMS over the left frontal cortex can sing the words they previously couldn't say. Could it be
therefore that the right hemisphere has a role in the processing of
music?

Neuropsychology has provided the answer. Maurice Ravel was
a composer in the impressionist movement who is probably best
known for his 1928 orchestral piece "Boléro" which, incidentally,
he didn't rate calling it "a piece for orchestra without music"!
However, in 1932, Ravel got knocked down by a taxi and most
probably suffered brain damage to his left hemisphere as a consequence. He became aphasic yet his ability to recognize melodies
remained intact. Even though he could still compose music, he
was unable to transpose it to paper as this required the lesioned
part of his brain. The involvement of the right hemisphere in the
processing of music is therefore long established. But does it have
any role in language? We now know through imaging techniques
that the right hemisphere has rather rudimentary language ability
with respect to comprehension and production, but it does make a
contribution to understanding the emotional content in language,
which can also be described as the musicality of our voices. This is
called prosody and is very important in puppetry when it is sometimes possible, knowing the context of a situation, to decode the
non-word language of a character. Think of The Clangers or Sweep

from Sooty and Sweep fame. Oftentimes the "actors" producing the sound for the characters work to a script and once you become attuned to the musicality of their voice and given a context, you can easily work out what they are saying. I'm sure I could now have a full scale conversation with Sweep because I have done so much ironing whilst watching his escapades on DVD. There is an episode of The Clangers called "The Iron Chicken" in which a doorway is supposed to roll back, but it gets stuck. The Clanger, climbing out of its hole says "doo, do do. Do d-d-doo do do-do" in Clanger-speak, which, it is well known in cartoon circles, stands for "oh sod it. The bloody door's stuck again". The Clanger then proceeds to kick the door and it continues to open. It's easy to spot once you know. Prosody is also very important in voice over work for movie trailers as the emotion must drip from the narrative (Don't believe me? You Tube the "Love in the Time of Cholera" trailer!). Sometimes, the words are incongruent with the prosody, for example if somebody says "I'm so happy" in a mournful tone. Do you believe the words or the emotional content? We now know that the emotional content is processed in the area analogous to Wernicke's area in the superior temporal gyrus but in the right hemisphere and so we need both the left and right hemisphere to properly and fully process all aspects of language.

## Feeling curious?

*Oxford Handbook of Auditory Science: The Ear, The Auditory Brain, Hearing.* Edited by David Moore, Paul Fuchs, Alan Palmer, Adrian Rees & Christopher Plack 2010; Oxford University Press. *An all-encompassing and study-based read with excellent coverage across three volumes.*

Gregory Hickok & David Poeppel (2007) Opinion: "The Cortical Organization of Speech Processing". *Nature Reviews Neuroscience* 8: 393–402 doi:10.1038/nrn2113. *A history of research into language processing and production in the brain.*

*A video of a patient with Wernike's aphasia* from the University of Wisconsin, Madison Physiology Department. http://www.youtube.com/watch?v=aVhYN7NTIKU

*A video of a patient with Broca's aphasia* from the University of Wisconsin, Madison Physiology Department. http://www.youtube.com/watch?v=f2IiMEbMnPM

Sophie K. Scott, Ingrid S. Johnsrude (2003) "The Neuroanatomical and Functional Organization of Speech Perception". *Trends in Neurosciences*, 26: 100–107. *This review article traces what functional imaging tells us about how speech is processed in the brain.*

CHAPTER **6** **Moving on**

The way we move around the world seems to be quite a subconscious process. Once we learn how to walk or bring a fork up to our mouths, we don't really have to think about how to do it every time. But if we are doing something new for the first time, we are all fingers and thumbs, be it playing darts or dancing the tango, or both at the same time. Perhaps that's a bad idea. So, the involvement of different regions of our brain in movements depend on whether the task is novel or not but it is not just well-defined movement regions such as premotor cortex, motor cortex, brainstem, cerebellum and basal ganglia that are involved. Sensory information such as touch, muscle position and vision are also required to guide our movements as well as our vestibular system for balance.

Balance cannot be over-rated as to its value in fluid motion. The vestibular system is so called because the organ that governs our sense of balance is in the vestibulum in the inner ear and is called the vestibular organ. It consists of three fluid-filled semicircular canals and also the utricle and saccule which together are called the otolith organs, positioned adjacent to the cochlea (see Figure 6.1). Their function is to tell us where our body is with respect to gravity and also to detect changes in the direction and speed of head movements. To help achieve this, the semicircular canals are positioned in three different planes to reflect the directions in which we move about, side to side, up and down, and backwards and forwards. They are filled with endolymph and lined with hair cells so that when the head moves, the endolymph in whichever semi-circular canal relative to the plane in which we moved is disturbed thus bending the cilia on the ends of the hair cells.

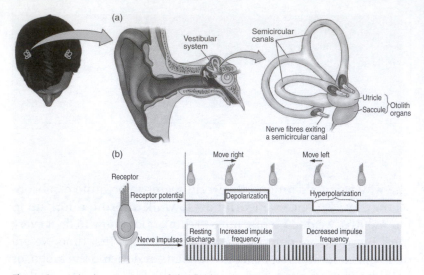

**Figure 6.1** It is the movement of the fluid in the semi-circular canals that allows our brain to detect what direction we are pointing in at any given time. From *An Introduction to Brain and Behavior*, Third Edition by Bryan Kolb and Ian Q. Whishaw © 2011 by Worth Publishers. Used with permission.

As with audition, the bending of the cilia is translated into receptor potentials in the hair cells with bending in one direction causing an increase in activity and bending in the other direction decreasing activity. The semicircular canals are connected at their ends on the utricle (as it looks like a little uterus) and underneath the utricle lies the saccule (little sac). These otolith organs are a little bit different in their action; they also contain hair cells with cilia tips but they are embedded in a gelatine-like substance on top of which lie tiny granules of calcium carbonate called otoconia. Whereas the semicircular canals detect the rotation and the acceleration of the turning of the head in any direction, the utricle and saccule's job is to respond to tilt angle and vertical and horizontal acceleration and so are active when we are static also. When the head is tilted backwards for example, the otoliths are pulled back by gravity and they in turn pull on the gelatine below thus activating the cilia.

The resultant action potentials from both the semicircular canals and otolith organs are carried via the vestibular nerve to the brainstem, cerebellum, thalamus, eye muscles and cerebral cortex.

The variety of places that the information about the head's (and therefore body's) position in space gives an indication of how important it is for many functions. In fact, one of the most important is that of eye-movements as it is very important to keep a stable visual image even though you may be jumping around like a looney tune. The vestibulo-ocular reflex (VOR) acts via the brainstem on the six extra-ocular muscles that move the eyes; when the VOR senses a rotation in the head, it tells the eyes to make compensatory movements in the opposite direction so that we don't see a blurry image. The same principle works for our skeletal muscles. If our body leans one way, our compensatory mechanisms make sure that we don't overbalance by activating muscles in the other side of the body via the activity of the vestibular system and cerebellar and cortical motor systems.

In fact, compensatory movements based on visual information can actually bypass our vestibular system. In the early 1970s David Lee from the University of Edinburgh came up with an idea for a swinging room; the walls and ceiling move independently of the floor on which you are standing. If the room is swung away from you, the visual impact of this over-rides your vestibular knowledge that you didn't move and the result is that you sway forward to correct the imbalance. For sure, there is an aspect of this that is related to the fact that we really don't expect rooms to move around us. But the mismatch between what we can see and what our vestibular system is telling us is thought to underlie motion sickness. So, if we are bumping around in an airplane for example because of turbulence, our vestibular system will be screaming signals about our body position to our brain. 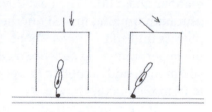 However, our eyes will be getting very stable images as everything inside the plane is strapped in and not moving with respect to everything else. This is called the sensory conflict theory; the visual information is not backing up what the vestibular system is saying and is prevalent in cars, boats and any other situation in which our bodies are being moved for us by a vehicle for example. Symptoms include dizziness and nausea possibly induced by changeable activation of the autonomic nervous system that controls our body organs; in this case, our gastrointestinal system is particularly affected. However, this can't be the entire story as blind people also experience motion sickness and we experience it even when our eyes are shut tightly. The inner ear is vital however as without the vestibular organs, motion sickness cannot develop.

Vertigo is caused by the abnormal distribution of otoliths embedded in the gelatine of the utricle and saccule. In this case, head tilts can lead to disorientating misperceptions of where the head is and how much it has moved thus leading to unsteadiness. One of the treatments for vertigo is medicine to control the nausea but another treatment which tries to right the cause of vertigo is "particle repositioning manoeuvres", which involves a series of abrupt changes in body and head position and is aimed at dislodging the displaced otoliths from their abnormal locations to more correct areas of the utricle or saccule. These kinds of movement are common to something most of us have done for fun, like riding roller coasters. In fact, temporary bouts of vertigo and/or motion sickness can be induced by roller coasters; next time you go to a theme park, check out how many people can walk in a straight line when they disembark from a fast ride. This was never more evident to me than after a particularly crazy coaster I once rode. Every time I opened my eyes (about three times) I was upside down; it was extremely fast and threw you every which way with lots of rotations and loop the loops. I threw up in every restroom I passed for at least an hour and a half. The next day, as it happens, I was doing some astronaut training to feed another passion of mine which is astrophysics and space travel. As part of the training we were offered the opportunity to experience a gyroscope, an apparatus that spins you around and around in lots of different planes. Astronauts use it to train their bodies how to cope with zero or minimal gravity, as the vestibular organs usually work with gravity to provide information to the brain. They have a competition between the trainee astronauts as to how long they can stay on the gyro and how many

maths problems they can solve while doing it. It was explained to us that if we had problems with our vestibular system, we should not ride it but then, fate intervened. The trainers explained that the gyro shouldn't induce motion sickness as because it was moving us in every direction, the fluid in our semi-circular canals and the position of the otoliths would be relatively stable. My inner physiologist didn't believe this however; so despite my exploits the day before, I decided to try it out for myself to test my hypothesis. I lasted less than 45 seconds on the instrument of torture, made all the more uncomfortable by the fact that when you scream STOP, it takes another 45 seconds for the gyro to actually stop. That was another restroom I became very familiar with. I was beginning to think a day wouldn't go by on that trip without me throwing up. Now, I'll concede, there may be a reason for the training, as it may take time for the vestibular system to get used to such movements. Irrespective of this, current astronauts on the International Space Station intermittently report space sickness, which is just like our more earthly motion sickness in its effects. Oooh, vomit in zero gravity...how very attractive. But the moral of this story is thus: don't believe everything rocket scientists tell you. They don't know everything. Neuroscientists do.

There also seems to be an aspect of personal control here. The driver of the car in which all of the passengers are groaning and begging for a throwing up party is rarely affected. In contrast, pilots sometimes experience motion sickness as forward acceleration and upward head tilt will lead to the same response from the otolith organs making pilots think they are going into a steep climb when they are in situations of poor visibility. The pilot then goes into a compensatory dive, which may of course be disastrous. Nowadays though, airplanes are so automated that there are warning signals for everything save for when the pilot needs a pee and so the incidence of this false-climb illusions is thankfully rare.

So, now that we know how important the vestibular system is to our movements, let's think about how we actually move. Say for example I wanted to pick up this mug that I have beside my laptop (see Figure 6.2). The idea occurs to me via activity in my prefrontal cortex; I fancy a drink; there is a beverage in my mug that will do nicely thanks. I then need to clap eyes onto the mug, get some visual information as to where it is. Frontal lobe areas such

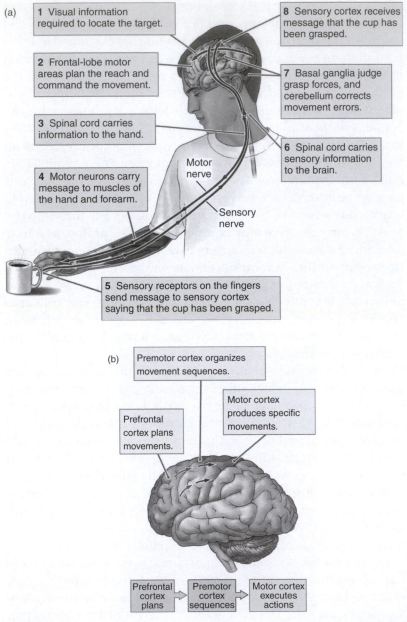

(a)

**1** Visual information required to locate the target.

**8** Sensory cortex receives message that the cup has been grasped.

**2** Frontal-lobe motor areas plan the reach and command the movement.

**7** Basal ganglia judge grasp forces, and cerebellum corrects movement errors.

**3** Spinal cord carries information to the hand.

**6** Spinal cord carries sensory information to the brain.

Motor nerve

**4** Motor neurons carry message to muscles of the hand and forearm.

Sensory nerve

**5** Sensory receptors on the fingers send message to sensory cortex saying that the cup has been grasped.

(b)

Premotor cortex organizes movement sequences.

Motor cortex produces specific movements.

Prefrontal cortex plans movements.

Prefrontal cortex plans → Premotor cortex sequences → Motor cortex executes actions

**Figure 6.2** What happens when you want to pick up a mug. The prefrontal cortex decides you'd like a drink, the premotor cortex organizes the movement sequence required to bring that about, then the motor cortex sends signals down the spine to the muscles. Equally important is the sensory information that comes back up from the hand. From *An Introduction to Brain and Behavior*, Third Edition by Bryan Kolb and Ian Q. Whishaw © 2011 by Worth Publishers. Used with permission.

as the supplementary motor area and pre-motor area then make a plan as to all of the things that need to happen in order for me to be able to lift that mug. The primary motor cortex (in the pre-central sulcus) then sends signals to the required muscles via the spinal cord in the right order for me to bring that about. I reach for the mug and the sensory receptors in my fingers send a signal to my somatosensory cortex (in the postcentral sulcus) via the spinal cord saying that the mug has been touched. Information is also fed back to the basal ganglia to judge the grasp force that is required (depending on the weight of the mug) and the cerebellum, which corrects movement errors. Seems pretty simple huh? Well, in essence, it is. But its beauty also lies in its subtlety.

Step by step, the simplicity of the system shines through. We decide we want to do something, we do it, the action feeds back to tell us whether we did it right or not. But, our movements are really fast and so all of them can't require this serial processing that is reliant on feedback. In 1951, Karl Lashley from Harvard University proposed a theory that holds to this day: our fluid movements are brought about by sets of instructions carried out by the brain called motor sequences and as one sequence is being executed, the next is being prepared. So we can think about movement production in our brain as being a series of movement sequences that are prepared and executed. This explains why when you are throwing a punch for example (or even something less violent), after a particular point in time, you can't stop the movement, because the sequence has already been executed. In the lab, we test this using perturbation experiments. We get our participants to point to one light in a row and then at the very last second, close to or just after the onset of movement, we change the light they have to point to. Depending on when we change the light, people either can't adjust their movement, or do so subconsciously and we can interfere with this at various stages by using TMS over different nodes of the movement network in the brain.

The prefrontal cortex (PFC) is mainly involved in our higher "thinking" and conscious functions and is very important in our voluntary actions. The more learned a movement becomes however, PFC is less involved and that makes sense as the more automatic a movement becomes, the less we have to think about it. So, the PFC plans the movement but if you have damage to this region of the brain, you can simply react to stimuli, but there is little discrimination about what you should react to, or not as the case may be. PFC therefore also evaluates what the best plan of action would be. This information is then sent to the supplementary motor (SMA) and premotor (PMA) areas. The SMA is located towards the back (posterior) of the frontal lobe but anterior to the pre-central sulcus. It also extends to the medial surface and is superior to the PMA, which lies underneath. The difference between the two areas lies in the fact that SMA is much more active in the initiation of movement sequences under voluntary control (damage here results in patients being unable to initiate voluntary movements); and PMA is more active when the motor sequences are guided by external stimuli, so like dodging a ball for example. Lesions to the PMA result in an inability to make complex movements such as retrieving an object with two hands. These two areas (often lumped together under the term "pre-motor cortex") are more active however when a movement is novel as opposed to learned. In essence, they put the plan coming from PFC into action by specifying the types of movement that are necessary for the planned action. Some of the most specialized movement sequences we make are those involved in speech, and this function also has dedicated premotor regions. Broca's area in the frontal lobe is the premotor area for speech that contains the motor programs for speaking words but there is also a supplementary speech area for vocal initiation.

The pre-motor cortex also shows activity via mirror neurons that become active when you are just looking at somebody carrying out an action. First discovered in the 1980s, Giacomo Rizzolatti and colleagues at the University of Parma found that neurons in the premotor cortex of monkeys responded when monkeys were looking at other monkeys carrying out intentional acts. Later, neuroscientists like Marco Iacoboni at UCLA and Vilayanur Ramachandran from UC San Diego used fMRI to show that the system can also be found in humans and believed that the discovery of mirror neurons heralded The Next Big Thing in neuroscience. It's not hard to see why. Neurons that respond not just when we act ourselves but also when we see the actions of others could underlie how we learn to move about and how we should arrange our lips to produce sounds via imitation but also to learn what facial expressions go with what emotions...the beginnings of empathy. Mirror neurons have been purported to be part of the system by which you put yourself in other people's shoes, the reason why you wince when you see somebody fall off their bike. Indeed, some people feel this activation as actual pain, as if the movement had actually been carried out by them. Called synesthetic pain, and as with other forms of synesthesia it is most probably resultant from abnormal cross-talk between brain areas: in this case a mismatch of internal intention and sensory input. The argument that deficits in the mirror neuron system could underlie social affective disorders such as autism has rumbled on over the years and its role has never been fully accepted as being separate to the neural machinations that must take place for the correct visual perception of movements.

What is clear is that electrical activity is seen in the pre-motor cortex about 55ms before the primary motor cortex (M1) becomes active, consistent with the fact that the pre-motor areas send instructions to the part of M1 that will execute the motor plan; i.e. the face area for speech, the leg area to kick a ball etc. The neurons of M1 send signals to the muscles via the brainstem and spinal cord and is located in the pre-central gyrus just anterior to the central sulcus. Without M1 we could not execute skilled movements as the premotor cortex just organizes complex movements; it doesn't specify how they should be carried out. If a patient has a lesion to M1 then they will be unable to perform precise movements such as the pincer grip with the thumb and forefinger. Instead, they will have to rely on more generalized movements like the whole hand grip instead.

Just like the somatosensory cortex, M1 has a topographical organization with an area of the pre-central gyrus devoted to different areas of the body. Those that require more precise control have bigger areas and so the area devoted to the face (for speaking) or the fingers (for dexterity) is larger than the area devoted to the thigh for example. I like to play a game in my lab when I am looking at a subject's MRI scan to guess whether or not they are right or left handed (as if they are right handed the area of M1 devoted to the hand will be bigger in the left hemisphere and vice versa if they are left handed). I can also spot good piano players as often their M1 region for hands will be very well developed bilaterally. Equally, the representations of the fingering digits in cellists, violinists and guitarists of the left hand in the right hemisphere are larger than the corresponding representations in non-musicians. I digress. We have the primary motor cortex map because of the groundbreaking electrophysiological work of Wilder Penfield, who founded the Montreal Neurological Institute at McGill University in Canada. What made Penfield different from other neurosurgeons of his era (the 1950s) is that, along with his colleague, Herbert Jasper, he applied electrical currents to the exposed brains of patients who were undergoing neurosurgery to remove the locus of their epilepsy. We've seen in the previous chapter how valuable this technique is when it comes to sparing language functions. Called the Montreal technique, it became the bench-standard for surgeons and to this day, many patients are kept awake during neurosurgery to map the function of regions of cortex surrounding the damaged area to cut down on side effects and tell the surgeon what they must spare if at all possible.

Different views abound as to what exactly activity in the primary motor cortex commands our muscles to do. However it would seem that M1 as a whole not only tells which muscles to contract thereby controlling force and direction of movement but it also responds to the type of movement required. Much of this work has been done by eavesdropping on single or small numbers of neurons in the monkey M1. Such studies have found that even if you want to move only your little finger, much more M1 than just the bit for your little finger is activated. But it makes sense that other areas of the hand motor cortex are active in order to keep the other fingers still, and so a much more intuitive interpretation is that the little finger movement is caused by an increase in the little finger area's relative activity rates. Given this, it is surgically possible to implant multiple tiny microelectrodes into the M1 of a paralysed patient or amputee to record the neural firing that occurs when the patient thinks about moving part of the body. The electrical signals can be translated by computer software to move a cursor on a screen. The next step would be to hook up these electrical signals to a prosthetic arm that could work in response to the motor commands coming from the patient's brain. It was possible for Anakin Skywalker right? Of course, that's not to say everybody who gets a bionic limb turns into Darth Vader... There is a technological bottleneck to getting that far because as we are beginning to see, the brain's control of the body doesn't just come from one area and for complex movement reproduction we would need to take input from all of these regions together. Some simple bionics can utilize the severed nerve endings of an amputated limb for example, but in cases of more systemic motor neuron degeneration this is not possible and therefore we must resort to taking input from the brain. As science fictioney as it sounds, one way forward would be through an EEG-based brain–machine interface. Certainly, Kenji Kansaku's group in the National Centre for the Rehabilitation of Persons with Disabilities in Japan agrees and can already use such machines to guide participants around virtual environments. If you think this sounds like a movie about blue people with extraordinary pony tails then you'd be right. But this is just one example of the half step that exists between what we know about how the brain works, and what we can do with it. Movement is actually one of the easier functions to work with as it has clearly demonstrable effects.

As paralysis shows however, you can have all the activity you like in the motor cortex, but if you have no way of getting that signal to the muscles, you are scuppered. Axons from neurons in the primary motor cortex project directly, and indeed indirectly, to motor neurons in the spinal cord via the corticopinal tracts that track through the brainstem and down to the spinal cord. It is at the level of the brainstem where the neurons from the left hemisphere that control limbs and digits cross over to the right side of the body to join the lateral corticospinal tract. The rest of the neurons that control midline areas continue on down the ventral corticospinal tract (see Figure 6.3).

This representation is also preserved in the spinal cord with limbs and digit neurons being at the lateral extreme of the cord with the midline muscles being in the centre. Different parts of M1 project to different areas of the spinal cord with motor neurons in the cervical (neck) level sending its neurons out to the muscles of the hand and arm while those in the lumbar region control the foot and the leg. The motor cortex neurons exit the spinal cord through the ventral horn of the spine; remember, all of the sensory neurons follow a pathway through the dorsal horn of the spine.

One motor unit in the spinal cord can innervate many muscle fibres (via branching axon terminals) within a single muscle. A signal being sent from the brain to a muscle requiring a lot of

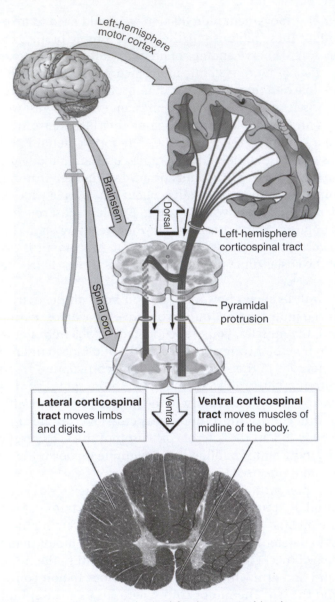

Left-hemisphere motor cortex

Brainstem

Spinal cord

Dorsal

Left-hemisphere corticospinal tract

Pyramidal protrusion

Ventral

**Lateral corticospinal tract** moves limbs and digits.

**Ventral corticospinal tract** moves muscles of midline of the body.

**Figure 6.3** The neurons that are destined for the arms and hands cross over to be carried in the most lateral part of the spinal cord. Neurons going to the midline structures are carried in the ventral corticospinal tract. From *An Introduction to Brain and Behavior*, Third Edition by Bryan Kolb and Ian Q. Whishaw © 2011 by Worth Publishers. Used with permission.

force will therefore "recruit" more muscle fibres. Motor neurons release the neurotransmitter acetylcholine where the neuron meets the muscle (imaginatively named the neuromuscular junction) which causes the muscle to contract through excitation-contraction coupling. The bones of it are thus: the action potential arriving at the neuromusclular junction causes an EPSP (an excitatory graded potential) in the post-synaptic (muscle) membrane which causes the release of calcium from the sarcoplasmic reticulum in the muscle which makes the filaments in the muscle slide pass each other, thus contracting the muscle. As we talked about in Chapter 2, there are many venoms that biting animals like snakes inject that interfere with this process, with the main aim being that prey cannot run away and will hang around for dinner. To be dinner, that is. Yes, dinner is a dangerous time of day, because you can also unwittingly poison yourself through badly stored or cooked food. The botulism (Clostridium Botulinum) toxin is a case in point. Its name stems from the Latin "botulus", which means sausage and is found in soil all over the world. This is not because this nasty little bacteria looks like a sausage under a microscope, even though it does; it is because one of the earliest known culprits of poisoning due to botulism was from a large blood sausage in Germany in 1793, which was shared by 13 people all of whom got sick and six of whom died. The botulism bacteria thrive in any oxygen-free environment (like that found in sausage or soup or stews for example) but its Achilles heel is that it can't survive heat. So, if you heat up your stew before you eat it and eat it piping hot, you'll be ok. But it's a clever, vicious little bug and can live in spore form to survive the heating. As soon as your soup has cooled a bit, those spores will begin to germinate back into being botulism again if the food is infected. Botulism poisoning presents with the symptoms of blurred vision, a "thick tongue", problems with swallowing, droopy eyelids and finally, respiratory failure. Each of these symptoms can be tracked back to botulism's ability to block the acetylcholine receptors at the neuromuscular junction thus bringing about skeletal muscle paralysis. It will also paralyse internal muscles such as that of the diaphragm, the big muscle in your chest that works as a bellows to make you breathe, thus leading to the respiratory failure. The fatality rate from botulism is now thankfully relatively small due to the invention of anti-toxin;

however, as it comes from horses, the cure can, in itself, have all sorts of side-effects. Without the anti-toxin, assisted breathing with a respirator for a few weeks should keep you alive long enough for the bacterial infection to abate. Up until the 1980s the mortality rate was 50%! This doesn't seem to have put people off getting themselves injected with pharmaceutical grade C. Bolutinum to paralyse the muscles of the face to lessen the appearance of wrinkles, enhancing youthful looks (and they may not be good, mind you). It does have therapeutic effects however in people with bladder control issues, muscle control (as occurs in dystonia) or even eyelid control problems.

Although the corticospinal tracts pass through the brainstem on their way to becoming the spinal cord, the brainstem is an important region in its own right for the production of movement. If we stimulate neurons here, we can induce species-specific behaviour such as pecking in a hen or grooming in a cat for example but stimulation can induce a whole set of movements depending on the circumstances. The brainstem also controls movements that are used in behaviours such as eating and drinking and the movements seen in sexual behaviour. Another behaviour the brainstem is important in is personal grooming. Think about your drying off routine after you get out of the shower or bath. It's always the same, be it a quick rub of your hair first and on down, but there is generally little variation. Even during the shower itself we tend to have the same routine. I know this because if I get interrupted during mine I get so mixed up (my brainstem automatic processes have been so rudely disrupted), I forget to wash the conditioner out of my hair only to realize what I have done from the slimy feeling on my head during my drying phase. For those of you who think in images, I humbly apologize; you didn't need one of me in the shower. Anyway, the brainstem is also important in organizing movement, particularly species-specific ones. In humans, damage here can lead to movement impairments whilst sparing cognitive and sensory abilities; however cognitive and sensory deficits can also be a consequence, perhaps because of disruption to the movement organization itself. For example, autism spectrum disorder can result from abnormally formed (or damage to) groups of neurons here hence the autistic person's need for well-defined routines as the brainstem is not working as well as usual to organize movements for them.

Feedback from the sensory receptors are almost as important for fluid movements as the movement signals themselves. Sometimes, this pathway can produce movement independent of the brain as in the spinal cord reflex that we talked about in Chapter 3. However, two brain regions, the basal ganglia and cerebellum, receive a copy of what movement should take place (from the pre-motor and motor cortex) and compare this with the movement that actually happened (via the sensory receptors). The basal ganglia represents a group of interconnected nuclei in the fore-brain, underneath the cerebral cortex (see Figure 6.4). It includes the caudate nucleus and the putamen (collectively known as the striatum), and the globus pallidus. Not strictly part of the basal ganglia but closely associated with it is the substantia nigra. It is collectively agreed that the basal ganglia is very involved in the calibration of movement force but the pathways by which it brings this about are complex and many theories abound; however it is widely accepted that there are excitatory and inhibitory pathways by which the nuclei can modulate force.

The connections between the areas of the basal ganglia are curious. The activation of the striatum has an inhibitory effect on the globus palladus. The neurons from the globus palladus that synapse on the thalamus release GABA, the main inhibitory

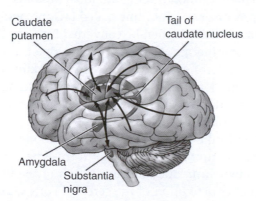

**Figure 6.4** The basal ganglia connects to the amygdala via the tail of the caudate nucleus and communicates with other regions such as the motor cortex and the substantia nigra in the midbrain. From *An Introduction to Brain and Behavior*, Third Edition by Bryan Kolb and Ian Q. Whishaw © 2011 by Worth Publishers. Used with permission.

neurotransmitter of the brain, and these are active all of the time. So, activation of the striatum inhibits the globus palladus which stops it from inhibiting the thalamus allowing the thalamus to talk to the premotor areas. In short, the basal ganglia allows a movement by stopping its inhibition. Take our lifting of the mug example. I own a mug (with a big chip in it) which looks much heavier than it is. When I first lifted it up in the shop, I applied the force related to how heavy it looked, as this information would have been fed into my basal ganglia along with other cortical information. When I actually lifted the mug, my somatosensory system fed back that it was quite light really and I had to adjust the force of my movement via the action of the basal ganglia. Not before I whacked it off the shelf above though. That is why I now own a chipped mug that is lighter than it looks.

The substantia nigra (so called because they look black under a microscope) in the midbrain also excites the striatum via its dopamine-releasing neurons; however these are the neurons that are killed in Parkinson's disease. The lack of input to the striatum results in decreased inhibition of the globus palladus in turn leading to over-inhibition of the thalamus and so decreased activation of the cerebral cortex. The symptomatic consequence of this is hypokinetic patterns of movements such as bradykinesia, or slowness of movement as well as akinesia, which is the inability to initiate movements, amongst other motor symptoms. The administration of a precursor of dopamine called L-Dopa, which can cross the blood-brain barrier to then be converted into dopamine by the remaining dopaminergic cells, brings some relief from symptoms but it doesn't work for everyone. Also, since Parkinson's disease is degenerative and dopamine cells in the substantia nigra continue to die; no amount of exogenous L-dopa will help if there are no cells for it to be converted by or work in.

On the other hand, damage to the basal ganglia can also result in hyperkinetic symptoms such as choriform-type movements like writhing and twitching due to disinhibition of the thalamus and the resultant over activation of the cerebral cortex. Such involuntary and exaggerated movements are present in patients suffering from Huntington's disease in which there is widespread atrophy of the basal ganglia. Abnormal activity of the right hemisphere basal ganglia is associated with Tourrette's syndrome, which was first described by French neurologist George Gilles de la Tourette in 1885. Symptoms include uncontrollable and involuntary tics, which can represent skeletal muscles movements or verbal utterances.

Both patients with hypo and hyperkinetic disorders suffer from cognitive deficits also either in memory or problem solving and often have affective disorders such as depression as well. This reinforces the idea that normal function of the basal ganglia are important in mood (not surprising given the input to the striatum from the limbic system areas such as the amygdala and also the role of dopamine in motivated behaviour) and higher cognitive functions.

The cerebellum is the last piece of the jigsaw. Latin for "little brain", it can be found just underneath the cerebral cortex at the back of the brain sitting on top of the brainstem. Just like the cerebral cortex, it has two hemispheres and a lobe tucked up on its ventral surface called the floccular lobe (see Figure 6.5). The cerebellum actually contains about half of all of the neurons in the nervous system (thus denoting its importance!). The main part of the cerebellum can be separated into the spinocerebellum and cerebrocerebellum. The spinocerebellum is involved in the control of muscle tone and coordination. It plays a vital role in the timing of movements and maintains movement accuracy as it compares the movement that actually happened with the one it was expecting.

The cerebrocerebellum is involved in motor planning, learning and memory. It is where our stimulus/response associations are stored. If somebody throws a ball at you, the most natural thing for you to do is stick a hand out to catch it and you don't even have to think about it. If you are a top-grade pianist, it is this area which benefits from your practice; if you don't practice for a few days and as a result your movements feel a bit clunky when you try to play something, it is because the cerebellum is vital in maintaining your movement skill and you haven't kept it in tip-top form. For those of us who are not concert pianists, my point stands for things we do every day like texting on our phones or typing. Don't do it for a while and you will notice your skill is affected. The floccular lobe is also called the vestibulocerebellum because it receives input from the ear's vestibular system to control our balance, postural adjustments and also the coordination of eye movements that we

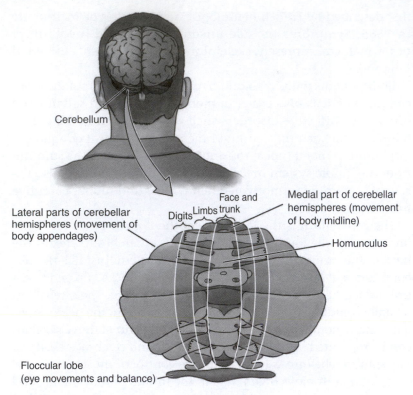

**Figure 6.5** The cerebellum helps to control various body movements and is also organized in a topographic way. The spinocerebellum is found in the medial section whilst the cerebrocerebellum is more lateral. The floccular lobe (also known as the vestibulocerebellum) looks after our balance and eye movements. From *An Introduction to Brain and Behavior*, Third Edition by Bryan Kolb and Ian Q. Whishaw © 2011 by Worth Publishers. Used with permission.

talked about earlier in this chapter. Just like M1 and the SSC, the cerebellum has a homuncular organization with the midline of the body represented by the centre of the cerebellum and the limbs and digits are represented by the more lateral parts.

As with other regions involved in producing a movement, damage to the cerebellum has given us clues as to what role it performs in movement. Cerebellar ataxia is a disorder in which movements cannot be coordinated and errors in trajectory cannot be corrected online. The easiest way to demonstrate this is via the finger-to-nose test. Patients often cannot accurately touch their nose with their finger and may stop short or miss the nose completely. This test may sound familiar to you as a field sobriety test…; indeed as the cerebellum is one of the first areas of the brain alcohol affects, it is an excellent test of impairment. Patients with damage to their cerebellum also cannot tap their finger in time to a metronome, denoting the role this area has on the timing of movements.

You'll remember from Chapter 4 that the dorsal stream pathway is important in translating our vision into an action making the secondary somatosensory areas found in the parietal lobe important for movement also. Not only does this region play a role in the transformation of visual information into a motor act (the visuo-motor transformation) but it also keeps track of which movements have taken place and which should follow. Damage here does not disrupt plans for making movements; rather it disrupts how movements are performed leaving them fragmented and confused. This disorder is known as apraxia, or the inability to make purposeful skilled movements. But the visual system has more basic control over what we do. You would pick up a full glass of milk differently to an empty glass of milk; hence the visual system feeds into the premotor areas and the basal ganglia particularly to adjust grasp and force parameters.

Even if you are thinking about making a movement, many of the areas talked about will become active in the brain. Sports scientists and sports people alike have mined this for its usefulness. Say you are a javelin thrower and you have hurt your arm three weeks before a big competition. You can't train with your arm; you have to wait for it to heal for two weeks. If you wait the two weeks and do nothing but watch daytime TV and eat pretzels, I guarantee that your performance when you start to train again will be appalling, even if you skipped the pretzels. But if you did some mental training, maybe for an hour a day, thinking about the actions involved in javelin throwing, throwing hundreds and hundreds of times, you will be keeping the brain circuits involved nice and practised. It makes a difference; athletes who carry out such imagery exercises are much less rusty than if they didn't maintain the neural circuits involved in the movements required. In fact, Steven Kosslyn and colleagues at Harvard University tested this in 1992. They got their participants to just imagine tensing and relaxing their right index finger for a few minutes a day. Four weeks later the strength of their index finger was increased by 20% purely due to the improvement and efficiency of connections between the areas of the brain we've talked about in this chapter. That is my kind of exercise! In fact, it is in the speed of connections that makes professional sports people much better than us mere mortals. Peter McLeod from Oxford University has long been fascinated by the game of cricket as many postural changes have to take place in a very short period of time in order for a batsperson to hit the ball. Also, since the ball bounces (unlike baseball) the batsperson has a tiny fraction of a second, less than 100ms, to do all of these calculations in order to get their body into the correct position to hit the ball to some part of the field where it won't get caught. Some players report seeing the ball as if it were a football; they have their "eye in" and it is easy to hit. Other players who mainly bowl all the time report not seeing the ball at all as it looks like a marble to them. So, there could be a perceptual aspect to their skill. It turns out however that the perceptual pickup between professional and novice players doesn't differ, but professional players react much faster by over 200ms, which can be attributed to the better flow of information through the neuronal circuits of the motor system. Could we all be international players with a bit of practice?

## Feeling curious?

Balance: In Search of the Lost Sense by Scott McCredie. 2008; Little Brown Book group. *A balanced account of problems with balance with good reference to underlying neural mechanisms.*

The Frontal Lobes and Voluntary Action by Richard E. Passingham. 1995; Oxford University Press. *A thorough and engaging account of the role of frontal lobe systems in movement.*

Daniel M. Wolpert, Jörn Diedrichsen & J. Randall Flanagan (2011) "Principles of Sensorimotor Learning". *Nature Reviews Neuroscience* 12: 739–751 doi:10.1038/nrn3112. *An up-to-date account of what we know about how we learn movements.*

Mirrors in the Brain: How Our Minds Share Actions and Emotions: How Our Minds Share Actions, Emotions, and Experience by Giacomo Rizzolatti, Corrado Sinigaglia & Frances Anderson. 2007; Oxford University Press. *A book all about mirror neurons by those that discovered them.*

# 7   How do your neurons grow?

Even though all their embryos look the same early doors, mammals who are born live (and not in an egg for example) and suckle milk when they are born, show a remarkable variability in their rates of development and how fast they get on in life. Human babies seem relatively useless in comparison to a giraffe baby which can fall up to six feet to the ground after exiting its mum's birth canal, stand up and learn to suckle, walk and run all within an hour. Human babies can take up to 14 months (or even longer in some cases) to start walking solo, and even longer to start talking and putting words together in sensible orders. Now, admittedly, I have never heard a giraffe talk whilst I have been awake, which is not to say they can't communicate of course, but what factors might underlie the differences in how speedily newborns get their act together?

One candidate could be the gestational period. As you know, the human baby cooks for an average of 266 days or just under nine months resulting in a baby, which is around 7 pounds (3 kg) and 18 inches (46 cm) long. In contrast, the giraffe stays in the uterus for a whopping 425 days, around 14 months, is 100kg and can be up to 6 feet tall! On the other end of the scale, kangaroos give birth to their babies who are less than a gram in weight and only 2 cm long. Called a joey, the baby moves along into the mother's pouch where it can spend up to ten months feeding and getting stronger. Lambs are born after 150 days' gestation (about five months) and calves after 284 days (longer than the human baby). Both lambs and calves are very good at getting up and going quickly, so a relatively short gestational period wouldn't seem to be a great argument for why human babies are relatively useless at birth.

How about the time that these animals will roam the planet? If they are going to be around for longer, perhaps they can take longer initially for development. Typically life expectancy increases with size, but there is also thought to be a correlation with gestational period as longer cooking time may lead to longer life, but there is much variation. For example the average life expectancy for a dog or a cat is between 12 and 15 years. A sheep can naturally live for 12 years, a cow for 20 years without intervention. So perhaps size matters. What about the added impact of gestational period? Giraffes with their 425 days of pregnancy, live for 25 years whilst camels who are in-utero for 400 days can expect 40 years of life. Not so clear-cut. And of course, humans debunk both theories as with their 266 day gestation can live for 70 to 80 years on average whilst elephants who cook for 625 days live for a little less time than humans. So even though elephants are (most times) bigger than humans, their life expectancy isn't greater than that of humans. And we can't say from this that the time it takes for young animals to achieve adult function is dependent on how long they will live.

Of course, it could be that animals born in the wild must be aware and equal to the risk of predation and so have to be functional much quicker than humans. Indeed, infants born in a very immature state (as joeys are as well as rodent young) are kept hidden from view in pouches or undergrounds nests (or your roof, if you are really unlucky) until they are stronger and more functional. Humans have no natural predators so they can take their time learning the ropes. It could be as simple as that. But one possibility remains. The human being is the most complex organism on the planet, with a brain which is unsurpassed in the animal kingdom. Perhaps this is the reason our development takes so long. So, let's see whether evidence from our nearest animal relatives, the primates, can support this argument.

The *Pan* genus of great apes are our closest relatives genetically with a 95 to 99% similarity between the *Pan* monkeys and humans depending on which genes you look at. It comprises two species, the Bonobo (*Pan Paniscus*) and the Common Chimpanzee (*Pan Troglodytes*). Due to their endangered status and the fact that the only place they remain is in one part of the planet, the Democratic Republic of the Congo, bonobos are harder to document than chimps. However, they do, every now and again, hit the headlines as a belated signal to the feminist movement as they live in a matriarchal society in which sex is used for conflict resolution, post-conflict making up, bartering etc. In fact, it's fair to say that in bonobo society, sex (both homo and heterosexual) replaces aggression and we can only imagine the kind of world we would live in if this were a human trait. Just like humans, bonobos separate sex from reproduction, producing an offspring only every six to eight years despite their wildly adventurous sex lives. It is thought that these monkeys can live for up to 60 years in the wild, but evidence for this is hard to come by in these times of danger for the great apes.

Gestation periods amongst primates in general varies a lot but by and large, the higher up the evolutionary tree the monkey you are talking about is, the longer the time spent in utero. For example, the mouse lemur takes only 60 days to cook whereas the chimpanzee takes an average of 230 days, about a month shy of humans. Our next closest cousin, the gorilla (from the genus *Gorilla*), has a typical gestation period of 255 days but as with the general animal kingdom, there is only a weak correlation between primate size and gestation period. However, it compares well with human pregnancy which lasts about 266 days. Primate newborns are more developed than those of rats or puppies or kittens but are less developed than horses, cows and other quadrupeds we've mentioned already. In contrast to other primate species, chimps and gorillas need to support their young as they are not able to cling on to the mother's fur as well as say lemurs or monkeys. Chimp babies develop the grasping action within a few days though and can ride their mother's back jockey style with ease after about six months without the need for an expensive baby rucksack. Young chimps get around mostly by walking after four years of age, which is comparable to humans and in the wild, females reach sexual maturity after the age of 12 or 13, also comparable to humans taking the difference in lifespan into account. In a comparison carried out in 2010, Kim Bard from the University of Portsmouth and colleagues compared groups of chimps and human babies and discovered that the only difference was that human babies had less muscle tone than their chimp counterparts. She concluded that development was governed by a complex interaction between the

environment and genetics rather than genes alone, thus strength-
ening the view that the fewer predatory pressures you have, the
longer you can take to grow up.

But there is one other difference between primates and humans
and that is the complexity of our relative brains. Perhaps we have
more neurons to connect than they do and that's why it takes us
longer to develop purposeful movement…; perhaps our brains are
simply capable of more things that we know of such as complex
language, thinking, reasoning, and so it takes longer for us to
develop. Let's turn our attention therefore to how our brains get
from the A of conception to the Z of death and that might answer
our question.

Brain development doesn't actually start until the 23rd day post
conception (see Figure 7.1); before that, various things must happen to lay the foundations so to speak. When the female egg is
fertilized by the sperm it is now called a zygote, which has 46 chromosomes, 23 from the mum and 23 from the dad. It takes only
12 hours for the cell to start dividing and after a week, the embryo
has three distinct layers, which will go on to form all the tissues of
the body: the ectoderm is the outer layer, the mesoderm in the middle and the endoderm on the inside. The egg knows where these
tissues should be as each egg has a front and back, and a right
and left with different concentrations of chemicals in each place,
guiding the different kinds of cell development in each place. It is
the ectoderm that eventually forms neural tissue. The cell layers
continue to thicken and the ectoderm grows into a flat oval bunch
of cells called the neural plate, the first view of the developing nervous system. The edges of the plate, called the neural folds, then
push upwards due to asymmetric rates of division across the plate
and form the neural groove.

By day 23 the neural folds meet along their length and the
groove becomes a tube and the brain and spinal cord develop from
its walls. The ventricles and spinal canal come from the cavity
inside the tube. The neural tube has three subdivisions, which will
later become the forebrain (cortex, basal ganglia, limbic system
structures, thalamus, hypothalamus), midbrain and hindbrain
(brainstem and cerebellum).

By the end of the eighth week (56 days) the embryo is recog-
nizable as a human but the brain is one half the total size of

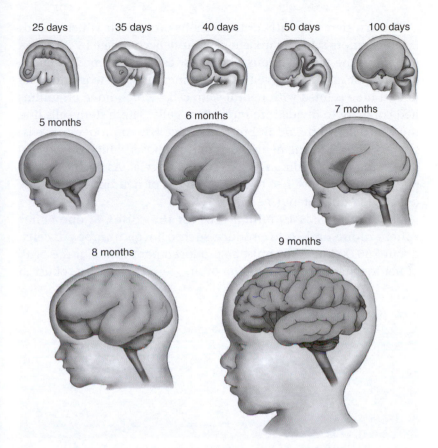

25 days   35 days   40 days   50 days   100 days

5 months   6 months   7 months

8 months   9 months

**Figure 7.1** Embryonic brain development from 25 days post conception to 9 months, or birth. Sulci and gyri don't develop until very late, post 8 months of gestation. From *An Introduction to Brain and Behavior*, Third Edition by Bryan Kolb and Ian Q. Whishaw © 2011 by Worth Publishers. Used with permission.

the embryo and other body organs are only at the first stage of their development. Post ten weeks of development, the developing human is called a foetus instead of an embryo. As for the developing brain, it is simply a case of carrying out six steps: cell birth, cell migration, cell differentiation, cell growth and maturation, synaptic rearrangement and cell death and finally myelination. Sounds straightforward enough, and it is, but as we shall see, there are a number of things that can go wrong along the way that can lead to life-long and sometimes life-threatening congenital disorders.

The first step, cell birth, or to give it its proper title which sounds infinitely more sci-fi, neurogenesis, is largely complete by 20 weeks (except in the hippocampus where new cells are formed throughout life, not surprising given its role in memory and learning). The neural tube is lined with neural stem cells, which have an unlimited capacity to divide into more stem cells. These stem cells line the ventricles in the adult brain and give rise to progenitor cells, which in turn become neuroblasts and gliobasts, which are precursors to the non-dividing neurons and glial cells. As blast cells can only eventually give rise to different types of neurons or glia they are called multipotent (see Figure 7.2).

The brain needs 10 billion cells for the cortex of one hemisphere alone and so to produce such a large number of cells, about 250,000 neurons must be produced per minute at the peak of neurogenesis. The developing brain seems to be most robust to

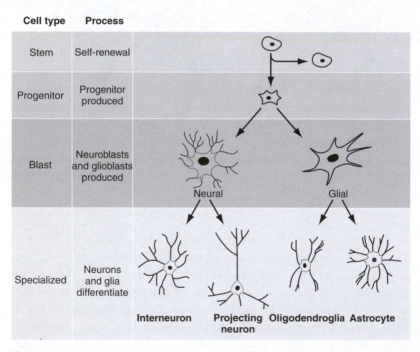

**Figure 7.2** Neurogenesis in the brain begins with the division of multipotent stem cells which become more specialized as they divide. From *An Introduction to Brain and Behavior*, Third Edition by Bryan Kolb and Ian Q. Whishaw © 2011 by Worth Publishers. Used with permission.

injury in the early stages of neurogenesis as it would seem that more neural cells can be produced to compensate. However, after neurogeneis is complete, the chances of a noxious stimulus harming the developing brain and resulting in impairments of function is much higher.

The newly born cells must then move to the correct location by a process called cell migration. This process begins shortly after the first neurons are generated but it continues for six weeks after neurogenesis is complete. Cells destined for the cerebral cortex are formed in the ventricular zone (the walls of the neural tube) at the posterior end of the tube and this area may be further subdivided based on where the cells formed there will be going. For example, Pasko Rakic and his colleagues from Yale University have found an area of the posterior ventricular zone whose neurons will go to the visual cortex, and another whose cells will go to the frontal cortex. These cells migrate along radial glial cells which acts like a scaffolding, guiding them along the length of their fibre to their correct destination in the cerebral cortex. The cortex has six layers and they are formed from the inside out from layer VI to layer I, with cells destined for layer I having to tramp through the other layers to get there. The layers are not of equal thickness and it's not really known how the system knows that a particular layer has enough neurons before the next layer is populated but the best bet is that it happens according to timeframes in that all cells destined for a particular layer move at the same time. It may also be that cells "talk" to each other via intracellular mechanisms in order to discourage overcrowding for example.

If cells don't migrate to their correct location, brain function in later life will be disrupted leading to disorders ranging from epilepsy to schizophrenia. There is increasing evidence that the abnormalities in the arrangement of neurons, particularly in the frontal lobe, observed in schizophrenic brains are associated with disturbances of brain development which could in turn be caused by an environmental insult during pregnancy for example. Indeed, the correlation between trauma during pregnancy and incidence of schizophrenia in the ensuing baby is high; in fact after epidemics of flu there seems to be a higher incidence of schizophrenia in the population. Schizophrenia can also be caused by some type of abnormal gene activity. One controversial example is the presence of a gene mutation in the *PCM1* gene in some populations of schizophrenic patients. This gene is involved in the cell division that mostly happens in adolescence and its abnormal activity means that the number of cells in the frontal cortex is altered. This could explain why the disease most often strikes at adolescence as this is the area developing most at this stage.

Once cells have migrated to their correct location they have to undergo cell differentiation in which the cell can turn into any one of a variety of different neurons, be they motor, sensory or interneurons or glial cells such as oligodendocytes or astrocytes etc. How does a stem cell know whether to turn into a neuron or a glial cell, and what type of neuron or glial cell to turn into? The answer to this lies in which genes the cell uses. The chromosomes of each cell contain about 100,000 genes. Each gene contains the code to make a particular protein. The cells know what to turn into based on which of its genes are expressed and which are turned off, i.e. which proteins will be made, thus defining the function of the cell. Stem cells that can be found in embryos at earlier stages of development can give rise to any type of tissue because none of their genes is turned off. Such stem cells are called pluripotent or totipotent. These are the cells that are so hotly debated in the use of stem cells in medicine as their removal usually leads to death of the embryo. In the past, they have been harvested from aborted embryos; however medical science has removed the need for this as it is now possible to take a multipotent (a cell that can turn into a tissue of a particular type like any type of blood cell for example) stem cell from a tissue of the adult body (bone marrow, skin, teeth for example) and encourage it to turn into any cell the body may need. The implantation of a stem cell into any tissue causes it to differentiate into the cell type of the surrounding tissue, a fact that has been used to great effect in the treatment of tendon damage in racehorses and sports people alike as well as in neurological disorders such as Huntington's disease or Parkinson's Disease for example.

Stem cells are being used in experimentation related to finding ways of resolving genetic abnormalities via genetic engineering or gene therapy. It involves playing with the expression of genes to turn them on or off thus resulting in a particular set of proteins being created (or not). This can then alter physical or behavioural traits. The oldest means of influencing genetic traits is selective breeding; however a more recent approach has been that of cloning. Cloning entails undifferentiating an adult cell so that it expresses all genes (so acts like a pluripotent stem cell) and can become anything. The DNA from this cell is then injected into an egg cell that has had its DNA removed (remember, the egg cell has DNA only from the mother's side; the injected DNA is from a cell that has two sets of chromosomes). This egg cell is then introduced to a surrogate's uterus and it grows in the normal way. The most famous example of this was Dolly the sheep, born on 5 July 1996, created by Ian Wilmut, Keith Campbell and colleagues at the Roslin Institute in Edinburgh. She had three mums; the sheep who provided the DNA (from a mammary gland cell, and as urban legend would have it, hence the name Dolly, as in Dolly Parton, with me?), the sheep who provided the egg to house the DNA and the sheep who grew the egg in her uterus. Dolly died on Valentine's Day 2003 making her a little over six-and-a-half years old. The average life expectancy of a sheep is 12, so did the fact that the sheep who provided the DNA was herself six years old when she donated have a bearing? Perhaps. Dolly showed signs of premature ageing and was already as arthritic as an older animal. Eventually, the lung disease she developed (again common in older sheep) became too much and she was put to sleep.

You can see how cloning is controversial; could the world cope with another one of you? Would you like to play with the genes that are expressed and maybe change your hair colour, or your height for example whilst you are still in a petri dish? In fact it would be pretty impossible to create an exact copy of you. Many cloned animals look nothing like the adults whose DNA they came from. This is because of epigenetics, factors that affect gene expression without changing the DNA sequence. So you have the same DNA but you look totally different because some different proteins are in action and can happen because of the prenatal but also the postnatal environment. This pretty much nixes the plot of many sci-fi B movies. Even the behaviour of mothers to their offspring can change what proteins are expressed without changing the DNA structure of the individual.

For example, an elegant set of experiments carried out over the past ten years by Michael Meaney and Ian Weaver at McGill University in Canada has shown that licking and grooming of rat pups by their mother led to the release of serotonin (the happy hormone) in the hippocampus, which in turn leads to the switching-on of the gene which inhibits the stress response. These happy pups grow up to be calm rats in direct contrast to the non-licked pups who grow up to be skittish. The crucial point here is that all the pups are genetically identical but their behaviour is shaped by what gene proteins are turned on.

The value of creating "á la carte" babies in which you can choose such things as hair colour, or even sex pales into insignificance when you think of what we could do in the case of genetic disorders. Gene therapy aims to solve problems created by abnormal genes before they have a chance to cause physical or behavioural problems. For example, Huntington's disease (HD) is caused by an abnormality to just one gene (called the huntingtin gene), which leads to too much glutamine being present in the huntingtin protein. These abnormal huntingtin proteins clump together, selectively damaging neurons and causing them to die. As more and more cells die in the brain, it leads to the cognitive and motor deficits seen in an HD sufferer. The post mortem brain of a HD patient has large areas of atrophy evident and so it is no surprise that HD sufferers live only for 15 to 20 years post symptom onset. A person with the gene has a 50/50 chance of passing it on to their offspring and because symptoms do not manifest themselves until at least the age of 35, the chances of sufferers having had offspring by the time they realize they have the disease are high. As mentioned, stem cells could be used in this case to repair damage caused by the disease and their use is also prevalent in research carried out to modify the abnormal huntingtin gene.

Other genetic disorders are caused by aberrations in part of a chromosome (on which the genes sit) or even an entire chromosome. Down's Syndrome results from one parent passing on two copies of chromosome 21. People with Down's Syndrome have characteristic facial features, short stature and are susceptible to mental retardation i.e. they score less than 70 on intelligence tests, they have limited mental capacities and difficultly dealing with day-to-day aspects of living. However, improved education for children with Down's syndrome shows that they can compensate for their disability. Although testing can now identify such genetic abnormalities, it remains to be seen whether and how medical science can use genetic engineering to stop such disorders having the debilitating effects that they do by repairing the chromosomal abnormality.

Cell differentiation is generally complete at birth but cell growth and maturation continues throughout childhood and even in some cases into adulthood. Now that the cell is in the correct place and has differentiated into the cell type it should be, in the case of neurons, it needs to connect up to other neurons. The growing tip of an axon is called a growth cone (a name coined by Santiago Ramón y Cajal, who invented that really important stain from Chapter 1) and it uses chemical signals in the embryonic environment to guide it to its correct destination among the millions of nerve cells now present all over the brain. These growth cones respond to two types of signal. Firstly, cell-adhesion molecules are released from the target cell to provide a surface to which the correct growth cone can stick. If it is the wrong growth cone, the cell adhesion molecule will repel it. The second signal is tropic molecules which act like big "over here" or "go away" signals. Cajal predicted the existence of the tropic molecule but only one, the netrin (from netr, meaning "one who guides" in Sanskrit), has been found so far. In an example from vision, at this stage axons from the retinal ganglion cells in the nasal retina cross over to the opposite side of the brain at the optic chiasm, whereas axons from the retinal ganglion cells in the temporal retina do not. Without doubt this is a happenstance correctly carried out by the action of cell adhesion and tropic molecules.

You'll remember that neurons connect with other neurons via dendrites, which synapse onto other neurons thus meaning those two neurons can now communicate. Well, neurons begin with simple dendritic trees, which become progressively more complex with age. To continue with the tree theme this is called dendritic aborization. Synaptic contacts are evident in the human foetus at five months of development and are seen between the deepest cortical neurons by seven months. The number of synapses made by axons increases rapidly after birth also. This increase in complexity of neurons is reflected in the overall shape and size of the brain which begins to form sulci and gyri just to fit all of this neural tissue in at seven months.

Neurons often make too many synapses during fetal development. After birth there is the need to rearrange the connections between neurons and remove unwanted connections. During this period of synaptic rearrangement, neurons that do not project to the correct location undergo cell death as do any neurons that are not used (i.e. connect to nothing). This process is sometimes called synaptic pruning, appropriate given the tree theme we seem to have going on. I get a bit carried away with my pruning shears in my garden, but the brain is just a bit more selective using a variety of means by which to influence the process such as genetic signals, experience, reproductive hormones and even external signals such as stress. Up to 42% of all synapses could be eliminated with 100,000 synapses being terminated per second, on a principle of the survival of the fittest. To use another example from vision, we know that in the developed primary visual cortex, the inputs from the left and right eye are kept nice and separate from each other, but in babies, before synaptic rearrangement takes place, the inputs are all intermingled and higgledy-piggledy (an underused scientific term). No wonder babies have such poor vision. No surprise then that the bringing to order of these inputs is coincident with improvements in their visual abilities.

Cells that don't connect to anything undergo apoptosis or programmed cell death. They basically kill themselves by having their lysosomes (which usually break down waste materials and cellular debris) blow up. They know to do this because they are not receiving neurotrophic factors, which regulate a cell's survival. Not to be confused with tropic molecules, these factors are released by target neurons and are taken up by pre-synaptic axon terminals. So a neuron can contain only neurotrophic factors if it is in a stable synapse with another neuron. The more synapses a neuron makes, the more neurotrophic factor it will take up and the less likely it will be to blow up.

The last stage involves glial development and myelination. The birth of most glial cells found in the brain (oligodendrocytes and astrocytes) begins after most neurogenesis is complete at 20 weeks. Oligodendrocytes form the myelin that surrounds the axons in the brain. As you already know, a myelin sheath insulates the nerve signal much in the same way as the insulation works on electrical cable. This means that the action potential can travel much faster down the axon as it doesn't have to regenerate itself at every point; it can jump between nodes in the sheath (saltatory conduction). The myelination of the brain varies between areas with myelination beginning just after birth and continuing until at least 18 but more likely up to 23 years of age. Areas such as the visual cortex, and motor cortex and language areas are relatively quick to myelinate with areas of the frontal cortex being the slowest. The development of behaviour has been shown to correlate with the myelination of neuron. For example, a group of axons in the motor cortex become myelinated at around the same time that infants can reach and grasp objects with the whole hand. Another set of neurons that control fine finger movements become myelinated at the same time that the pincer grip develops and your child is now able to pick up his or her cereal piece by piece and fling it at you. Good times. In contrast, the frontal lobes don't myelinate fully until much later. This being the decision making, reasoning and higher cognitive control areas that allow you to foresee the consequences of your actions, do you think its state of unmyelination could have anything to do with the lousy decisions you made when you were a teen (even though, respectfully, you thought you knew it all)? Bad decisions and risky behaviour result from an immature prefrontal cortex, which we all have until probably our early twenties. Great excuse huh?

The developing foetus is obviously at great risk from damage throughout the period of gestation. In fact, as Lewis Wolpert, a highly regarded developmental biologist from UCL, puts it: "It is not birth, marriage or death, but gastrulation [early development of the embryo] which is truly the most important time of your life." For sure, if something goes wrong in the very early stages, the embryo won't even be viable and will cease to develop. But there are many external factors that can affect any of the stages of development we talked about above and this will cause problems later in life. Aside from the genetic factors we've touched on, and although the placenta does a good job of shielding the embryo from many noxious substances, the developing brain is very susceptible to malnutrition and hormonal imbalance such as low thyroid hormone levels, infections that cause fever, and toxic chemicals. This latter issue is never so evident as in Fetal Alcohol Syndrome (FAS) in which babies born to alcoholic mothers have a typical pattern of physical and mental retardation. Children with FAS may have abnormal facial features such as unusually wide spacing between the eyes and a range of brain abnormalities related to cell growth and maturation such as small brains with abnormal gyri, neurons with short dendrites and little arborization and a significantly reduced corpus callosum. Related to these brain abnormalities are certain behavioural symptoms such as learning difficulties and lowered intelligence scores as well as hyperactivity and other social behavioural problems. In 2010, Suyinn Chong and colleagues from the University of Queensland found that such changes may be coincident with changes in gene expression in the mouse foetus leading to a model of how alcohol affects the developing brain at a molecular level. This may lead to the finding of Robert Berman's group in UC Davis that the action of neurotrophins in the fetal brain exposed to alcohol is decreased. As a result of this, neurons can't form stable synapses and eventually the neurons commit suicide by lysosome. However, it is not just babies born to alcoholic mothers that are at risk. FAS has recently been expanded to Fetal Alcohol Spectrum Disorders (FASD), which describes a range of behavioural and cognitive effects in children. This is related not only to the quantity of alcohol drunk by the mother but also to the stage of development in which it was consumed. Excessive alcohol in the early stages of embryonic development will lead to structural deformities, but alcohol consumed in later stages will affect the growing brain such that cognitive deficits will be seen during childhood and later life. FASD has been used to explain attentional and other behavioural problems in children as well as various learning difficulties for example. Indeed, good general advice to expectant mothers nowadays is to never drink alcohol during pregnancy with some countries even going so far as to arrest expectant mothers caught drinking alcohol in public. Advice is not restricted to alcohol however. Cocaine use in pregnancy has been linked to lower IQ scores and hearing deficits. There is also a correlation of attention deficit disorder, aggressive behaviour and impaired memory and intelligence with the ingestion of nicotine from maternal smoking during gestation according to an analysis done of the relevant literature by Karen Linnet and colleagues from Denmark in 2003.

So, the human newborn brain is a product of all of these issues prenatally, but what influences brain development after birth? The brain quadruples in size and there is an explosion in our range of functional abilities, but what drives it in one direction over another? This has been a debate since time immemorial: nature versus nurture. Is our behaviour purely a product of our genetics and how we are wired up or is our behaviour (and the wiring that causes it) susceptible to the environment and experiences we have growing up? Well, because there are no genetic factors that have ever been studied independently of the environment and there are no environmental factors that function independently of the human genome, the current thinking is that a trait emerges only from the interaction of a gene and the environment in which it lives. And so, our personalities, intelligence, likes and dislikes are determined by the lives that we lead making the whole idea of "the way I was made" pretty redundant. In fact, Patrick Bateson, a zoologist at Cambridge University, has a lovely way of describing the fact that humans (and all other animals) start their lives with the capacity to develop in any number of ways. He calls it "the developmental jukebox"; the individual has the potential to play a number of different developmental tunes. But it is the environment in which the individual is growing up that picks out the tune. This doesn't mean that genetics haven't got a part to play; they do. In fact, it is your genes that determine what kinds of developmental tunes are stored in your jukebox from which the environment can select; epigenetics can take care of the rest.

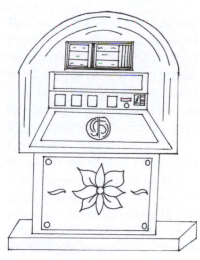

Brain plasticity refers to the lifelong changes in the structure of the brain that accompany experience. This term suggests that the brain can be moulded (like plastic) into many different forms and changes in behaviour can be correlated with the development of the brain. The importance of good nutrition for brain development is well established with poor childhood diet being linked to deficits in brain development, learning and behaviour. Obviously, if the components required for construction of dendritic trees, neurotransmitters, neurotrophic factors etc. are not consumed in the diet, neurodevelopment will suffer with predictable effects on behaviour. The world in which the child lives also has a part to play. Brains exposed to different environmental experiences are moulded in different ways and as different cultures create different environmental experiences we would expect differences in brain structure across different cultures. For example, neuroscientists Trey Hedden and John Gabrieli from MIT got a group of Americans and a group of East Asians to solve basic puzzles whilst in an fMRI scanner in 2008. The American brains had to work harder (i.e. frontal areas related to mentally demanding tasks were activated) than those of the East Asians' when carrying out relative judgements whilst the East Asian brains found the absolute judgements more challenging. Trey and John attributed these differences to differences between the two cultures. Psychology research has shown that American culture focuses on the individual and independence is valued; therefore Americans would have little problem with absolute judgements and would be wired to do these tasks quickly and efficiently. East Asian culture, in contrast, is more community-focussed and emphasizes seeing people and objects in context and so they would find relative judgements easier but absolute judgements harder, with this prediction reflected in their brain activity. It is not so much that people from different cultures see the world any differently (as the brain activity associated with this function is similar cross-culturally) but the way they think about it may vary.

The effects of experience on the brain and behaviour have been extensively studied by placing laboratory animals in different environments. In a classic study carried out by Donald Hebb in the 1940s, the ability of rats to navigate mazes was correlated with the complexity of the environment in which they were raised. Rats raised in complex environments solved mazes more quickly than rats raised in standard laboratory cages. In fact, rats raised in enriched environments showed greater levels of dendritic arborization and bigger glial cells in their brains. On the basis of these findings the suggestion first arose that

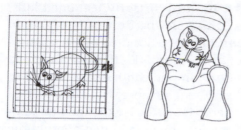

people raised in enriched environments would maximize their intellectual potential whereas people raised in impoverished environments would not. This theory does seem to hold true as there have been cases of babies raised in environments with little or no stimulation or in the presence of abuse or neglect and these can be expected to be at a serious disadvantage in later life. One well-publicized example of this is the case of the Romanian orphans. In the 1970s, the communist regime then governing Romania outlawed all forms of birth control and abortion. The result was that thousands of unwanted children were placed in orphanages in which the children had virtually no environmental stimulation. An adoption programme began in the late seventies to place these children with new families all over the world but up until then the kids had had little or no individual attention. Despite being loved and doted upon by their new families, many of these children have grown up with profound social and emotional problems that have never been truly overcome.

The normal social behaviours of children are learned through imitation of adult behaviour and this could be either good or bad. In 1961, Albert Bandura investigated the influence of adult behaviour on children aged 3 to 5. Children who viewed adults being nice towards an inflatable doll called Bobo were, in turn, well behaved, gentle and non-aggressive towards the doll. However, if they viewed the adult being violent towards Bobo, the children did exactly the same thing. The kids had no empathy for Bobo, their frontal lobes were unmyelinated and therefore their rationalization abilities and sense of right and wrong were not yet formed. In contrast, adults with fully developed frontal lobes don't imitate violent adults. The closest imitation was when a child observed an adult of the same sex. The finding that children imitate what they see adults do in person also holds for children imitating what they see an adult doing on television and even in video games. Aggression caused by violent video games has been confirmed not just in younger children but also in early teenaged kids. Researchers such as Jeanne Funk from the University of Toledo have discovered that the brain changes associated with it are two-fold: it can lead to decreases in brain activity in areas linked to self-control, focus and concentration and can make children less emotional when confronted with real violence, which could lead to inappropriate and unsafe behaviours. Such experimental findings have directly informed the introduction of age-appropriate guidelines in movies and computer games. From a neurodevelopmental point of view, parents would do well to make sure their kids stuck to them.

There are other, horrific, single case studies of children being raised in entirely impoverished environments that show the same, or worse, effects as those seen in the Romanian babies. In the case of Genie, rescued at age 13 from an extraordinarily deprived environment, her language and other forms of self-expression and communication were completely undeveloped. After rescue however, and even with intense effort, there is little chance of improvement. Why is this? If the brain has the ability to learn and is malleable (or plastic), then why can these individuals who grew up in deprived environments not "catch-up"? The reason is because we have critical periods for development of each of our major functions. This is the time of our life when a behaviour is most susceptible to the influence of the environment. We have a critical period for learning language, for example. Anyone witnessing language development in a child can't help but be amazed at how quickly learning takes place. This is in contrast to adult acquisition of a new language which can be a painfully slow business that never produces full fluency (Obviously, some people have an aptitude for languages and don't have this problem. The rest of us just live in envy). It would seem that our ability to score well on tests of English grammar and vocabulary decreases after the age of seven. Jacqueline Johnson and Elissa Newport from the University of Illinois tested the language abilities of a variety of non-native English speakers new to the United States in 1989 and found that fluency decreased as a function of their age on arrival in the US. If they arrived after the age of seven, they could not achieve the language abilities of a native English speaker. This explains why people raised in situations of extreme deprivation will never achieve more than the very basic rudiments of language.

Culture also has a big effect on your language abilities. For example, adult Japanese speakers can't reliably distinguish between the sounds associated with r and l. However, four-month-old Japanese infants can make this discrimination just as well as four-month-old English speaking children can. Therefore, the latter inability is acquired and the reason is because the phonemic distinction between r and l does not exist in the Japanese language. There is a similar example from the Irish language. When "th" occurs in Irish it is pronounced "h" and not "thhh" as in English, sticking your tongue between your teeth and spitting all over everyone in the process. Although the Irish language is not generally in everyday usage in Ireland (albeit it is compulsory to learn it in school), Irish people have real trouble with "th"; it comes out as a hard "t" unless much concentration is engaged. You'll know what I mean if you ask the next Irish person you meet to say "thirty three and a third". But they might add some more choice words on the end for your delectation.

Most babies begin producing speech like sounds, or babbling, at about seven months and this is thought to be an important precursor to good speech development. This is around the time that the language areas are under development, including the arcuate fasciculus, which links Wernike's Area (for the comprehension of speech) with Broca's area (the production of speech). In congentially deaf babies however, this can't occur as there is no speech comprehension and as a result they show deficits in their vocalizations. They therefore often fail to develop language if they are not provided with an alternative form of symbolic expression such as sign language during their critical period. If they are exposed to sign language during this time, they show the same babbling activity as their hearing counterparts but use their hands instead!

We've already touched on the development of motor behaviours in babies but the development of balance and other athletic abilities are just as sensitive to the critical period regarding the maturation of the motor system and the connection of the cerebellum, basal ganglia and motor cortices into a functional loop. Adults who were not very physically active as kids may find that their balance is appalling in later life. I'm probably one of those.

Critical periods also exist for vision. Animals raised in the dark have normally developed eyes but they are functionally blind because their brains have not developed to understand the meaning of images. In humans, congenital cataracts which are removed after the critical period do not result in a restoration of vision as the visual system did not develop properly due to a lack of sensory input from the eyes. A common occurrence in children is amblyopia or dull vision. This occurs when the eyes are not properly aligned during a critical period of postnatal life. Called a strabismus, because the eyes do not see the same visual image, the brain suppresses the input from one of the eyes, resulting in dulled vision in that eye. Not only is input suppressed but over time the terminations from that eye in the visual cortex begin to retract. The solution is to patch the dominant eye to encourage normal connection of the non-dominant eye with the visual cortex, but this should work only if it is done during the critical period of development of binocular vision, up to the age of two. However, some success has been seen in its treatment up to the age of six, suggesting some plasticity outside of the critical period.

Visual development as a whole is gradual in the infant brain. This means that their behaviour based on what they see is incremental. At one month, the contrast sensitivity is so low (because of the cross talk between inputs from the left and right eye in V1) that it is impossible for a baby to distinguish facial expressions. I have no idea why human adults therefore continue to make goo goo faces at newborn babies; they have clearly no clue as to what the adults are doing. It is however possible for them to see high contrast areas such as the contour between the hair and the forehead and in fact this is how most babies recognize their mums. But in general, at one month, their vision is slightly worse than an adult's night vision. At three months, the contrast perception has improved such that the perception of facial expression is possible. Children have very good recognition abilities and can even tell the difference between lemur faces. Obviously we can't ask the infant what they are seeing/perceiving so we sneakily play on the fact that babies will prefer to look at something they have never seen before. If they recognize a picture of a face as new, they will look at it longer than if they don't. If they think they have seen it before, they will quickly get bored and look away. Babies tested in this way seem to be able to tell the difference between separate lemur faces, something adults have trouble with. Lo and behold, as the visual system develops, we lose this ability to recognize different lemurs in order to focus on human faces more.

Using the same kinds of experimental process it is possible to determine that four-month-old infants categorize colours the same way as adults do and at the same time gather a good understanding of motion. It is also around this time that depth perception comes online. Before this time, the eyes don't converge or diverge according to depth in order to get both eyes on the target. In fact a depth cue used by adults to denote the third dimension called occlusion can't be used by infants until five to seven months of age. For example, if I am standing in front of a table, occluding some of it from your view, you will know that the table is behind me and not (as in a baby's view) that the table is part of my body. This is the underlying principle of why the game peek-a-boo works on so many levels. Now you know.

Therefore, as children grow, the environment has the ability to direct the genetic orchestra to result in the symphony of behaviours that enlighten adult life. That's my take on Bateson's developmental jukebox idea. Like it? Took me seconds.

## Feeling curious?

*Building Brains: An Introduction to Neural Development* by David Price, Andrew P. Jarman, John O. Mason & Peter C. Kind. 2011; Wiley-Blackwell. *An in depth examination of all stages of neurodevelopment.*

*Epigenetics: The Ultimate Mystery of Inheritance* by Richard Francis 2011; W.W. Norton & Co. *A look under the lid of genetics into the argument of nature vs nurture.*

*Plasticity, Robustness, Development and Evolution* by Patrick Bateson & Peter Gluckman 2011; Cambridge University Press. *Further argument supporting the developmental jukebox.*

Richard E. Brown & Peter M. Milner (2003) *Timeline: The legacy of Donald O. Hebb: more than the Hebb Synapse. Nature Reviews Neuroscience* 4: 1013–1019 (December 2003) doi:10.1038/nrn1257. *A great biopic article detailing the contribution of Donald Hebb to neuroscience which entailed more than demonstrating the value of enriched environments.*

Jacqueline Johnson & Elissa Newport (1989) "Critical Period Effects in Second Language Learning: The Influence of Maturational State on the Acquisition of English as a Second Language". *Cognitive Psychology* 21(1): 60–99. *This paper presents the study discovering a critical period for second language acquisition in immigrants to the USA.*

Mark H. Johnson (2001) "Functional Brain Development in Humans". *Nature Reviews Neuroscience* 2: 475–483 doi:10.1038 /35081509. *This article is particularly useful for its discussion on how to scientifically investigate baby behaviour, a problem which is the absolute opposite to trivial.*

# CHAPTER 8 Oh DO behave!

Everybody behaves differently, and our reactions to situations are never the same either. It's one of the things that makes us unique. So, does this mean that all of our brains produce our behaviour in different ways? Not really; it's just that our behaviour is modulated not only by our experience, what we have learned and what we remember, but also by our emotions. We'll cover these two issues in later chapters, but first, let's spend some time delving into how the brain produces our general behaviours.

How much control do you think you have over your behaviour? Most of the time, people think that we do what we do because we want to, we have complete control and use our free will to great effect. We decide what we do and when we do it. But now we know that there are many factors influencing our behaviour. For example, a number of processes happen in our bodies to keep our temperature or the level of glucose in our blood regulated, and we are not even aware of them until we get the urge to take off a coat or eat something. So, is it our decision to eat a hamburger or is it the natural conclusion of our unconscious processes? You don't actually have as much "free will" as you think you have. Okay, perhaps I'll have to convince you.

The types of behaviour in which our lack of conscious control is most apparent is in our regulatory behaviours. These are the ones that keep us alive and so include temperature regulation, eating, drinking, that kind of thing. They are also called homeostatic mechanisms, those that keep our operating levels within normal parameters. Our non-regulatory behaviours are more amenable to top–down control and these include behaviours such as parenting, aggression, sex and other behaviours on which our very survival does not depend. In the following chapters, we will look in more depth at selected regulatory (sleep) and non-regulatory (sex) behaviours as well as investigate the role of emotion and learning and memory on our actions. But first, it would be really useful to understand what the causes of behaviour are and the neural mechanisms that underlie all of our behaviours.

What would happen if no behaviour was required of us at all? The need for us to behave in some shape or form really becomes obvious only when we forbid any kind of behaviour at all. In the 1950s, Donald Hebb and his colleagues at McGill University in Canada investigated this by putting human participants into extreme isolation conditions. It was completely dark so the subjects couldn't see anything. They wore headphones that piped white noise into their ears constantly so that they couldn't hear anything other than that. Somatosensory information was restricted by making the participants wear big cuffs over their hands, legs and arms to minimize tactile stimulation. Perhaps needlessly to say, the participants became distressed very quickly. In an environment where no behaviour is allowed and there is no stimulation, people begin to hallucinate after 30 hours. It is as if, in the absence of sensory input to the brain, the brain will make some up with which to stimulate itself. Therefore, stimulation is an important reason as to why people behave the way they do; it is not stimulation for stimulation's sake; it actually works to keep our brains sharp. The isolation experiment participants were tested on verbal fluency skills, higher reasoning skills and memory tasks, amongst others, before entering isolation. Following the isolation period they did much worse on these tasks than they did before and so it can be concluded that stimulation helps create connections and keeps information flowing around the brain at an effectual level. Sensory deprivation can dramatically impair this process. Thus, our need for stimulation, in addition to our homeostatic mechanisms, are important drivers of our behaviour. Psychologists Robert Butler and Harry Harlow from the University of Wisconsin, Madison came to the same conclusion based on studies of sensory deprivation in monkeys around the same time. Monkeys who were placed in a dimly lit room with a small door that could be opened to view an adjoining room would spend much of their time opening the door to see what was going on in the other room. They'd even learn to solve puzzles or do other tricks to gain access to the door. The more stimulating the environment in the other room was, the more incentive the monkey had to open the door.

The centre of all behaviours in the brain is the hypothalamus, my favourite part of the brain. So indulge me whilst I tell you how fabulous it is and why. The hypothalamus lives just below the thalamus and in tandem with the pituitary gland controls the hormonal environment of the body. It has a number of centres or nuclei which are specific for different aspects of our behaviour. Many of the nuclei in the hypothalamus are so called because of where they are located. The dorsal hypothalamus lies to the top whereas the posterior hypothalamus lies to the back etc. The suprachiasmatic nucleus lies just above the optic chiasm of the visual system and the preoptic area lies just in front of the input of the visual pathway's entry into the brain at the optic chiasm.

The pituitary gland (see Figure 8.1) has an anterior lobe called the adenohypophysis and a posterior lobe called the neurohypophysis. The adenohypophysis is connected to the hypothalamus

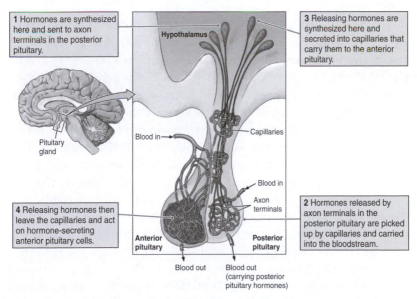

**Figure 8.1** The hypothalamus sends axons via the hypothalamic-hypophyseal tract to the posterior pituitary gland but the releasing hormones destined for the anterior pituitary are carried there by the hypothalamic-hypophyseal portal system. From *An Introduction to Brain and Behavior*, Third Edition by Bryan Kolb and Ian Q. Whishaw © 2011 by Worth Publishers. Used with permission.

by a blood stream (called the hypothalamic-hypophyseal portal system). Neurons of the hypothalamus secrete hormones into this portal system to regulate the secretions of the anterior pituitary. For example, thyrotropin-releasing hormone (TRH) stimulates the release of thyroid-stimulating hormone (TSH) from the anterior pituitary, which in turn causes the thyroid gland to release thyroid hormone, which is very important in stimulating your metabolism. Another hormone released by the hypothalamus is gonadotropin-releasing hormone or (GnRH), which stimulates the secretion of follicle-stimulating hormone and luteinizing hormone from the anterior pituitary, two hormones involved in reproductive and sexual behaviour. Other releasing hormones exist for growth hormone, adrenocorticotropic hormone (ACTH) and prolactin, which have roles in metabolism and reproduction. On the other hand, the neurohypophysis or posterior lobe of the pituitary gland is connected via neurons to the hypothalamus. The posterior lobe releases only two hormones (anti-diuretic hormone and oxytocin) that regulate fluid balance and lactation/bonding behaviours respectively.

The activity of the hypothalamus is in turn ultimately controlled by the levels of hormones it manages in the blood. For example, a rise in thyroid hormone in the blood tream feeds back to the anterior pituitary to halt release of TSH. Less TSH reaching the thyroid gland means less release of thyroid hormones into the system. This is an example of a negative feedback inhibition and is common to all hormones involved in the hypothalamus–pituitary axis. When levels of thyroid hormone fall too low, more TSH is released. This mechanism is common to many behaviours we carry out every day. For example, let's look at how the brain can drive our behaviour to eat. In the 1950s it was found that electrical activation of the lateral hypothalamus stimulated feeding but that stimulation of the ventromedial hypothalamus inhibited feeding. Similarly, damage to the lateral hypothalamus in rats causes them to stop eating whereas damage to the ventromedial hypothalamus results in voracious feeding (but only if the food is good!). And so, a very simple mechanism of the lateral hypothalamus being responsible for "eating on" and the ventromedial hypothalamus being responsible for "eating off" was suggested. Now we know that damage to these areas and others such as the periventricular or arcuate nucleus can cause a range of difference effects from changes in taste and attractiveness of food, to metabolic rate changes, to the levels of glucose and lipids present in the blood.

We could accurately think of the hypothalamus as a sensor for the levels of glucose and lipids in the blood. The fun starts at the arcuate nucleus, which can react to good tasting food to stimulate your hunger, but will also react to the presence of ghrelin, which is released by your stomach when you are hungry. Ghrelin is also responsible for the muscle contractions that cause your stomach to growl with hunger, usually at the most inopportune moments. Also in the arucate nucleus are neurons that respond when you have eaten; these are called satiety signals. Blood glucose and cholesystokinin (CCK) released by the intestines when they are full are short term signals that causes the release of insulin to pack the excess sugar away in stores. A longer-term signal of satiety comes from leptin which is released by body fat. The activity of the arcuate hypothalamus satiety neurons is passed on to the paraventricular nucleus, which also works to limit food intake: problems here result in overeating. The hunger neurons in the arcuate nucleus will normally inhibit the paraventricular nucleus satiety cells but again, if the arcuate nucleus sends signals when it shouldn't (e.g. when a meal has just been eaten) and the satiety actions are blocked, extreme overeating will ensue.

The arcuate nucleus also seems to project to the lateral hypothalamus where a hormone called hypocretin increases the persistence in seeking food after a prolonged period of food deprivation but will also respond to the taste incentive of a particular food. Think of this the next time you are stuffed after a meal at a restaurant and your waiter asks if you want to see the dessert menu. It would be rude not to of course. Then you spy chocolate fudge cake on the list. What do you do? You kick your lateral hypothalamus into gear. Hypocretin has the power to override the satiety indicators meaning you can "find room" for your dessert even though you are not in the least bit hungry. And so it is clear that the lateral hypothalamus has much to do with our taste. Indeed, when the lateral hypothalamus detects hunger, it sends a signal to the brainstem to make the food taste better by altering the salivation response to the different tastes and can alter higher brain regions' activity in response to the sight, smell or taste of food.

It's true what they say; hunger is a great sauce. The lateral hypothalamus, through its action on the anterior pituitary gland, works to increase insulin secretion in preparation for packing that sugar away and also acts to increase digestive secretions via the autonomic nervous system. Last but not least, it has an important role in ingestion and swallowing, obviously essential for feeding.

As for the ventromedial hypothalamus (VMH), as already mentioned, damage in this region can cause serious overeating and weight gain. In humans this can lead to a 10kg increase in body weight each month. Weight will eventually stabilize but at a higher level and food intake will go back to normal. It may in fact be that in contrast to the paraventicular area in which damage causes rats to eat larger meals, damage to the VMH leads rats to eat more frequently. The VMH would seem to have a role in regulating stomach motility and secretions as damage causes an increase in their rate and stomach empties faster than normal so the rat is ready to eat again quicker. The damage also increases insulin production meaning that more of each meal is stored as fat so it is not the overeating that makes it fat; it's the abnormal storage of blood sugar that does the trick. And because there is low blood sugar all the time, the rat is hungry. What a vicious circle!

Given the range of areas, just even within the hypothalamus, and the number of hormones and neurotransmitters involved, it is clear that problems relating to food intake such as anorexia and obesity could result from disruption to any of these areas in humans. However, even given our knowledge of what damage to these regions, particularly the lateral and ventromedial nuclei, causes in animals, little is known about their impact in human behavioural disorders. The role of other factors such as the emotional aspect of feeding and taste no doubt have an impact, and indeed, these factors are harder to quantify. There is some evidence from Francisco Vaz and colleagues at the University of Extremadura, Spain, that food does not taste as good to anorexic people, food being actually aversive and distasteful. This could be linked to a malfunctioning lateral hypothalamus or arcuate nucleus but the cause of the aversive behaviour is unclear.

Cognitive factors are also important in the control of eating. For example, just thinking about a favourite food is enough to make us feel hungry. Similarly, external sensory inputs in the form of images of food or the food odours trigger a feeling of hunger. The neural events that underlie these events must therefore include the sensory regions of the brain. However, two other areas appear to be important: the amygdala and inferior prefrontal cortex. Damage to these areas changes food preferences and eating patterns with damage in the right hemisphere sometimes resulting in a rare disorder called Gourmand Syndrome in which patients display a preoccupation with food and a preference for fine dining.

The sense of satisfaction that comes from that "full feeling" is an important aspect of the control of our eating behaviour as it is indicative of the reward we get for resolving the drive to eat. This is mediated by the reward system in the brain, which releases the neurotransmitter dopamine into our limbic system. With such a reward, we are encouraged to carry out the same actions the next time our lateral hypothalamus is activated. Also activated is the serotinergic system in which serotonin is the neurotransmitter, which acts in the limbic system to bring about feelings of happiness. There is evidence that the brains of overweight people have more serotonin receptors than normal, but it is unknown whether this is a cause or effect of obesity; it could even be genetic. In effect it means that these people must eat more in order to activate all of these serotonin receptors and feel the happiness food brings; this point reinforces the emotional impact of food. Stimulating serotonin receptors chemically in obese patients has had some degree of effect in that they have to eat less in order to feel satisfied leading to the conclusion that this system has a role to play in satiety.

Another regulatory or homeostatic system over which we have no conscious control but which is vital for our survival is fluid regulation. This time, it is the hypothalamus and the posterior pituitary that are involved. Despite our best efforts to evolve an outer layer of skin which is to all intents and purposes impermeable to water (Imagine going swimming if it wasn't. Messy!), we still lose fluids from the skin via sweat and from the respiratory system. However, the main way we lose water is via the urinary system in the kidney, which is very important in regulating the extracellular fluid (in both blood plasma and tissues) environment of the body. In the process of urine formation, the kidneys regulate the volume of blood plasma, the concentration of waste products in the blood and the concentration of electrolytes such as sodium and potassium amongst others. We know from Chapter 2 that Na$^+$ and K$^+$ are very important for our nervous system to work; without their close regulation, we couldn't have action potentials, and so, there is no way we could function at all. The main organ that the posterior pituitary has to work on with respect to fluid regulation is therefore is the kidney.

In the case of eating, the hormones that trigger the feeling of hunger lead to the behaviour of feeding. In fluid regulation, there are two different states that can signal that more water is needed (i.e. thirst). These are called hypovolemic thirst resulting from low extracellular volume and osmotic thirst resulting from a concentrated extracellular fluid. Hypovolemic thirst results from serious blood loss or fluid loss through diarrhoea, vomiting or bleeding. The blood vessels in the body are therefore not as full as they should be, so the first thing that happens is a dip in blood pressure. This drop is detected by pressure detectors in the blood vessels called baroreceptors, which cause the heart to decrease the release of atrial natriuretic peptide (ANP). ANP normally reduces blood pressure, inhibits drinking and promotes the excretion of water and salt from the kidneys. In the case of hypovolemia though, these are the last things you want so stopping the release of ANP is the first important step. The autonomic nervous system informs the brain of the state of affairs, triggering the limbic system to act on a drive to drink and also to eat salty food. In fact, our food preference for salty foods is increased through activity of the lateral hypothalamus. Replacing the water without replacing the salts (like NaCl) that have been lost in the blood too would result in blood that wasn't concentrated enough. As you will remember from Chapter 2, the body likes a concentration balance and in this case, salts would leave the cells to add concentration to the plasma, which would be entirely counterproductive. So we are driven to avoid this by the drinks and foods we ingest.

Another response from the brain results in the release of antidiruetic hormone (ADH – also known as vasopressin) from the posterior pituitary as diuresis is the production of urine. ADH is produced in the hypothalamus and stored in the pituitary. ADH increases the reabsorption of water from the kidney, thus decreasing the amount we lose in the urine. In diabetes insipidus ("passing bland", not to be confused with diabetes mellitus, or "passing sweet"), the release of ADH ceases leading to an inappropriate loss of water in the kidney and pale, very diluted urine which is produced in great quantities. The old test for diabetis insipidus was to taste the urine; if it tasted bland and insipid then this, along with the symptom of extreme thirst, was taken as evidence of the disorder. To modern GP's eternal gratitude, there are now other tests that can be done to diagnose this problem which is easily treated with the administration of ADH. The kidneys also have a hormonal part to play. The decreased blood volume leads to the release of the hormone renin into the circulation, which reacts with a protein called angiotensin to form angiotensin I, which is then converted to angiotensin II. As its name suggests (angeion is Greek for "blood" and tensio is Latin for "tension"), this causes blood vessels to constrict in order to maintain blood pressure or else all your blood would pool in your feet. Angiotensin II also acts on the preoptic area of the hypothalamus to promote drinking to redress the balance.

Osmotic thirst is thirst that results from overly concentrated extracellular fluid, perhaps by having a very salty meal. This causes water to be pulled out of the cells so that the inside and outside of the cell can be in concentration balance. The thirst is triggered to stop the cells from becoming dangerously depleted of water or dehydrated. In the 1950s, osmosensory neurons that react to the concentration changes in the extracellular fluid were found in the preoptic area and the anterior hypothalamus as well as the supraoptic nucleus. Most cells will try very hard to maintain their water content but osmosensory neurons swell up or shrink according to concentration changes. Their cell membranes have mechanically gated ion channels that respond to these different shapes leading to the activation of the hypothalamic-posterior pituitary pathway to release ADH to conserve water at the level of the kidney when there is high concentration. The feeling of thirst which then causes the drinking behaviour is therefore common to both hypovolemic and osmotic thirst and involves the same regions of the brain involved in the regulation of feeding.

Temperature regulation also relies on the activity of the hypothalamus, specifically the preoptic area and the anterior hypothalamus. The body likes a stable temperature of around 37°C (98.6°F). In 1981, D.O. Nelson and C. Ladd Prosser from Ohio State

University found that this area of the green sunfish monitors body temperature partly by monitoring its own temperature. These cells transduce small changes in blood temperature into changes in their firing rate. In fact, if you heat up the preoptic and anterior hypothalamus, the animal will pant or sweat. This latter study was carried out by Evelyn Satinoff from the University of Delaware in rats; I've never seen a panting fish. Equally however, if she cooled this area, the rat shivered, even in a warm room. She also found that rats would do tasks to get hot or cold air depending on whether this area was cooled or heated respectively.

The activity of the preoptic and anterior hypothalamus is reinforced by the temperature information these areas receive from the skin and spinal cord. The detection of temperature however is an entirely different thing to actually being able to raise or reduce temperature. It would seem that the activation of the cold-detecting neurons in the anterior hypothalamus causes the medial preoptic area to discharge thyrotropin-releasing hormone to the anterior pituitary that brings about the release of thyroid-stimulating hormone (TSH) which acts on the thyroid gland to release thyroid hormone. This hormone is really important in regulating our metabolic rate, too much and our heart and respiration rates increase, our bodies go into overdrive, too little and our metabolism goes to sleep leading to weight gain and lethargy. When we are cold however, an increase in metabolism is good as the burning of glucose by our cells creates heat. The sympathetic nervous system is also activated resulting in the release of noradrenalin which constrict blood vessels and blood vessels are diverted away from the skin. We also experience piloerection (or goosebumps, but piloerection sounds better), which helps us trap a layer of air the body has warmed around our exposed bits. All of these actions result in non-shivering thermogenesis. We all know the value of a good shiver however and this will also result in thermogenesis due to the action of our muscle activity. Shivering is mediated by the lateral hypothalamus. Without these areas of the hypothalamus however, shivering and panting behaviours are minimal, so all the animal can do is move to a warmer or colder environment which is a behaviour governed by our higher brain regions such as prefrontal and motor cortices. On the other hand, if the heat-detecting neurons of the anterior hypothalamus are activated by a rise in temperature, the preoptic area reduces the TSH release, blood vessels are diverted to the skin to lose heat, the lateral hypothalamus initiates panting in animals or causes humans to sweat (or glow if they are a lady). The higher cortical areas prompt us to move to cooler areas or sit on an air conditioning machine.

Sometimes however, it is advantageous for our body to be at a higher temperature than usual. We all have had experience of when we have some kind of infection and we get an ensuing fever. This is because certain types of bacteria grow less vigorously in a hotter environment and fever also enhances the activity of the immune system. This isn't unique to humans or even mammalians; fish and reptiles will also try to find a warmer area to produce a feverish body temperature when they are laid low with a lurgy. The mechanism for the increase in body temperature in relation to infection is relatively simple and has been delineated by the aptly named Michael Lazarus and colleagues from Harvard University. It turns out that the body's immune response to infection sends signals to the hypothalamus via the autonomic nervous system which increases the release of prostaglandins (which are local acting messenger molecules that almost all cells in the body are capable of producing). The medial preoptic area of the hypothalamus has receptors specific for prostaglandins and in mice that have been bred not to have these receptors in this area, fever does not happen. Therefore, the direct action of prostaglandins in the medial preoptic area leads to an increase in temperature creating a new set temperature of around 39°C (up from 37°C). If you get colder than that, the shivering and non-shivering thermogenesis behaviours will be initiated. All of those extra duvets, hot water bottles and layers of pyjamas are ways to increase your body temperature to fever proportions. If your temperature exceeds this, you will perceive this as too warm and have a bit of a sweating session, always added entertainment when ill…not. However, we can take it  too far. A fever above 39°C (103°F) is likely to be harmful whereas a fever above 41°C (109°F) is life-threatening.

Hopefully you can see by now how integral the hypothalamus is to our regulatory behaviours with different areas multitasking for different tasks, but it is also very important in non-regulatory behaviours as we shall see. On its own, the hypothalamus can initiate behaviours, but these behaviours are much more likely to be carried out again if we get a validation effect, in other words, a reward. We all use reward to improve our behaviour and the behaviour of others. How many times do you see parents rewarding kids for good behaviour? Some would call it bribing...; either way, it works. The body bribes us too; it rewards the behaviour that brings about a positive situation such as eating a meal after a period of hunger, having sex, passing a test etc. So what is the neural basis of "the rush" feeling you get when you've done something good?

The first clue to the presence of a reward system came from studies in which rats would press a bar to deliver a brief burst of electrical activity to specific sites in the brain. Despite the fact that they were zapping their brains albeit with low-level stimulation that mimics the brain's own electrical activity, rats went back to that bar to stimulate these sites more and more. They were clearly getting a pleasurable feeling from it. We now know that there are many areas of the brain that will maintain self-stimulation and that these are linked to many of our behaviours. Sometimes in the animal kingdom however, the reward system can lead to bizarre behaviour. Why does your well-fed cat bring you a mouse they caught and proceed to disembowel it before your very eyes? It's not because they are hungry. It is because cats have a brain circuit that rewards killing prey. This is an evolutionary throwback and makes sense in the days before Whiskas; these drives encourage cats to hunt and so not starve to death and it is not unique to cats in the animal kingdom.

The dopamine-producing cells in the midbrain form a particularly important node in the reward network. Indeed, dopamine is believed to be central to circuits mediating reward. When animals engage in behaviours such as feeding or sexual activity, there is an increased activity of neurons in the brainstem. These neurons project to other areas in the limbic system. Drug addiction is caused by a similar train of events that reward instinctual behaviour such as eating. Most addictive drugs work by altering levels of neu-rotransmitters, mainly dopamine in the limbic system's reward circuitry. However, unlike motivated behaviour, addictive drugs cause changes in the receptors to which they bind, making them less sensitive. This creates tolerance (the need to take sequentially larger amounts of drugs to produce the same effect) and addiction based on withdrawal effects (the feeling of unease when the sub-stance is removed).

Disruption to the reward system can leave people with a seem-ingly limitless appetite. They can never get enough of whatever they are hooked on: sex, food, risk or drugs and it can mediate regulatory and non-regulatory behaviours. Depending on which part of the reward system is most affected, a person may display anything from mild anxiety, and irritability to eating disorders, drug addiction and gambling. Obsessive compulsive disorder (OCD) is characterized by the feeling that something is not quite right in which people fail to generate the feeling of satisfaction when something has been done. Unsurprisingly, the biological basis of OCD has been linked to the serotonin system in the brain. People in the modern world often confess to being addicted to adrenalin. People who bungee jump, parachute jump, go surfing or zorbing or do all manner of other life-threatening (a.k.a. fun) activities can need more adrenalin to get a "buzz" than others. Adrenalin is released by the adrenal glands in response to stress and is mediated by the sympathetic nervous system. It is not how-ever the adrenalin that people are addicted to; it is the intense reward via the dopaminergic system provides them when they live to tell the tale, commonly called the "buzz". It is probably more accurate to say that they are risk-addicted. It may not make sense to you or me, but from an evolutionary perspective however, the risk of hunting a Woolley mammoth and perhaps dying in the process, had to be weighed up with the benefit of feeding the family throughout the winter. The underlying basis of this addic-tion is common to other behaviours such as gambling and shop-ping. Addiction to risk can therefore over-ride the self preservation instinct. It's also clear that risk is inherent and a major component of other addictive behaviours such as gambling (and going shop-ping on the first day of the sales...).

## Feeling curious?

*A total isolation experiment was carried out for a Horizon documentary in 2010. The BBC Worldwide YouTube channel has full coverage of the effects of isolation on behaviour.* http://www.youtube.com/view_play_list?src_vid=jfdN_megX4E&annotation_id=annotation_6316 32&p=0DCDF28C82617678&feature=iv

*Human Physiology* by Stuart Ira Fox. 2010; McGraw Hill. *Any basic physiology text book will give you more depth on the endocrine system and its value in regulating our internal behaviours but this book is a favourite of mine.*

*Eating Disorders and the Brain* edited by Bryan Lask & Ian Frampton. 2011; Wiley-Blackwell. *This book takes a thematic approach with chapters covering investigation, cause, effect and treatment of eating disorders written by experts in the field.*

Steven E. Hyman & Robert C. Malenka (2001) "Addiction and the Brain: the Neurobiology of Compulsion and Its Persistence". *Nature Reviews Neuroscience* 2, 695–703 doi:10.1038/35094560. *An article which discusses drug addiction however the underlying mechanisms can be applied to many different compulsions.*

*Understanding Drugs and Behaviour* by Andrew Parrott, Alun Morinan, Mark Moss and Andrew Scholey. 2007; John Wiley & Sons. *This book describes how classes of drugs affect the brain and so subsequent behaviour.*

# 9 Just sleep on it

Our lives are ruled by rhythm, and I'm not talking about "Dad dancing at weddings" rhythm here. These rhythms take the form of cycles, peaks and troughs of activity throughout the day, month or even year. In the natural world the tide goes in and out every day. Women have a monthly menstrual cycle up until the menopause (menopausal men buy motorcycles). The sleep/wake cycle is generally thought to be our most important daily cycle, and is known as a circadian rhythm. This is the rhythm that gets disrupted if you fly to another time-zone, particularly if you fly east. When everybody is ready for bed, you may be in the middle of the afternoon in your cycle and it takes time to adjust. Our sleep/wake cycle is very constrained to the day/night cycle of the sun and indeed light does control this circadian rhythm. Zeitgebers (meaning timegivers) are environmental events that entrain biological rhythms and light from the sun is our most important Zeitgeber. But what would happen if we lived in a nuclear bunker and we had no light cues at all? What would happen to our biorhythms then?

It turns out that in the absence of external environmental cues, we have a perfectly functioning biorhythm, but our sleep/wake cycle would last for 26 hours and not the 24 that we usually have to match the day/night cycle. This endogenous circadian clock seems to be located in the suprachiasmatic nucleus (SCN) of the hypothalamus. If the SCN is disconnected from the rest of the brain, its neurons continue to show fluctuations of neuronal activity that match the circadian rhythm. Damage to the SCN causes animals to continue to eat, drink, exercise and sleep but they do so at haphazard times and so the SCN is not just a biological clock but acts as a pacemaker for other rhythms too. The location of the SCN (see Figure 9.1) also explains how light can entrain our

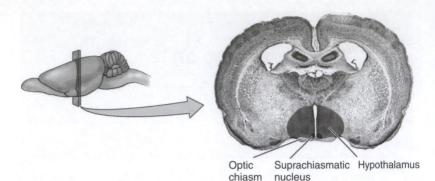

Optic     Suprachiasmatic   Hypothalamus
chiasm   nucleus

**Figure 9.1** The SCN interacts with the hypothalamus and our visual system to entrain our circadian rhythm. From *An Introduction to Brain and Behavior*, Third Edition by Bryan Kolb and Ian Q. Whishaw © 2011 by Worth Publishers. Used with permission.

endogenous rhythm as it receives direct input from the retina (the retino-hypothalamic pathway mentioned in Chapter 4) allowing light to direct the rhythmic activity of the SCN.

Light also modulates the amount of two different hormones in the body that have direct effects on the brain: serotonin and melatonin. When light levels decrease, serotonin is converted into melatonin in the pineal gland and released into the blood stream, which in turn promotes sleep by acting on the inhibitory mechanisms in the brain, in effect slowing us down. In contrast, in high light level conditions, the pineal does not convert serotonin into melatonin and so we are more alert and have more serotonin in our systems. Light/dark cycles change throughout the year however and through many winters in the high latitudes, light levels and duration of light in a day can be considerably lower. In animals, this circannual rhythm triggers hibernation or migration but in humans it also results in measurable effects. Seasonal affective disorder (SAD) is triggered by decreased light levels altering the biorhythm of humans to trigger hibernation-like behaviour. The pineal gland converts serotonin into melatonin causing sufferers to feel constantly sleepy and the decrease in serotonin leads to depressed mood.

SAD was first described by the Roman scholar Jordanes in the 6th century in his writings about Scandinavia. In fact, 9.5% of people in Finland suffer from SAD every winter but the Icelandic people (at the same latitude) seem to be immune. This may be due to the amount of fish present in the Icelandic diet, which is rich in Vitamin D. The best way to get Vitamin D is by absorption through the skin from sunlight and it has a very important role in the absorption of calcium from our diet through our gut. As you now know, calcium is not only important for healthy bones and teeth, but also nerve conduction (Chapter 2) and so a lack of Vitamin D will result in impaired neural activity. Therefore SAD may be caused by an interaction between lack of light (causing an increase in melatonin which makes us lethargic) and a lack of Vitamin D, so treatment of this disorder is most effective when both of these issues is addressed. Increasing the amount of Vitamin D in our diet is the easy step, but we need to be a little more creative when playing with the retino-hypothalamic pathway as the NHS will not pay for winter holidays to sunnier climes, more's the pity. A bright sunny day has an intensity of 100,000 LUX (a measure of light intensity) and the ambient light in our homes and offices reaches only around 500 LUX. However, treatment with a light which reaches intensity of 10,000 LUX can have the desired effect on our retino-hypothalamic pathways, telling our SCN it is daytime and also telling our pineal gland to decrease production and release of melatonin. Twenty minutes to half-an-hour of exposure to a light of this brightness a day during the autumn and winter should do the trick.

Circadian rhythms are becoming increasingly important in medicine with the discovery that many treatments such as those for cancer or heart disease are more effective if drugs are administered at the time of day at which they may be optimally incorporated into the body. There is a strong correlation between time of day and cardiovascular events, which often coincide with the early morning surge in blood pressure at (on average) 6:45am. In fact, a link has been made between body clocks that misfire due to genetic causes and heart disease. The circadian clock directly controls a gene that regulates the production of aldosterone, a kidney hormone which regulates how much water we keep and how much we excrete; its activation at the incorrect time can cause water retention. This leads to an increase in blood volume and therefore an increase in blood pressure. Shift workers, long-distance flight crews and people with sleep disorders have a heightened risk of heart problems and so this strengthens the link between the role of this biorhythm and health. Other bodily

functions which peak and trough during the day include testosterone secretion which is greatest at 9am. Our best coordination will be achieved at 2:30pm with our fastest reaction time
happening an hour later. Our highest blood pressure occurs at
6:30 pm followed 30mins later by our highest body temperature.
Melatonin secretion starts at 9pm and ends at 7:30am the following morning.

One group of people for whom normal timings do not stand
however is teenagers. The adolescent body clock is shifted forward
by at least an hour in that melatonin is not released until 10pm.
This leads to a state of chronic jet lag as melatonin is still being
released as the school day starts. Not only have studies shown that
teens learn best in the afternoon but given how important sleep
is to learning, depriving school-goers of even part of their sleep
period could be detrimental. Some schools have taken steps to
accommodate this biological oddity by starting the school day at
10am and this has had the effect of slashing absentee rates and
improving learning.

When we finally do settle down to go to sleep, the rhythm of the
brain's activity changes over the course of the night. We can measure this using electroencephalography (EEG) by fitting subjects
with close fitting caps with electrodes all over it so we can listen to
the electrical activity of the brain. This results in squiggles or waves
that are drawn on a pen recorder (or a computer screen nowadays)
which resemble the recording that you see in all of those earthquake disaster movies that are on TV in the afternoon. Not that
human brain function can be compared to an earthquake, but
I digress. Clearly, we don't get a bolt of electricity every time we
touch our head; these brain "waves" are very small. Therefore, the
hard technical part of recording them is not just in their detection
but their proportional amplification so that we can actually see
them. Such a machine was first developed by Hans Berger from
Bavaria, Germany in 1929. He was incredibly secretive about his
work, developing his brain-listening technique in his garage whilst
giving decoy lectures on telepathy! Hans tested the machine on his
son and readily identified alpha ($\alpha$) waves and beta ($\beta$) waves that
occurred while the boy was awake. If his son was concentrating on
a task, the beta waves were more common. These are small waves
in amplitude (low voltage) and there would be between 13 and

30 per second. The unit for this is Hertz, Hz for short. If his son was just having a bit of a relax, the waves got bigger and slowed down to a rhythm of between 8 and 12 Hz, which is an alpha rhythm.

Therefore, when the subject is awake, the brain waves are small but frequent. As the person goes into deeper sleep, brain waves get bigger and are slower. There are four definable stages of sleep as well as a stage of Rapid Eye Movement (REM) sleep that we cycle through throughout the night. In stage 1 sleep the EEG shows very irregular, low-voltage (or small) waves. There is less activity than the alpha waves seen when one is relaxed and awake but more than the other stages of sleep, it's called a theta (θ) rhythm and has a frequency of 4–8 Hz. Stage 1 happens when we are just dropping off. Stage 2 of sleep contains two characteristic brain patterns called K complexes and sleep spindles. Sleep spindles are indicative of the rhythm that the thalamus is trying to set to calm down and synchronize activity across the brain and a K complex is a high-amplitude spike in activity. K complexes are more likely to happen in the earlier cycles of sleep and result from the brain processing information from inside and outside of the body to decide whether or not we need to walk up i.e. whether there is danger for example. In fact, sudden stimuli like a loud bang can effect K complexes in any stage of sleep.

Stages 3 and 4 represent slow wave sleep characterized by delta (δ) waves in the EEG which have a frequency of less than 4 Hz. At this point, the activity of the entire brain is highly synchronized and very little sensory information gets to the cortex, if any at all. During these stages, the body temperature decreases, the heart rate declines, levels of growth hormone increase (which is why sleep is so important for children's natural development). Stages 1–4 of sleep are called non-REM or NREM sleep for pretty obvious reasons (See Figure 9.2).

We have 20-minute bursts of REM sleep every 90 minutes or so but these REM intervals get longer over the sleep period with much of our total REM sleep occurring in the latter half of the night. So what makes REM sleep different? Well, as the name suggests, our eyes move during this phase of sleep. This was discovered in the 1950s by a couple of scientists in America, Nathaniel Kleitman and Eugene Aserinsky, who were measuring eye movements to see when people went asleep. They assumed that eye movements

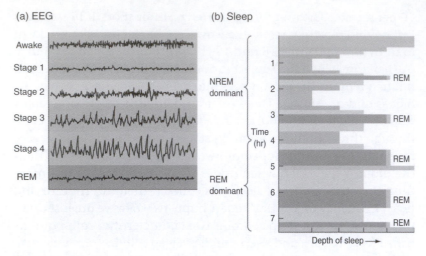

**Figure 9.2** The stages of sleep and how they are represented in EEG. We get a greater proportion of REM sleep as the night goes on, our deepest sleep (stage 4) occurs early in the sleep cycle. From *An Introduction to Brain and Behavior*, Third Edition by Bryan Kolb and Ian Q. Whishaw © 2011 by Worth Publishers. Used with permission.

would stop when you fell asleep. But they found that there were periods during the night when people routinely moved their eyes. Assuming this was complete tosh and nonsense, they blamed their equipment and did a bunch of very careful experiments to investigate their initial findings. Lo and behold, it turned out their equipment was functioning perfectly and we do have clearly definable periods when we move our eyes about, rapidly. So, they called it Rapid Eye Movement sleep. (Sometimes, the tosh and nonsense finding is true, and that's why I love them when they happen in my lab. Of course, sometimes they can lead you a merry dance down the scientific garden path but the fun is in the proving them right or wrong. Many of the scientific world's best discoveries have been made in this way, and some have been complete accidents of discovery.)

During REM sleep the EEG changes are striking. Brain activity now produces irregular, small amplitude, high-frequency waves that look much more like the waking EEG. Indeed, the brain is very active during this phase of sleep. Heart rate, blood pressure and breathing rate are all variable during REM periods. But one thing that is really remarkable is that this is the stage in which we are paralysed! Our body movements are inhibited; it's hard to tell with people, but if you have ever seen a sleeping horse you would know when he was in REM sleep as opposed to NREM sleep. Horses can doze standing up, and can sleep sitting down in that elegant way of theirs. But have you ever passed by a field where you think a horse is dead? He/she is completely flaked out on the grass? This horse is in REM sleep and no longer has the muscle tone to keep him/her upright. So, not dead, just sleeping. No need to crash the car looking.

As already mentioned, we cycle through the four NREM stages and REM sleep throughout the night. We start off in stage 1and slowly go through stages 2, 3 and 4 in that order. We spend longest in stage 4 in the early period of sleep and longest in REM towards the latter end but this can sometimes be dependent on how tired we are to begin with. The first cycle of sleep lasts about an hour and then we go back through stage 3, then 2 and then REM. The only time we have stage 1 therefore is at the very beginning of the sleep period. This sequence between stages 2 and 4 and back again with a bout of REM takes about 90 minutes.

You might notice that I haven't called REM sleep dreaming sleep. The temptation is there believe me. In fact, REM sleep has become synonymous with dreaming since the 1950s when Kleitman and William Dement found that people who were awakened in this phase reported dreams up to 90% of the time. Of course, this is not hard to justify as we can see much increased activity in the occipital cortex which would explain the visual imagery that we associate with dreams. It may be that the cerebral cortex is bombarded by signals from the brain stem (the origin of brain rhythms) and this generates a random collection of images from memory stores. But activity in the frontal areas, important for reasoning and decision making, is very low, hence the bizarro nature of some of our dreams. Because the frontal and parietal lobes are less active, the plot of the dream could be entirely preposterous and space could be represented in a strange way. (Ever had an upside-down dream?) Dreaming doesn't just happen in REM sleep; however, there is now evidence that dreaming also occurs in NREM sleep. Indeed, nightmares are most associated with this period of sleep and they tend to be logical and repetitive. This is, in fact, the phase of sleep in which night terrors happen, much more likely in children. If you wake people up from a phase of NREM they will be less likely to report dreaming; it does still happen but they are harder to remember.

So, how does sleep come about? The activity in our whole brain must be controlled and synchronized in order to create a neural environment in which sleep is possible. We have already mentioned the role of the SCN of the hypothalamus in the circadian rhythm and the pineal gland in the production of melatonin, but it is the action of melatonin on another area of the hypothalamus called the preoptic area that promotes sleep. Regulatory hormones are released from the hypothalamus which act on brainstem neurons to decrease the rate of their firing which then act on the neurons of the thalamus, perched on top of the brainstem, to send out the sleep rhythms characteristic of the different sleep stages. Slow rhythms from the thalamus block the flow of sensory information to the cortex meaning we don't wake up at the slightest thing (remember K complexes also have a role in this) and it also explains how some people are able to sleep with their eyes open; the brain is simply switched off to the visual input. Inhibition of neural firing is mediated by the brain's main inhibitory neurotransmitter GABA without which sleep could not occur. Therefore, there are two aspects required for sleep to occur: the setting of a rhythm of activity by the thalamus and the action of GABA so that if localized brain activity does occur (perhaps in the auditory cortex after a loud bang which is able to over-ride the top-down blocking signals from the thalamus), it is not passed on to other areas. We know that when we are asleep, brain activity is not passed on to neighbouring regions from Marcello Massimini's work at the University of Wisconsin, Madison. Using EEG recording, he has shown that if he applies a TMS pulse to the awake brain, lots of different regions become active. If he does this while the subject is asleep, only the local area becomes active.

Another important neurochemical is adenosine, which acts as a neuromodulator; it has the power to amend the firing rate of neurons and indeed inhibits neurons that release the excitatory neurotransmitters ACh and noradrenalin. Since these neurons promote wakefulness, their inhibition will do the opposite. Interestingly, caffeine blocks the action of adenosine and this is why coffee keeps us awake. There may be direct links between the immune response to infection and the regulation of sleep. This explains why some people have the uncanny knack of being able to sleep when ill and wake up two days later just fine, while the rest of us have been awake to endure the sore throat, runny nose, mental confusion that occurs with a bad winter cold. But it turns out that there are things that we can do to promote sleep. A really interesting study published in 2011 by a group from the University of Geneva, Switzerland, found that gentle swaying can synchronize brain waves during a short nap. This explains why rocking a baby helps it get off to sleep or why a little nap is irresistible if you find yourself relaxing in a swinging hammock. This may be because of the anatomical links between the vestibular and somatosensory system and the emotional areas for relaxation or the hypothalamus and thalamocortical networks involved in the induction of sleep. The rocking has to be at a pretty gentle rate of 0.25 Hz. If 1 Hz is one rocking cycle (side to side and back) a second then 0.25 Hz is one cycle every 4 seconds. Hence, people don't fall asleep on swings as they tend to swing faster than that. Can you imagine? A carnage of sleeping kids slipping off swings all over the playground. Entertainment.

The counterpoint to sleep of course is wakefulness and since normal brain function depends on alertness, it is worth knowing what areas of our brain are involved in generating this state. The posterior hypothalamus promotes wakefulness through the reticular activating system (RAS) of the brainstem (see Figure 9.3) and is mediated in part by the action of two excitatory neurotransmitters: serotonin in the raphe nucleus and noradrenalin in the locus coeruleus. The rhythms from the thalamus to the cortex get faster and so the sensory input can now arouse us from our slumber.

Damage to the RAS results in coma as these regions are no longer able to convey the "wake-up" signal. During REM sleep, the acetylcholine neurons in the pons (part of the RAS) become active and firing rates of the raphe nucleus and locus corerulus decrease to nothing and so there is a semi-activation of areas of the brain. However, descending regulation, from the cortex to the cerebellum normally prevents us from moving whilst dreaming. If an area on this pathway is damaged in cats they can actually move during REM sleep. When they dream, they act out what they are doing, in which case they most often pantomime catching mice. Could

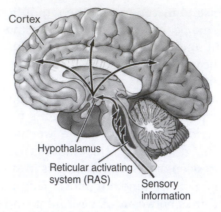

Cortex

Hypothalamus

Reticular activating
system (RAS)

Sensory
information

**Figure 9.3** The Reticular Activating System of the brainstem directly affects activity in the hypothalamus and so the rest of the cortex. Damage here results in the inability to wake up i.e. coma. From *An Introduction to Brain and Behavior*, Third Edition by Bryan Kolb and Ian Q. Whishaw © 2011 by Worth Publishers. Used with permission.

there be a learning or practice function for sleep? We'll talk about this a little later.

As you'll have realized by now, the hypothalamus doesn't just send all of its signals to the pituitary. It also has pathways that lead into the cortex. For example, neurons releasing the neurotransmitter histamine extend from the hypothalamus throughout the cortex which promote wakefulness, particularly during arousal and alertness. If you take anti-histamines therefore for a rash, allergies, an itch or an insect bite, you may become drowsy as one of your components of the alertness system is absent. However, there are now anti-histamines on the market that don't cross the blood-brain barrier and so don't have the unwanted effect of falling asleep at the controls of your forklift truck that the advice leaflet warns of. Another pathway from the hypothalamus, specifically the lateral and posterior hypothalamus, releases the neurotransmitter hypocretin to the basal forebrain and this is an important pathway in staying awake (as opposed to waking up). As soon as we go to sleep, the levels of hypocretin drop. The basal forebrain neurons project to the thalamus and the cerebral cortex. Some of these release acetylcholine, another excitatory neurotransmitter important in maintaining correct brain activity seen in a normal EEG pattern. Therefore, if hypocretin levels drop, this acetylcholine system is not activated and so our brain activity becomes less active.

Our individual sleep cycles may be related to the proteins that are produced by our genes and these in turn are determined by our genetic makeup. How our genes work and when our genes work may be dependent on our surroundings however and we know that this gene expression changes according to our sleep pattern (this field of enquiry that stands on the shoulders of genetic science is, as you know, called epigenetics and investigates the partnership between our genetic makeup and the environment). Many sleep disorders, or parasomnias, are particular to the phase of sleep in which they occur. For example somniloquay, or sleep talking, occurs during non-REM sleep as does somnambulism, or sleep walking, characterized by the acting out of complex behaviour while sleeping. Happily, the prevalence of sleep walking tails off after the age of 11 years; however, people have been known to drive, do laundry or even cook and eat large meals with no conscious awareness whist asleep and will wake up with no memory of the event. In fact, there is some recent evidence from Christina Gurnett and colleagues from Washington University that there

may be a chromosomal link to sleep walking. There seems to be a rift between mind and body in these cases: the cerebellum, which controls automatic movement and coordination, is active however the frontal and parietal lobes, corresponding to reasoning and conscious control of movement are dormant. EEG readings of sleepwalkers show a combination of delta waves and higher frequency "wakeful" waves.

Another parasomnia more prevalent later in life is sexomnia. Again people have no conscious control and do not remember their actions either with a partner or by masturbation. There is the danger that partners can be physically harmed in this way but there is also emotional and relational harm. If your partner is having a very fulfilling sex life while they are asleep, even though they are not aware of it, their rating of their desire for sex decreases as their sex hormones involved in libido have been "used up" so to speak. Therefore, you would seem to be superfluous to their sexual needs.

Yet another sleep related incident that may be harmful to relationships is hypnagogic myolonic twitch or "Hypnic jerk". That falling feeling that you get just when you are dropping off to sleep is also something that happens in the early NREM phase of sleep. Don't worry, it's not just you. Up to 70% of people do it and it can happen at least a couple of times a night. As the muscles relax just after you go to bed, somatosensory information about muscle tone is relayed to the brain. The changes in muscle tension are quite like those seen or felt when we are falling (Through space. You'll know what I mean if you have ever bungee jumped, and if you haven't, what's stopping you? It feels just the same as a hypnic jerk that you have probably already experienced!) and so the brain misinterprets the body's signals to make you believe you are falling. It tends to happen more often the more tired you are, and it's prevalence has been linked to people who are sleep deprived and are trying to fall asleep or who suffer from anxiety caused by not being able to fall asleep. The medical profession isn't worried and various sleep researchers see it as being a normal part of the shutting down procedures the body goes through in order to prepare for sleep. It's not dangerous, unless of course you are a poor unfortunate sitting in a cramped plane seat beside an habitual hypnic jerker on a long-haul flight. Keep tight hold of your peanuts. That's good advice in any walk of life I find.

Disorders related to the REM period of sleep can lead to some disturbing effects. Narcolepsy is when people fall asleep at inappropriate times and go straight into REM sleep and is characterized by excessive daytime sleepiness. It has been found that narcolepsy sufferers have a decreased number of hypocretin-releasing neurons in the hypothalamus. Since these neurons promote wakefulness, narcolepsy sufferers are unable to control their alertness thereby falling asleep at inappropriate times. The administration of modafinal, a drug which increases the hypothalamic histamine input and noradrenalin release from the locus coeruleus, helps improve wakefulness by decreasing the brain's reliance on the hypocretin pathway. There may be an autoimmune cause for narcolepsy although a genetic pre-disposition as well as exposure to a particular virus is also a theory as to its prevalence. Cataplexy is a form of narcolepsy in which an awake person suddenly loses all muscle tone in response to anger, surprise or laughter. They go straight into a hallucinogenic form of REM sleep but are fully conscious at the same time. Sleep paralysis is also coincident with narcolepsy in which a person has entered REM sleep but has partially awakened i.e. only part of the sleep regulatory system we talked about above is working. Because it occurs in REM sleep, the body is paralysed but the person is fully conscious. Happily, introducing a stimulus that over-rides the top–down thalamic blocking of sensory information can resolve this situation. A gentle touch to the person in sleep paralysis should arouse them. No thumping allowed.

The function of sleep as a whole is a complex and undefined issue. One of the earliest theories was that sleep happens as a result of a lack of sensory stimulation (i.e. night-time). But in isolation experiments with absolutely no sensory input, subjects spend less, not more, time asleep. So now we are left with three main theories. The first is that sleep is a biological adaptation to conserve energy to cope with times when food is scarce. Animals hunt or gather food at the optimal time for their species, be that in the day or in the night (for nocturnal animals) and sleep the rest of the time. But the amount of sleep could also be influenced by whether an animal is a predator or prey and so a balance must be struck between the amount of time required to gather food and the risk of predation.

We all love a good night's sleep so it seems obvious that another reason that is perhaps more prevalent to humans as to why we sleep is that it restores our bodies and minds. Research is ongoing to prove this intuitive link. Sometimes, it is not supported though. For example, energetic activity prior to sleep encourages us to go to sleep earlier, but not to sleep for longer. Although we know that we feel grotty when we have not slept well, or could not sleep for whatever reason, sleep deprivation studies have not clearly identified any function for which sleep is essential although cognitive performance is impaired the longer one is deprived. This clearly has impacts on professions in which long shifts are required such as emergency room doctors for example.

So why do we feel so bad if we haven't slept? Recent studies show that the immune system acts as if it is under attack when the body is sleep deprived; it's the same kind of reaction the body has to stress. There is a sharp increase in Nitric Oxide Synthase, which makes nitric oxide, which is a strong predictor of heart disease and other stress related illnesses. It just so happens that nitric oxide prompts recovery sleep. A study by a team of scientists at the Karolinska Institute in Sweden led by John Axelsson have discovered that pictures of people who have been awake for 31 hours are rated as being less attractive than pictures of the same people who have just arisen from an eight-hour sleep. So perhaps there is something in this beauty sleep thing ... Jim Horne from Loughborough University believes that women need more sleep than men as women multi-task and use more different parts of their brain, thus requiring the reset function more than men. Jim concedes however that if a man has a job that requires the juggling of lots of different tasks against a time constraint however, he may need as much sleep as women routinely do. Gerhard Kloesch and colleagues at the University of Vienna have shown that no matter which sex needs more sleep, men who sleep with partners get less out of it even though they report that they sleep better with a partner. Even without sex, their sleep is more disturbed than when they sleep alone and this has knock on sleep deprivation effects. Women's patterns are also affected but they have more deep sleep periods than men.

The third reason put forward as to why we sleep comes from the observation that sleep is important in memory consolidation. Non-REM slow wave sleep has a role in hippocampus-dependant declarative memory for events (see Chapter 11) and according to Olaf Lahl in 2008, even a six-minute nap improves verbal recall performance! I suppose this means it is a good idea to nod off during one of my lectures...; REM sleep on the other hand seems to be very important in the learning of procedures. Our learning of movements required for piano playing and driving for example gets a boost following a period of REM sleep as opposed to the passage of time without sleep. Indeed, imaging studies show that the brain areas active in the learning of the movement are also active during REM periods in the following sleep period. Napping with REM sleep can also make you less sensitive to other's emotions. Matt Walker from the University of California discovered that people were significantly more sensitive to angry or fearful faces as the day wore on. But if his subjects were allowed a 90-minute nap at lunchtime in which they managed to achieve REM sleep, they were less sensitive to angry and fearful faces and more receptive to happy faces! Therefore, REM sleep may allow our emotional reactions to reset to the baseline we experience early in the day.

Yawning is something that we all do when we are tired but what exactly does yawning do for us? It seems pretty well accepted that yawning is a quick and easy way to get more oxygen into the body and for your brain this will have the happy consequence of making you more alert. This explains why we yawn when in a stuffy environment as much as why we yawn when we didn't get enough sleep last night. Also, if you watch a movie with lots of people yawning in it, you will yawn. This works even if the person you are talking to over the phone yawns or even if your dog yawns. Your dog will yawn if you yawn too; I yawn when my dog yawns. In fact, all this talk of yawning may be making you yawn right now. It's always been thought that how much you can be infected by yawning is a measure of your empathy. However, in really fun experiment in 2007, a father and son duo Andrew and Gordon Gallup from the State University in New York placed cool packs on subjects' heads while they were watching movies of yawning people. The subjects yawned less frequently than if they didn't have the cool packs on. So this can be taken as evidence that yawning also has the effect of cooling your brain, perhaps independent of oxygen, thus making you more alert. But why do we all yawn together? Yawning is a brainstem function, the evolutionarily oldest part of the brain. If we think about how humans have evolved over thousands of years, various mechanisms have evolved to ensure our survival. Contagious yawning may be one such mechanism to improve group alertness when the group is off hunting a woolly mammoth or something. Even in today's day and age, army parachutists report having a good old group yawn before they jump out of the plane. I might have a jolly good scream too while I was at it.

Although sleep is a vital neurobiological function, it has always been thought that due to our lack of consciousness, the brain is relatively dormant throughout a sleep period. As we have seen however, nothing could be further from the truth. The activity required to send us to sleep, keep us asleep and wake us up again involves coordinated activity in widespread regions of the brain, both cortical and sub-cortical so it is no longer accepted as the passive process it was originally thought to be. Although one of the reasons for sleep is energy conservation, the sleeping brain uses 65 calories an hour to keep us ticking over; this is in comparison to the 95 calories an hour it takes to do a crossword. Suffice to say, the brain never switches off completely.

## Feeling curious?

Erik D. Herzog (2007) "Neurons and Networks in Daily Rhythms". *Nature Reviews Neuroscience* 8, 790–802 doi:10.1038/nrn2215. *A comprehensive review of what makes us tick.*

*Sleepfaring: A Journey through the Science of Sleep* By Jim Horne. 2007; Oxford University Press. *An entertaining account of all things sleep related including parasomnias.*

Katharina Wulff, Silvia Gatti, Joseph G. Wettstein & Russell G. Foster (2010) "Sleep and Circadian Rhythm Disruption in Psychiatric and Neurodegenerative Disease". *Nature Reviews Neuroscience* 11, 589–599 doi:10.1038/nrn2868. *An article which seeks to disentangle the cause and effect of sleep disorders and neurobiological problems.*

Andrew C. Gallup & Gordon G. Gallup (2007) "Yawning as a Brain Cooling Mechanism: Nasal Breathing and Forehead Cooling Diminish the Incidence of Contagious Yawning". *Evolutionary Psychology* 5: 92–101. *The Gallups' experiment investigating yawning, thermoregulation and how you catch a yawn.*

R. Allada & J.M. Siegel (2008) "Unearthing the Phylogenetic Roots of Sleep". *Current Biology* 5;18(15):R670–R679. *A cross species investigation of the reason why we sleep.*

# 10 Let's talk about sex

In the past couple of chapters, we have talked about behaviours that we are driven to complete but for the most part happen outside of our conscious control. In this chapter we will begin to explore the role of the brain in non-regulated behaviours, those that we do not rely on for our survival, and a good example of this is sexual behaviour.

The word "sex" in fact applies to much more than copulatory activity. It is the definition of whether we are genetically male or female; this is called our genotype. Every cell in our body which is not involved in reproduction (i.e. the oocyte or egg from the female or the sperm from the male) has 23 pairs of chromosomes, 46 in total, half from the paternal side and half from the maternal side. One of these pairs is the sex chromosomes. There are two types of sex chromosomes referred to as X or Y because of their appearance. The female has two X chromosomes and the male has one X chromosome and one Y chromosome. The oocyte and sperm cell are different in that each of these has only 23 chromosomes. Therefore, the fertilized egg will have 46 chromosomes in total, 23 from the mother and 23 from the father.

We are therefore a product of our genotype (whether we are XX or XY) but there is another side to the story. We are also susceptible to the action of sex hormones pre-natally and the proportion of sex hormones post-natally. The production and release of sex hormones post-natally is governed by the brain, and just the same as regulatory behaviour, the hypothalamus has a big role to play. But let's start our story from the beginning.

In the days following fertilization of the oocyte by the sperm cell, otherwise known as conception, the egg begins to divide, slowly growing. By 21 days it is a ball of cells with a tiny heart which begins to beat at this stage. At this point and all the way to the sixth week, the embryo is identical regardless of whether it is XX or XY and has the potential to become either male or female; and the precursor tissue for making either the testes or ovaries is present. The male reproductive system results from the Wolffian ducts, which have the potential to develop into the seminal vesicles, prostate and vas deferens, all components of the testes and penile structure. In contrast, the Müllerian duct gives rise to the development or the uterus, oviducts (fallopian tubes) and upper part of the vagina in females.

In the sixth week, something must happen in order to differentiate the embryo into male or female and that something is the activation of SRY, a gene located in the short arm of the Y chromosome and so only present in XY or male embryos. SRY stands for sex-determining region of the Y chromosome and its action causes the release of a chemical called testis-determining factor which causes the foetal gonadal tissue to become testes. If SRY is not activated, the foetal gonadal tissue develops into the female ovaries, which start producing oestrogen at around 12 weeks.

It is at this stage that genetic influence over development yields importance to hormonal control. The initial hormones that organize the reproductive organs into male and female are released by the developing organs. The male testes produce two hormones, the androgen testosterone and Müllerian duct-inhibiting hormone. Testosterone is made from progesterone, which is ultimately made from cholesterol (yes, it is good for something). By the action of an enzyme called 5-α-reductase, testosterone is turned into a more powerful androgen called 5-α-dihydroxytestosterone and this hormone is very important in the differentiation of the penis and scrotum. The enzyme aromatase also acts on testosterone to create estradiol, which has a vital role in the masculinization of the male brain. What is really interesting about this process is that numerous things have to happen to make a foetus male starting with SRY through the action of androgens and Müllerian-duct-inhibiting hormone. If SRY is not activated, the female ovaries and external genitalia develop with relatively little fuss.

But what if things go wrong at this stage? Usually the genotype (our genetic makeup) and phenotype (or how your genotype is expressed, such as hair colour, sex etc.) are aligned in that individuals with XX chromosomes end up as females and XYs end up as males. However, there are a variety of genetic mutations that result in an ambiguous sexual phenotype. As already mentioned, the female egg and the male sperm have 23 chromosomes each, one of which is the sex chromosome. The egg cell always contains an X sex chromosome but the sperm cell could contain an X or Y chromosome. If a Y sperm cell fuses with the egg, the genotype of the resulting embryo will be XY. On the other hand, if the sex chromosome in the fusing sperm is X, a female XX will result. One developmental problem that occurs due to abnormalities at this genetic stage is Turner's syndrome. This happens if an egg is fertilized by a sperm which has lost its X chromosome or if the egg cell had lost its X chromosome. The resulting embryo will therefore have only one X chromosome. The genotype for this is XO. The correct development of the female ovaries requires the genes that are present on two intact X chromosomes, but despite this, the baby appears female in phenotype (because there is no Y chromosome). But because the ovaries did not develop properly, this can affect the production of hormones released at puberty leading to problems with menstruation, stunted growth and non-development of the breasts along with webbing of the neck and heart abnormalities. Turner's syndrome is not inherited and happens in 1 out of every 2,500 live births due to a random event in the production of the egg or sperm cells. Some of its symptoms can now be controlled by the administration of exogenous hormones by endocrinologists.

Even if there is a normal genotype, another problem may occur due to abnormally high levels of circulating androgens that results in a masculine phenotype of XX individuals. Called Congenital Adrenal Hyperplasia (CAH for short) it happens because the foetal adrenal glands lack an enzyme needed to make cortisol (a hormone which helps the body cope with physical stress) and aldosterone (a hormone important in the balance of salts in the body). The inability to produce these hormones results in the over secretion of androgens. If this happens at the stage of the differentiation of the female genitalia (week 6) it will result in the masculinization of the female genitalia, leading to the newborn having a small penis and a poorly formed scrotum. The internal organs are usually intact and normal as the androgens are released too late to affect their development. Therefore CAH results in an XX female who has normal gonads (ovaries) but masculine genitals and these individuals are sometimes referred to as pseudo-hermaphrodites.

What is a parent to do in this case? Do they raise the child as a boy or a girl? There are reports of these children being happily raised as boys in the past; however problems arose at puberty which would fail to follow the masculine pattern. Nowadays however, these kids are more likely to be raised as girls and treated with hydrocortisone to inhibit the production of androgens (and restore normal levels of cortisol). In some cases, surgery may be required early in life (3–6 months) to alter the genitalia to resemble the normal female. It would seem that in many cases, regardless of treatment, that girls with CAH will grow up with some masculine behaviours and will be described as "tomboys" by their parents and so the pre-natal circulating hormones, even if they are corrected post birth, can have an effect throughout the life of an individual most likely through their action on the developing brain which we shall talk about shortly. CAH can also happen in XY boys, but the problems associated with it are relatively minor in that they enter puberty at a much earlier age, developing body hair and a deep voice sometimes as early as two years old. The penis will be bigger than normal and the muscles will be defined well, and early.

Another problem related to circulating levels of androgen is Androgen Insensitivity Syndrome (AIS). This occurs when the developing foetus is not responsive to the circulating levels of androgens in an XY genotype resulting in the feminization of the male foetus. Although the SRY gene still works and the testes develop (thus inhibiting the Müllerian or female development), the lack of androgens means that the external genitalia are not formed properly (remember the androgen dihydrotestosterone was particularly important for this). The result is a male pseudo-hermaphrodite which looks like a girl due to the lack of male external sex organs. These children are often raised as females with problems detected only when menstruation does not happen at puberty. There is very little the medical profession can do about this as neither surgery nor hormone replacement can reverse its effects. This doesn't seem to be a problem however, as AIS individuals identify themselves as being females anyway due to the lack of masculinization of the brain by the androgen estradiol. But those with AIS will never be able to bear children of their own.

Now that we know what differences there are in the development of the male and female, it's not hard to accept that these hormones will have had different effects on the brain. For example, estradiol (derived from testosterone) is important in masculinizing the brain. As you know, estradiol is a form of oestrogen. So why does the oestrogen being released by the female ovaries not masculinize the female brain? Well, the reason is because oestrogen is bound into an inactive form by alpha fetoprotein in both sexes. The estradiol comes from converting testosterone into estradiol by aromatase, which is released by the hypothalamus and limbic system in the brain. Therefore, you need testosterone to begin with, i.e. from the male testes.

So, are female brains different from male brains? The short answer is yes and some of these differences point to behaviours that are more likely to be male over those which are female. Darwin dubbed these sex-based differences "sexual dimorphic behaviours" and the regions that differ in the male and female brains are dubbed sexual dimorphic regions. So here is the first big difference between the male and female brain. At birth, the size of the preoptic nucleus in the hypothalamus is the same in males and females but the action of estradiol post-birth results in the male nucleus growing to several times that of the female brain. The eventual size of the preoptic nucleus is correlated with testosterone levels and sexual activity in males later in life. As we found out in Chapter 8, the preoptic nucleus is also very important in temperature regulation during illness. It creates the conditions that make fever possible. Could it be that the male's bigger preoptic nucleus is the basis for "man flu"? We have no evidence yet; I'm just throwing it out there. Other differences between the male and female brain includes the INAH3 (3rd interstitial nucleus of the anterior hypothalamus), which is twice as large in males as females. Also, the suprachiasmatic nucleus (SCN) region of the hypothalamus has twice the number of neurons in the male brain as the corresponding female region.

As you can see, all these regions are areas of the hypothalamus and I think I nattered on enough about how brilliant this area of the brain is in previous chapters but it really is!). Given that the hypothalamus controls the levels of hormones in our body and these in turn affect our behaviour, having differences between males and females here will mean the two sexes definitely won't act in the same way, in some instances at least. The hypothalamus releases gonadotrophin-releasing hormone (GnRH) to the anterior pituitary which in turn release follicle-stimulating hormone (FSH) and luteinizing hormone (LH), which have actions in both the male and female reproductive system. The hormones are released cyclically in females however leading to the menstrual cycle. As FSH and LH act to develop and release oocytes, which in turn release varying levels of oestrogen and progesterone (which prepare the walls of the uterus to receive the oocyte), the release of FSH and LH is governed by a negative feedback loop related to the levels of oestrogen and progesterone in the blood at any one time.

In the female menopause, when there are few oocytes left, FSH production and release increases because its release does not result in an oocyte-producing oestrogen. Therefore, there is no signal to inhibit its release. There is also evidence that as the number of oocytes declines, the release of another ovarian hormone called inhibin declines, prompting a boost in the release of FSH, high blood levels of which is indicative that a woman is in menopause. The ovaries also release testosterone but only about 14% of what would be found in the male body. Its role in the female is to maintain muscle and bone mass and contributes to the sex drive or libido. After menopause however, testosterone release decreases by one-third. The symptoms of menopause generally include the inability to regulate temperature (hot flushes), mood swings, sleep disturbances, changes in metabolism and weight gain and more frequent urination. Therefore, the change in reproductive hormones and their feedback on the anterior pituitary and hypothalamus

seems to have wider effects on other behaviours, some of which are regulatory in nature.

Is there such a thing as the male menopause? Well, in men, it is the release of testosterone that is regulated by FSH and LH from the anterior hypothalamus. When testosterone levels drop, FSH and LH levels increase and vice versa in a negative feedback loop. Testosterone levels do drop as men age but unlike the female, there is not a well-defined period in which hormone production stops completely. Men can reproduce throughout their lives as, unlike the ovaries and the egg, the testes does not run out of the main ingredient it needs to make sperm. Low testosterone levels may reduce the sperm count but may also affect men in that they develop erectile dysfunction and experience an increase in breast size as well as a loss of body mass and muscle tone. It may also cause hot flushes, increased irritability and an inability to concentrate, all symptoms in common with the female menopause. The link between these latter symptoms and the decrease in testosterone are still controversial but it would seem that some men do experience a change in their reproductive hormone milieu akin to the female menopause. In men however, it is more accurately called the "andropause".

Back to the differences in male and female brains and the effects they have on behaviour. One of the main differences is how males and females conduct themselves during sex. There are many examples of this in the animal kingdom but one of the most obvious can be seen in the behaviour of rats. When the female rat is ready to mate, she displays proceptive behaviours such as ear wiggling, hopping and darting about. Admittedly, these are behaviours that a bunch of frisky teenagers down your local town centre may display late on a Saturday night…; but let's stick with rats for now. The female rat then adopts a lordosis posture in which she arches her back and elevates her rump. This is mediated by the ventromedial region of the hypothalamus, which has many oestrogen receptors and so this behaviour will be carried out when

oestrogen levels are high. Lo and behold, oestrogen levels are at their highest around the time of ovulation. If the female has sex with a male at this time, the chances of fertilization and subsequent pregnancy are high.

The actions of the female prompt the male to mount the female and begin to mate and this action is mediated by the preoptic region of the hypothalamus (which is much bigger in males than females). In fact, the "sex action" of an animal can be dissociated from the motivation to have sex. If the preoptic area of the hypothalamus is damaged, males will not mate with females but will continue to show interest in them. For example, monkeys with lesions to the hypothalamus will not mate with receptive females but will masturbate while watching them from across the room. A classic experiment to investigate sexual motivation involving rats required a male rat to press a bar to gain access to a receptive female. The female literally drops through a trap door into the male rat's cage! A rat with a lesion to the hypothalamus will continue to press the bar to gain access to the female but he won't do anything when she gets there. On the other hand, a rat with a lesion to the amygdala doesn't have the motivation to press the bar to get access to the female but if that female is placed inside the cage with the male, he will mate with her. And so it would seem that the hypothalamus is central to sexual behaviour whereas the amygdala is involved in the motivation aspects of sex.

The amygdala is one of a wider range of structures called the limbic system that is very important in emotion and reward and we will talk more about this in Chapter 11. We all think about sex; we may occasionally dream about it. These behaviours involve the action of the hypothalamus and limbic system but they surely involve other regions of the cerebral cortex in humans at least. For example, visual imagery about sexual activity must include activity in visual cortex. We can examine this question not just by getting people to think about sex but also to achieve orgasms in an fMRI scanner. As scientists, we often moan about the fact that the questions we are interested in are just not sexy enough for the public to care about, but this is a definite exception! Beverly Whipple of Rutgers University has examined various aspects of the female orgasm and has discovered that a multitude of brain regions are involved from the hypothalamus, through the limbic system, including most areas of the cortex as well as the basal ganglia and cerebellum. Bruce Arnow and colleagues from Stanford University discovered activation in similar regions when heterosexual males were sexually aroused whilst watching erotic videos. We can also investigate what happens to sexual behaviour following brain damage. Lesions to the frontal lobe are just as likely to result in a loss of inhibition about sexual behaviour as they are to produce a loss of interest in sexual behaviour. This is indicative of the moderating influence the frontal lobe has over the activity in the amygdala. Lesions to the left dorsolateral prefrontal cortex are more likely to result in aggressive sexual behaviour and dysfunction of the frontal lobe can lead to a condition called erotomania in which a sufferer believes that another person is in love with them the way they are with the object of their affections.

Our experience with sex as well as imaging studies and neuropsychological investigations indicate that the successful completion of sexual behaviour is accompanied by a reward, called the orgasm. This is caused by the release of the neurotransmitter dopamine in the reward circuits of your brain and the feeling of relaxation and bonding with your partner is caused by a release of oxytocin from your posterior hypothalamus. Oxytocin has a chemical structure that closely resembles endorphins, which are the brain's natural pain killers. This explains two oddities of human behaviour. People who have suffered chronic pain for years can suddenly be cured or at least have their pain relieved by falling in love and this is no doubt due to the ability of oxytocin to block pain signals like endorphins do. Equally, new lovers feel agitation when they are separated and this may be caused by their desire to increase their oxytocin levels. Along with the activity in the dopamine reward system, the lovers show signs of addiction (in this case, to love) and cannot cope with the withdrawal of the closeness of their partners. Most times, the frontal lobe kicks in to rationalize the situation, so this doesn't last.

One factor that is outside of our control is the effect pheromones have on our behaviour. Olfactory receptor cells are used to detect odorants (smells) but they can also detect pheromones.

These chemicals are not perceived consciously as smells but they nevertheless influence behaviour. Processed by the vomeronasal organ in the nose, they directly activate the amygdala and the hypothalamus. Pheromones explain why a bunch of women living together will coincide in their menstrual cycles (called the Witten effect) and these chemicals may be produced in the armpit. We know this because Michael Russell and colleagues from the University of California swabbed the armpits of women and swabbed the result in turn on the upper lip of a second woman. The second woman synchronized her menstrual cycle with that of the first. Pheromones also explain why you could be incredibly sexually attracted to a member of the opposite sex you can't stand as they transmit information about the immune system of the emitter. Claus Wedekind and colleagues at the University of Bern in Switzerland got men to wear the same T-shirt for two nights in a row and took blood samples so that the genetic make-up of their immune system could be determined. Then, they got women, whose own immune systems had been examined, to smell the T-shirts and say which one they liked best. It turned out that the women preferred the T-shirt from the male who had the most dissimilar immune system to them. This preference would be highly beneficial to any potential offspring as a mix of immunity genes that are more wide ranging would give them protection to a wider range of diseases.

We have covered the differences between men and women's brains with respect to sexual behaviour, but is there a difference between the sexes for other behaviours and tasks? The obvious difference is aggression in that males tend to be more aggressive than females and this can be neatly correlated with the levels of circulating androgens in the system which, for example, act to decrease the amount of serotonin release. As we will discover in Chapter 11, serotonin acts to reduce aggression and so a decrease in serotonin will lead to an increase in aggression. It is also a widely held belief that men and women think differently with a wide range of tests showing that women generally do better in tests of verbal fluency whilst men do better on tests of spatial reasoning. One possible explanation for this is evolutionary. Males have tended to range over larger territory in order to catch prey and so greater spatial abilities would be advantageous. It might also be argued that females were left behind in social groups and thus were more likely to develop more advanced tools for social communication. Is there any basis for these theories in the human brain however? Although women's brains tend to be slightly smaller than males (possibly due to the effect of androgens on the male brain), MRI has uncovered some other more subtle differences. The inferior parietal lobe, an area known to be involved in spatial and mathematical abilities, is bilaterally larger in males over that seen in females. On the other hand, two areas involved in language, Broca's area in the left inferior frontal lobe and Wernicke's area in the left superior temporal lobe, are bigger in females than in males. Also, the posterior end of the corpus callosum (the big tract of nerve fibres that link the hemispheres) is relatively bigger in females once you take the larger size of the male brain into account. It is this difference and the proposed increased connectivity between hemispheres in the female brain that may be the source of some of the more subtle differences in cognitive ability between males and females. Using fMRI, we can see what parts of the brain are active during the processing of a task the subject is given to do in the scanner. The female brain seems to be bilaterally active, especially for language tasks whereas the male brain showed activity only in the left side. This added "brain power" that women devote to language tasks may explain why they are better at such tasks and the finding may also explain why strokes which cause damage to the left side of the brain are more likely to cause profound language deficits in men as opposed to women. However, Markus Hausmann and colleagues from Durham University have found it may be that the female brain becomes less lateralized (and shows more bilateral activity) according to the level of sex hormones at any particular time leading to changes in abilities across the men-strual cycle. So it may be true that women are bad at parking, but don't get carried away boys, this only happens for a limited time during the menstrual cycle. Limited. Got it?

Differences in the structure of the hypothalamus may form the basis of sexual orientation and sexual identity or gender (a person's sex being their genotype and their gender being the sex that person identifies themselves as). Much of the work on sexual orientation has been done in homosexual men. As already mentioned, the suprachiasmatic nucleus (SCN) of the hypothalamus has twice the number of neurons in the male brain than the corresponding region in the female. However, the SCN is twice as large in gay men as in heterosexual men. The functional significance of this difference is unclear but it may have resulted as a by-product of the lack of pruning by lower levels of circulating androgens in early brain development. The SCN is involved in the regulation of the sleep/wake cycle and biorhythms. Indeed, there is some evidence from Dick Swaab from the Netherlands Institute for Brain Research that male rats with an abnormal SCN caused by deprivation of testosterone in early development make advances towards male and female rats early in their active period of the day but veers towards female partners as the day goes on. There is absolutely no evidence to date that this has been replicated in humans.

Another region, the third interstitial nucleus of the anterior hypothalamus (INAH3) is twice as large in males as in females. But the INAH3 is half the size in the homosexual male brain as that in the heterosexual male brain, but on average is still bigger than the heterosexual female region. This area has more cells with androgen receptors in men than in women and again seems to be related to lower level of circulating androgens in early development. In contrast, there is some evidence that homosexuality in women results from an increase in circulating androgens in early development, but little has been done examining the difference between the gay and straight female brain. The increased androgen view is supported however by the increased proportion of homosexual females that result from congenital adrenal hyperplasia (remember, these foetuses are exposed to high levels of androgens), but clearly not all homosexuality in females can be explained by CAH.

There may be a genetic cause of homosexuality via influence of a gene which is sex linked to the tip of the X chromosome called Xq28, which could cause the difference in circulating androgens in early brain development which leads to these sexuality dimorphic regions. There is no difference between homo and heterosexual levels of circulating hormones post puberty.

Using MRI in 2008, Ivanka Savic & Per Lindström from the Karolinska Institute in Sweden showed gay women have asymmetric brains like straight men (who seem to have larger right hemispheres). In contrast gay men have more symmetric brains like straight women (during most of their menstrual cycle!). Interestingly, it is possible to link the behaviour of gay men and women in times of crisis to how their limbic system is wired up. The amygdala of straight women and gay men connects to areas of the brain that manifest mood, fear and anxiety. The amygdala of gay women and straight men connects more to sensorimotor system and striatum of the basal ganglia leading to a much more action-related response. Put in real life terms, if a gay man or a woman were accosted by a robber demanding their money, much screaming may result. However, if the same situation were to happen to a gay woman or a man, they would probably bop the robber one instead. Of course, reality is not as clear cut as this study doesn't take into account the modulating influence of the frontal lobes. Phenotypical sex and sexuality occur on a continuum on which every point is represented and there are many points of intersection between the male and female, gay and straight brain. What is interesting is that variants of structural differences in the brain are evident at these points.

Transgender individuals feel strongly that their gender (whether they identify as a male or female) does not match their sex and this, is also generally assumed to be caused by a disturbed interaction between circulating hormones and brain development. Some structural differences, specifically in the connections between the amygdala and the hypothalamus have been found by Swaab and colleagues. The tragic case of a boy being raised a girl in the 1960s after a botched circumcision destroyed his penis at the age of 7 months particularly resonates with the hypothesis that circulating androgens in the prenatal brain determines sexual identity. Even though Bruce became Brenda following a castration at 18 months carried out on the advice of a doctor specializing in sex changes called Dr. John Money, Brenda always showed male-specific behaviours, like standing up whilst urinating etc. Although sworn to secrecy by Dr. Money, Brenda's parents could see how unhappy she was becoming living as a girl and at aged 14 told her the story. From that day forward, Brenda became David and lived his life as a man, had reconstructive surgery, married a woman at 25 and although he could have no kids of his own, he happily helped raised his three new step-children. Although David had much less circulating testosterone (since the castration), he still identified himself as male due to his prenatal development and it was not possible to change this by rearing him as a boy (and so it can be concluded that rearing was not decisive in gender identity).

Other issues correlated with sexual orientation include parental stress and birth order. It is known that parental stress alters sexual development in lab animals. Stress releases endorphins in the brain which decreases the effect of testosterone in the hypothalamus of the developing foetus. Corticosteroids are also elevated leading to decreased testosterone (remember, the opposite was true in congenital adrenal hyperplasia). Nadezhda Nosenko and Alexander Rezinkov from the University of Kiev have suggested that these lower levels of testosterone lead to the changes in brain structure prevalent in the gay male brain we have already discussed. Interestingly, two-thirds of women who gave birth to gay sons confirm their hypothesis and admit to being under some form of stress during pregnancy; however, these findings could be merely subjective.

Meanwhile, a Canadian neuroscientist called Ray Blanchard has noted that the prevalence of homosexuality is higher among men who have an older brother and that this finding is restricted to boys who are right-handed. It is thought that this may account for one in seven homosexual males and Anthony Bogaert thinks there could be a link with the immune system in that a mother's immune system may react against a protein in a son and then attacks subsequent sons to alter their development. Supporting this hypothesis, homosexual sons born later in the time line are also smaller than their older brothers. Taken together, all these findings indicate that whatever the cause of homosexuality, people are born that way and choice is not a factor.

Another related non-regulatory behaviour, parenting, also relies on areas of the hypothalamus for its initiation but is triggered by the circulating hormones in the body, just as sexual behaviour is. Prior to giving birth, the mother rat's brain increases its sensitivity to estradiol in the medial preoptic area and the anterior hypothalamus. Remember from Chapter 8 that these are the areas intimately involved in the regulation of feeding, drinking and temperature? It would also seem that antidiuretic hormone released by the supraoptic and periventricular nuclei of the hypothalamus and stored in the posterior pituitary in male prairie voles prompts good pair bonding with his female and exemplary helping behaviour in the rearing of their young. What does this mean for humans? For sure, giving birth to a baby and the hormonal changes that happen along with release of oxytocin from the posterior pituitary promotes good parenting behaviours. However, it would seem that the hormonal changes seen in new parents are not contingent on the pregnancy itself; simply the behaviours required to look after a new child can stimulate their production thus explaining how adopted children can still have excellent parents.

## Feeling curious?

*Delusions of Gender: The Real Science Behind Sex Differences* by Cordelia Fine. 2011; Icon Books. *A robust and entertaining account of what the differences in brain development between boys and girls actually mean for sexually dimorphic behaviours.*

Larry Cahill (2006) "Why Sex Matters for Neuroscience". *Nature Reviews Neuroscience* 7, 477–484 doi:10.1038/nrn1909. *This article seeks to tackle various misconceptions in the topic of sex differences in the brain.*

James G. Pfaus (1999) "Neurobiology of Sexual Behavior". *Current Opinion in Neurobiolology* 9(6):751–58. *Review article covering the brain's involvement in all aspects of sexual behaviour.*

*Gay, Straight, and the Reason Why: The Science of Sexual Orientation* by Simon LeVay 2010; Oxford University Press. *A thorough account of the history of research into homosexuality and the current thinking on the issue.*

De Vries GJ, Rissman EF, Simerly RB, Yang LY, Scordalakes EM, Auger CJ, Swain A, Lovell-Badge R, Burgoyne PS, Arnold AP. (2002) "A Model System for Study of Sex Chromosome Effects on Sexually Dimorphic Neural and Behavioral Traits". *Journal of Neuroscience.* 22(20):9005–14. *This article delves into the theory that genes sitting on the sex chromosomes have an effect on behaviours that are different between males and females.*

# 11 Second that emotion

Most of everything that we consciously do has some emotion attached; either emotion has a role in how we act or there is an emotional impact of what we do. All of us have also experienced the physiological effect our body has in response to emotion, such as shaking hands, thumping heart or whatever. So it won't come as any surprise to you that emotion requires the involvement of much of our brain. But knowing what parts of the brain do what in emotion is the easy part of this story. The hard part comes from trying to understand which comes first: the perception of an emotional situation or the physiological response to it.

This argument has been rumbling on since the mid-to-late 1800s and frankly, there is support for the two main sides. The oldest view comes from William James, an American philosopher, in 1884. Around the same time, the Danish psychologist, Carl Lange, came up with pretty much the same theory and so it is called the James–Lange hypothesis. In short, it purports that the physiological changes come first and we use these to perceive emotion i.e. "my heart is thumping therefore I must be in fright" or "I am crying therefore I must be sad" or "my hands are shaking, I must be nervous". If you only consciously perceive emotion based on the physiological responses feeding back to your brain then people who have a severed spinal cord must feel very little emotion right? Well, in 1966, an American psychologist who worked for the VA Paraplegia Service, George Hohmann, investigated this very issue. He discovered that the lower the severance of their spinal cord, the less effect it had on their emotion presumably because the brain still had much of the body to listen to. Those men who had damage to the spinal cord higher up with little peripheral sensation did notice a difference. It was as if their emotions were dulled, their anger had no "heat", with anger being more mental than before. Spinal cord transaction doesn't abolish emotional perception though and so this evidence supports the James–Lange model to a degree, but it does not tell us whether perception of emotion or the physiological response comes first, just that the perception feeds off the physiological response and possibly vice versa.

The other main view is that of the Cannon–Bard model, double barrelled again because Walter Cannon's theories were further investigated by his Harvard colleague Phillip Bard. This theory holds that the perception of an emotional stimulus and the physiological response occur separately and independently. The model is even more specific; the thalamus acts as the gateway for the sensory experience and sends two signals, one to hypothalamus to activate the autonomic nervous system responsible for the physiological response and another for the perception of the emotion in the cerebral cortex. The evidence that prompted this theory came from research carried out in the 1920s. Cannon showed that if you inject adrenalin into people thus giving them the physiological effects of activation of the autonomic nervous system, no perception of concurrent emotion occurs. People didn't suddenly get afraid or angry or display any other emotion. They just coolly commented that their heart was racing off its own accord. How interesting that must have been for the subjects!

Another way that you can induce a physiological response without the perception of emotion is to present a stimulus such as an angry face to subjects and you immediately mask it by a picture of a neutral face. This means that viewers don't have a chance to process them properly and so they never reach conscious awareness. The angry faces, albeit brief, are linked with a stimulus such as a mild electrical shock, something that will activate the autonomic nervous system. After a while, even though people are not given a shock and even though the angry face is visible too briefly for conscious awareness, you still get a nice big autonomic activation! This led the experimenters Arne Öhman and Ray Dolan from the Karolinska Institute in Sweden and University College London to conclude that emotional experience is not a prerequisite for emotional expression, but as subjects did not report an emotion following on from the physiological response, they do not fully support the James–Lange theory either. But the Cannon–Bard view of parallel and independent pathways is compatible with these findings. The common sense view, and the modern biopsychological view is that the perception of an emotional stimulus such as happening upon a black bear protecting her cubs in a clearing in the middle of Canada (you can't fault me for painting a detailed picture here) leads to an emotional feeling as well as a physiological response and these two aspects interact to help you make the correct decision (to get the hell out of there) and give you the energy to act on that decision (run as fast as your legs can carry you).

Others, like Guillaume-Benjamin-Amand Duchenne were interested in whether it was possible to induce emotional affect, specifically emotional facial expressions, without the underlying emotion. And so he resurrected Galvini's electrophysiological techniques to send electrical currents into the face of his subjects, with alarming and quite grotesque effects. Spectators loved it and Duchenne managed to isolate at least 13 emotional expressions by the judicious activation of just two muscles. His most successful subject was an old toothless man, sadly no oil painting, who very fortuitously suffered from a complete lack of sensory input from the face. Lucky boy. But Duchenne discovered that smiles resulting from real emotion use muscles of the mouth and eyes whereas fake ones only include the mouth muscles. Legend has it that around this time in the 1850s, big genuine facial expressions of happiness were called "Duchenne Smiles".

Happily, we are most interested in finding out what parts of the brain do what in generating emotions, from both the physical aspect and the mental aspect, the easy part of our story. We have mentioned much about the hypothalamus in previous chapters and talked about its role in the neuroendocrine system and homeostasis. But the hypothalamus also directs the goings on of the autonomic nervous system (see Chapter 2) via its connections with the spinal cord. Specifically, activation of the sympathetic nervous system will directly activate the medulla of the adrenal gland to release adrenalin which acts on lots of different systems in the body including the brain to increase alertness and give the body energy to deal with whatever it needs to. This is a very fast system and has not been dubbed the "fight or flight" response (by Walter Cannon as it happens) for nothing. Also via the sympathetic nervous system and part of the flight or flight response, heart rate increases, respiration rate increases, blood is diverted away from the skin to feed the vital organs (and so you go pale) amongst other things. But the hypothalamus is also involved in a slower pathway. Corticotropin-releasing hormone (CRH) is secreted by the hypothalamus to act on the anterior pituitary to in turn release adrenocorticotropin hormone (ACTH). ACTH then acts on the cortex of the adrenal gland to release cortisol into the blood stream. This acts on body systems including the brain to raise the alertness of the body by doing such things as encouraging the liver to release glucose and stopping the function of insulin (so that vital fuel is not stored away). This is the body's stress response which can happen in response to something good like organizing a wedding to something bad like organizing a funeral. It does not discriminate based on the underlying emotion. All in all, the hypothalamus is very important in the bodily expression of all emotions.

A collection of other regions in the brain are involved in the interpretation of emotion and together with the hypothalamus is called the limbic system. These regions were grouped anatomically by Paul Broca in 1878 who noticed that if you look at the medial surface of the brain (or cut the brain down the centre from front to back and have a look at the middle), there is a layer of cortex under the outer layer that looks different (the cingulate cortex), and inside that you have structures like the hippocampus, the amygdala, the fornix, the thalamus and the hypothalamus. He named this anatomical grouping the Limbic lobe as the Latin word for border is limbus but he didn't attach any common function to the collection.

In the 1930s and based on the work of Cannon, Bard and others, it was now pretty clear that at least some of these regions had a role in emotion and it was the American neurologist called James Papez who reckoned that these structures represented an emotional system. This made sense to him due to their position between the cortex and the hypothalamus. He identified the hypothalamus as the region involved in emotional expression as we have already discussed but that the cingulate cortex was the area most intimately involved in emotional experience with the higher cerebral cortex required for conscious interpretation of emotions, what Papez called emotional colouring. The communication between the hypothalamus and the cingulate cortex is bidirectional and so is compatible with both James–Lange and Cannon–Bard. Because Papez linked his emotional circuit to Broca's limbic lobe, the term limbic system is used for the loose collection of regions involved in emotion. That is not to say that these regions don't do anything else, we already know how busy the hypothalamus is with other functions. But one part that seems to be closely correlated with emotion is the amygdala.

Pretty convincing evidence that the amygdala is really important in emotion came in the 1930s when Heinrich Kluver and Paul Bucy removed the temporal lobes, including the cortex, the amygdala and the hippocampus of rhesus monkeys. These monkeys, who would usually be highly aggressive, became extremely docile. Given that their temporal cortex was also removed, and knowing as we do that this region is very important for object recognition, the monkeys had real trouble identifying things. They relied more on their somato-sensory system by touching everything and putting things in their mouths...; even when presented with a snake that monkeys are normally pathologically scared stiff of; instead they showed no fear. They also showed uninhibited sexual behaviour, try-ing to initiate intercourse with everything that moved and even didn't move, like chairs for example. This pattern of behav-iour was termed Kluver–Bucy syndrome. But the problem with this study was that  the entire temporal lobe was removed, so it was very difficult to attribute emotional disturbances to any of the specific areas in the temporal cortex. So, they set about making smaller lesions and soon found out that the important region in particularly the emo-tion of fear is the amygdala.

The amygdala can be found towards the front of the temporal lobe and it receives input from most areas of the cortex including the sensory areas (especially visual cortex) of the temporal and frontal cortex, other areas of the limbic system (like the hypothal-amus) and the olfactory bulb. This last connection is very import-ant; smells have the power to evoke powerful emotions. These can even interact with your hypothalamus to make you want to buy fresh bread when you walk into a bakery. Did you know that many convenience stores that do not bake their own bread release the smell of freshly baked bread into the atmosphere to play on your emotions to buy their bread? But it is also important to know when something is off and you shouldn't eat it. Its smell (and the activity of the amygdala) gives you that aversive feeling generally associated with the word "Ugh".

Therefore, the amygdala plays a role is keeping us safe from harm, minimizing our contact with dangerous animals, objects or places by producing the emotion of fear. This has an innate and learned component. For example, if you expose a rat to the urine of a ferret, the rat will display fear. But what if I told you that rat had never met a ferret, had never had a bad experience of a ferret and had no grounds on which to say a bad word of a ferret? This is an instinct, rats as a whole are petrified of ferrets. However, we can also learn to be afraid of certain things and this is really important for our survival. Our amygdala is vital to our memory of fearful and aggressive situations, so that we either don't put ourselves in that situation again or that we marshal the resources to deal with it. This has been demonstrated very easily using learned associations based on what Ivan Pavlov was doing late in the 1800s. He had a neutral stimulus which was the ring of a bell. Any time he rang the bell he gave his dogs something to eat. After a while, when Pavlov rang the bell, the dogs would salivate (even if there was no food). It's called classical conditioning and we will talk about it more, including the brain regions associated with it, in Chapter 12. If we pair a neutral stimulus such as a sound, with an aversive happening such as an electric shock, a rat will react with fear anytime it hears the sound even when there was no shock. It is the amygdala in this case which acts to link the neutral sensory stimulus (the sound) with other stimulus (such as a shock) which is directly associated with threat.

Damage to the amygdala in humans does not lead to the loss of emotions and so clearly it is not the centre of our emotion processing. But it does play an important part when emotional signals are subtle or unclear in any way. For example, an emotional judgement like how trustworthy one looks is based on a number of different cues, but people with damaged amydalae (plural as there is an amygdala in each hemisphere) regard all faces as being equally trustworthy, which sometimes leads to them asking for help from clearly shifty characters. Ralph Adolphs and Antonio Damasio from Caltech found that this was because a damaged amygdala leads to people being unable to focus their attention on emotion stimuli in the same way neurotypical people do. Normally, people will remember the emotional import of a story and forget the background issues, or will focus on the emotional words in a text. But people with amygdala damage will remember the irrelevant parts just as much as the emotional parts; there is no guidance of their attention by emotional aspects.

Just as with Kluver and Bucy's monkeys, the role of the amygdala in humans can also be localized to negative emotions: fear, disgust, aggression etc. Indeed, electrical stimulation of the human amygdala (during neurosurgery for example in which patients are typically awake anyway) results in fearful behaviours. More evidence comes from a case study in which a patient (called SM) had bilateral damage to the amygdala. When asked to rate the intensity of emotion in a series of photographs of facial expressions, she was impaired in the evaluation of a variety of emotional expressions but particularly anger and fear. Damasio, Adolphs and colleagues went a bit further and asked SM, who had a background in art, to draw different emotional expressions. She made really good drawings of most emotions but couldn't draw a fearful face because she said she didn't know what such a face would look like. When asked to try anyway, she drew a picture of somebody crawling away with their hair standing on end, but with little facial expression.

It turns out that people with damage to the amygdala don't look at faces normally and so don't pick up on the emotional cues the rest of us do. They focus almost entirely on the nose and mouth without looking at the eyes at all; such patients are noted for not making eye contact. If SM was explicitly asked to look at the eyes, she had no trouble recognizing fear at all. This is because happiness is expressed mainly with the mouth but if someone is afraid, this is best communicated through the eyes. There are cultural differences in this however. In 2010, Rachael Jack from Glasgow University investigated subtleties in emotional recognition between a group of people from East Asia and a group of Westerners. She found that East Asians were more likely than Westerners to read fear as surprise and disgust as anger. They focussed more on the eyes whereas Westerners focussed on the entire face including the mouth. Therefore, East Asians may use culturally specific decoding strategies and so are unable to distinguish between disgust and anger, fear and surprise, which may engage similar eye expression and so need the added cues from the mouth expression for their delineation.

The inability to detect another's emotional state sounds suspiciously like autism, one of the main symptoms of which is the inability to communicate and relate emotionally to others. So, could it be possible that autism is caused by a badly formed amygdala? In part, the answer is yes. Post-mortem studies have shown that autistic people have larger amygdalae, which is indicative that this structure did not form properly and that the correct synaptic pruning did not take place (see Chapter 7). fMRI studies have shown that the amygdala of autistic people does not get involved in facial recognition as it normally should. But there are other areas involved in autism. For example, areas of the brainstem important for controlling facial expression and relaying auditory input are smaller than usual and temporal, parietal and occipital lobes are bigger in the autistic brain, due to poor development, but possibly leading to savant qualities sometimes seen in autistic individuals. In contrast, the corpus callosum is smaller meaning that the communication between the hemispheres is impaired.

So even by looking at the limbic system in isolation, it is clear that the brain both interprets and generates all emotions, including those "of the heart". As you will know by now, there is nothing that grates on my nerves quite as much as Valentine's Day cards with big red (anatomically incorrect) hearts plastered all over them, or love songs extolling the state of the singer's pump apparatus when it comes to their feelings. It's your limbic system, got it?! In fact, when it comes to love, your brain shows different responses to friendship love and romantic love. When students who were newly in love were placed in an fMRI scanner by Semir Zeki

I Love You
from the
bottom
of
my...

Limbic System

and Andreas Bartels at UCL in 2004 were shown pictures of their lover as opposed to their friends, there was an increase in activity in the insula (deep inside the lateral sulcus) as well as the anterior cingulate cortex, areas which link emotion and bodily expression. In contrast, activity was less in the posterior cingulate cortex (important in awareness but also pain perception), the amygdala as well as the right frontal lobe (which tends to be involved in more negative emotions) when pictures of the friends were viewed as opposed to the lover. When we are in love therefore, we tend to be much more positive and this is not just due to the balance of activity seen in subcortical structures but the influence of the cortex too.

As indicated by the case of autism and as mentioned previously in this chapter, there are other areas of the brain that are very important in the emotional interpretation/expression functions in neurotypical people (see Figure 11.1). We have discussed how important the amygdala is particularly in negative emotions, and the hypothalamus to which the amygdala is connected in the bodily expression of emotions. But the cortex plays an incredibly important part in the evaluations of these emotions. If you get a paper cut and want to scream like a baby, what stops you? If somebody angers you to the point that you want to thump them, what stops you (usually!)? Your cerebral cortex, that's what. In fact, if you lesion the cerebral cortex and sever all connections to the hypothalamus, this results in extreme aggression to any external stimulus. This is called sham rage and demonstrates the importance of an intact cerebral cortex to interpret and control emotional states.

The frontal lobes are particularly important. This region has many connections with the limbic system and particularly the amygdala and hypothalamus. It doesn't just "do" emotion; it is also very important in conscious decision making, evaluation and judgement, self-awareness, abstract thinking and it also helps censor our behaviour. The most famous example of this point is that of Phineas Gage. Phineas was a foreman of a railway construction gang but in 1848 an accident happened. What a story! The job the 25-year-old Phineas and his team were engaged in was the clearing of land, flattening the ground for the ensuing track to be laid just outside the town of Cavendish, in the state of Vermont. On Wednesday the 13th of September, he was going about his

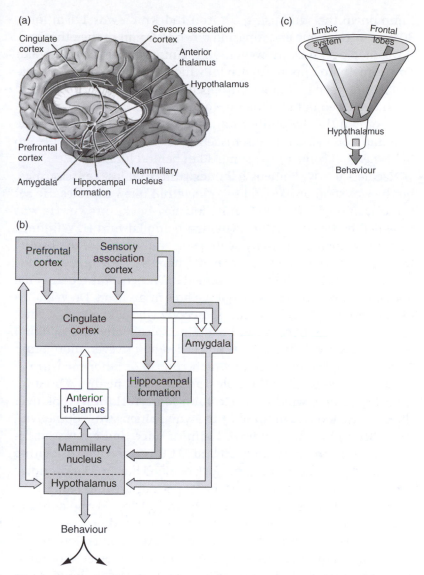

**Figure 11.1** The regions and pathways involved in the perception and production of emotions in the brain. From *An Introduction to Brain and Behavior*, Third Edition by Bryan Kolb and Ian Q. Whishaw © 2011 by Worth Publishers. Used with permission.

business using dynamite to blast rocks in the way of the new track. This required the boring of a hole into the rock, filling the hole with explosives, inserting a fuse into the dynamite and pouring sand on top to protect the mixture. The next thing to do was to tamp down the sand using an iron rod which was 1.1 m long, 30 mm thick at one end tapering down to 6 mm at the other end. It weighed over 6 kg. However, on the morning of this particular day, something apparently trivial which would have huge consequences happened. Phineas dropped his tamping iron. The sand hadn't yet been put into the hole and so a spark from the dropped iron ignited the dynamite and the resulting explosion sent the tamping iron flying through his left cheek bone and out of the top of his head. It came to rest some 30 m behind him.

Needless to say, Phineas fell backwards and lost consciousness but he was soon awake and talking within a few minutes. He sat upright in a cart for the ¾ mile journey back to town. He was attended by two physicians, the first being Edward H. Williams, who remembered distinctly seeing the "pulsations of the brain" from a distance as he approached. There was obviously a huge wound and as Dr. Williams examined it, Phineas was regaling the gathering crowd as to how he got the hole in his head. Dr. Williams didn't particularly believe that somebody who had endured what Phineas had described could be talking so cogently and so didn't believe his story. Phineas then proceeded to lose even more brain by vomiting, the pressure of which caused another measure of brain to squeeze out of the hole and fall onto the dirt. About an hour later, the town doctor, Dr. John Martyn Harlow, took over the case. He too was amazed at the way Phineas was coping with his injury; Phineas recognized him at once and expressed his hope that his injury wasn't too bad. At this stage he was getting exhausted presumably from the lack of blood but Dr. Harlow noted that although his pulse was 60 beats per minute and regular, he did look a bit of a state, covered as he was in "blood and gore".

Dr. Harlow proceeded to pack the wound and dress it as best he could. There was obviously a real danger of infection and so the wound had to be cleaned, drained and redressed regularly. The recovery was not without its low points however. Phineas was semi-comatose from the 23 September through to 3 October presumably due to pressure on his brain. His mood deflated; he seldom spoke unless spoken to. His friends assumed he was on his deathbed; they even had his coffin and burial clothes ready. But by 7 October, Phineas was beginning to rally and was able to walk around, even going outside. He promptly relapsed with a fever but by mid-November was up and about again with not even a pain in his head and was ready to return to his parent's house in Lebanon, New Hampshire. By December he was riding horses and was thought to be improving both mentally and physically.

The following April Gage returned to Vermont and visited Dr. Harlow who, despite noticing the physical effects of the injury like the loss of the left eye, a big scar, some paralysis of the left side of the face, was inclined to say that Gage had made a complete recovery. He had no pain, but did report "a queer feeling". Gage's old mates were not quite so impressed with his recovery; in fact Gage's personality was completely different to that of the man they remembered. Before the accident Phineas was hard working, conscientious, a caring and polite individual and his employers for whom he was laying the Rutland and Burlington Railroad held him in high esteem calling him "the most efficient and capable man". After the accident, Gage was petulant, childish, impatient and disrespectful, and so needless to say, he was not re-employed by the railway company. Gage often became inappropriately angry or emotional, didn't follow social mores, and was erratic and unpredictable. Perhaps the most important of his deficits was that he was unable to form or execute plans, could not foresee the consequences of his actions, nor did he seem to care. Dr. Harlow also saw the psychological change, saying: "The equilibrium or balance, so to speak, between his intellectual faculties and his animal propensities, seems to have been destroyed".

Gage became a drifter and appeared for a while in a freak side show at Barnum's American Museum in New York where he appeared to the paying public along with the tamping iron that injured him. He later worked in a livery stable in Hanover, New Hampshire and then as a stagecoach driver on the long-distance route from Valparaiso to Santiago in Chile. But his health began to fail in 1859 so he made his way to San Francisco where his mother and sister were. Despite a brief recovery, Gage was now suffering from frequent epileptic seizures and was working as a farm hand in Santa Clara. He died the following year, 12 years after his accident at the age of 38. He was buried with his tamping iron.

In 1867, Gage's body was exhumed and his skull sent, along with the tamping iron, to Dr. Harlow. He realized that the tamping iron had passed through the left anterior part of the frontal lobe including the orbitofrontal cortex. As a result of his prescient observations of Gage's behaviour, even in the 1800s it was known that the frontal lobe is important in the control of behaviour and planning, every respect in which Gage had changed. The skull and tamping iron ended up in Harvard Medical School where it is still on show and where Antonio Damasio used MRI to further define the affected brain areas. And so, almost 120 years later, the location of damage was shown to be not much different from Harlow's analysis save that both frontal hemispheres were severely damaged, but with the worst region of damage being in the left orbitofrontal cortex. This region has extensive links to the cingulate gyrus, amygdala and hypothalamus of the limbic system and also has a direct pathway linking it to brainstem nuclei in control of the autonomic nervous system.

Other examples of people with brain damage in the late 1800s and early 1900s confirmed the view that the frontal cortex was important in emotional control. In the early 1930s, John Fulton and Carlyle Jacobsen performed surgery on a highly volatile and emotional chimpanzee called Becky to remove both her frontal lobes. After the surgery, Becky was as quiet as a church mouse and extremely docile. They presented their findings at the second World Congress in Neurology meeting held in London in 1953 at which a Portuguese neurologist named Egas Moniz was also attending. This gave Moniz the idea that he could use this technique to treat emotionally disturbed patients. He called it psychosurgery and soon persuaded a neurosurgeon called Almeider Lima to perform it on a female patient suffering from severe depression and paranoia both of which are characterized by abnormal communication between the frontal lobes and limbic system. The surgery in those days required the drilling of holes in the skull and the injection of pure alcohol to kill the nerve cells and thus that area's links to other regions of the brain such as the limbic system. The surgery was deemed a great success and refined by the development of a leucotome which was a wand-like instrument that could be inserted into the brain. A retractable steel wire loop would open in the brain and could cut out cores of brain matter, effectively lobotomizing the patient. The results, according to Moniz, were remarkable, but doubt has been cast on Moniz's reportage; he provided little verifiable evidence regarding the patients' improvement and it is entirely possible that the surgery had little effect at all. In 1949, at the age of 76, Moniz received the Nobel prize for Medicine but unfortunately was rendered paralysed ten years previous when a paranoid patient who had not undergone surgery shot him four times in the back.

In the meantime, psychosurgery was further developed in the United States and in 1948 Walter Freeman developed the transorbital lobotomy in which a leucotome was held beneath the upper eyelid and then driven into the skull using a mallet. The leucotome was then wiggled about to cut the connections of the frontal lobe with areas of the limbic system such as the thalamus. In general, the mortality rate of this surgery was favourable (4%). Only 2% of patients saw no improvement, 41% greatly improved with the rest seeing a minimal improvement in symptoms. However, patients were also left with the side effects of frontal damage. They were listless, or had social difficulties or planning problems. It began to dawn on people that the disadvantages of the surgery outweighed the advantages.

During the height of psychosurgery, there is evidence that it was becoming an elective surgery, sometimes performed in the physician's office! An example of this point lies in the treatment of Agnes, a rather outspoken woman, who was married to an oil baron in the 1950s. Her husband could not countenance her constant butting in to his business affairs and wanted a docile wife who could serve his business partners at dinner parties but without offering her opinions on their decisions. He persuaded a psychosurgeon to perform a transorbital leucotomy in which Agnes's left frontal lobe was destroyed. Agnes immediately became more compliant, submissive and obedient and so her personality was completely changed such that her emotions were dulled. Indeed it was as if her capacity to understand her own emotions was lost. The left hemisphere would seem to be more important in the generation and interpretation of positive emotions and so damage here will result in a more negative affect. Agnes never smiled again except once when she was told her husband had died. He left her a wealthy woman but she soon lost it all as she could not organize her spending or plan what to do with her wealth. Happily, with the advent of more targeted treatments, with drugs to target the low serotonin levels coincident in aggression and depression and others such as benzodiazepines which selectively reduce the symptoms of anxiety by potentiating the activity of the brain's main inhibitory neurotransmitter GABA, there is less need for psychosurgery and so less than 100 of these operations are carried out each year.

These examples of interference with frontal lobe function tell us that frontal regions are very important in emotional control. Emotional responses are initiated by the amygdala and hypothalamus before information has reached the frontal lobes. However, the frontal lobes act to damp down or inhibit the emotional response if it is not warranted. There is some recent evidence that even the language areas of the frontal lobes (discussed in Chapter 5) can negate the negative emotions associated with pain. For example, swearing after injury interacts with our limbic system to lessen the pain. Richard Stephens and colleagues at Keele University have found that people who swear can keep their hands in a bucket of ice cold water for 50% longer than those who don't. However this does not extend to people who habitually swear anyway as swearing is emotional language that loses its emotional attachment if overused. So when it comes to pain, it pays not to be a regular potty mouth. Tantrums in children probably occur because their frontal lobes have not developed connections with the limbic system yet. Even teenagers whose frontal lobe neurons are not yet fully myelinated find it hard to control their emotions. If the normal connections between the frontal lobe and the limbic system fail to develop properly, phobias often arise. Say for example a child is attacked by a bird in childhood. A fearful emotional response mediated by the amygdala (just like our rat with the electric shock) will be linked to the sight of a bird. This cannot be rationalized by the frontal lobe as the connections do not exist yet. In later years however as the child grows into adulthood, the individual will forget the incident with the bird but may be left with at best an unsettled nervous feeling when they see a bird and at worst a phobia of birds otherwise known as orthiophobia.

We also know that emotions are not purely mental affairs. The sight of a bird will produce an autonomic response: sweaty hands, dry mouth, increased heart and respiration rates allowing the individual to run away or fight the bird. This is also the mechanism that underlies post-traumatic stress disorder (PTSD). Let's use the example of a soldier on patrol in a war zone. If an improvized explosive device (IED) goes off right beside our soldier, fear is an inevitable consequence. His amygdala has linked a loud bang or a big flash of light with fear. There is also a predictable autonomic response creating a bodily expression of his emotions. In later life, this soldier may be susceptible to episodes of PTSD where a loud bang or flash of light creates the same emotion and bodily affect the IED did. He starts to sweat, goes pale, his heart races etc. It may be that the reinforcement of the emotion of fear by the inordinate activation of the autonomic nervous system at the time of the IED has created this situation and it may not happen over one exposure to such dangers, but multiple episodes (not unusual for serving military). But if soldiers are administered beta blockers, which block the autonomic response in the hours following a trauma such as an IED going off beside them, the prevalence of PTSD is lessened. This is controversial though, as there is some evidence that cortisol levels (just one aspect of the autonomic response) are lower in people who suffer from PTSD immediately after a traumatic event and for weeks afterwards. It may be that the negative feedback loops the endocrine system relies on are impaired in some way. The effect of this is that these individuals are ill equipped to combat the stress they find themselves under. Either way, it seems PTSD is more prevalent in those who have a smaller-than-usual hippocampus (an area important in memory formation as we'll see in Chapter 12), which may explain the faulty linkage of bodily response to memories. Over a century after the debate first started, it would seem that emotional perception, interpretation and expression are interlinked and interdependent.

## Feeling curious?

*Descartes' Error: Emotion, Reason and the Human Brain* by Antonio Damasio. 2006; Vintage. *An entertaining account of the role of emotion in rational thinking debunking Descartes "I think, therefore I am" thesis.*

Emeran A. Mayer (2011) "Gut Feelings: the Emerging Biology of Gut–Brain Communication". *Nature Reviews Neuroscience* 12, 453–66 doi:10.1038/nrn3071. *The effect our digestive system has on emotions and vice versa.*

*Phineas Gage: A Gruesome But True Story about Brain Science* by John Fleischman. 2004; Houghton Mifflin Harcourt. *An accessible account of Phineas Gage's misfortune and the neuroscientific discoveries it fuelled.*

*Last Resort: Psychosurgery and the Limits of Medicine (Cambridge Studies in the History of Medicine)* by Jack D. Pressman. 2002; Cambridge University Press. *A thorough examination of the history of psychosurgery, its value and place in modern neuropsychology.*

Israel Liberzon, Chandra Sekhar Sripada (2007) "The Functional Neuroanatomy of PTSD: A Critical Review". Progress in Brain Research, 167, 151–69. *This review article evaluates the evidence for a neurological model of PTSD based on findings from neuroimaging.*

# 12 Memories are made of this

Do you remember what Chapter 2 was about? Stop flicking and answer the question. No? What if I said the word "neuron"? Would you remember then? Have I jogged your memory? Lots of the things that we learn about are like this. You will have made an association between Chapter 2 and neurons and remembered it, or you may not have bothered to make the association and forgotten, but when I prompted you by saying neuron, you may have remembered. We all have different interests and these determine the things we remember, but it isn't just about the memory aspect of it; it's about the learning too.

A vast amount of work has been done on learning and memory because it is so integral to our lives. You could say that it informs our brain development because it directs our plasticity, the changes and associations that happen between neurons because they are concerned with the same thing. It's very important not just in early life but later on too because we never stop learning. Remember the road system where you grew up? Is it totally different now? You had to learn to adapt to that. If you move to a new city you have to learn and remember your way around that. This is spatial memory and is just one of the aspects of memory that is possible. There are loads more. Some are simple, such as memory for faces, numbers or names. Some are much more holistic and require memory for lots of things all in one go, such as the memory of something that happened to you in your youth, otherwise known as episodic memory. So it can get a bit complicated. Psychologists have identified lots of different forms of memory and split them up according to different headings to make it easier (see Figure 12.1). But remember, they may not be mutually exclusive or entirely separate. There's declarative (or explicit) memory, where you remember

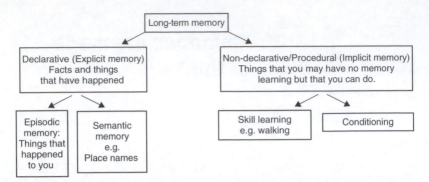

**Figure 12.1** How your long-term memory can be split up according to whether you are remembering facts or procedures.

a person, an event, a book etc. and there's procedural (or implicit) memory where you remember how to do things that you no longer need to devote any conscious energy to such as walking or driving a car. There is the episodic memory that we've talked about but that is a special form of declarative memory. Spatial memory is generally declarative but can become procedural if you take the same route every day.

You can also separate memory into how long you have to remember something for. All of the examples above are examples of long-term memory. Short-term memory will allow you to remember something for a few minutes but long-term memories have to be retained for a much longer period. And then there's working memory, allowing you to remember where you are so that you can use the information about what's come before to inform where you are going. I'm probably using a fair bit of that right now; it should cut down on any rambling, you hope. Now, you could have declarative or procedural short-term or long-term or even working memory. So, as you can see, all of these nominal divisions are linked and interrelated and make it all very complicated indeed. But such division of labour has allowed scientists to investigate aspects of memory (and learning) to try to understand each in turn. After about a century of such enquiry, we are only now getting to the point where we can begin to put it all together and neuroscience has helped us with that. If you look at a problem from the point of view of the brain, what different parts do, whether one part is involved in two kinds of memory for example, things get much simpler. It's almost as if brain activity can tell us whether the divisions cognitive psychology has established are actually treated as separate by our neurons or not. We're only beginning to get a handle on learning and memory looking at it from this angle and this chapter is concerned with what we know now.

Let's think about short-term memory first. Somebody calls out the number of a pizza shop to you and you have to remember it long enough to fish your phone out of the deepest darkest recesses of your pocket and punch in the number. You mumble the number over and over to yourself to keep it in your mind, or you might try to make complicated associations with the numbers (if it is 364 something you might think "well 6 is two times 3 and minus two is 4"). We are generally restricted to remembering a string of about 7–9 numbers but making an association such as this increases our capacity dramatically. This is much easier if you are an expert, and so making a sum out of it may be something a mathematician might do. Associational memory doesn't just apply to numbers. The pieces on a chess board can be much better memorized by a master chess player than a beginner, but only when the pieces reveal a strategy pattern in a realistic game.

Short-term memories are held only for a few minutes at most and are then discarded. The frontal lobes play a large role here. Once you have forgotten them, they are lost and no amount of hinting or prompting will help you get it back. It is possible to consolidate short-term memory into long-term memory; you can explicitly learn the pizza shop's phone number for example but short-term memory is not always a precursor on the way to learning something for the long term. And so in 1974, Alan Baddley and Graham Hitch came up with an alternative view of short-term memory called working memory. This covers the kinds of memory storage we need when we are working with information and need to hold it in mind. Remembering numbers to punch into our phone fits into this model but there are more taxing ways to test people's working memory capacity. One way of testing your working memory capacity is the delayed response task. You need to remember, say, a position on a map and after a given amount of time you have to pick out that position again. Using fMRI in 2002, Kat Sakai, James Rowe and Dick Passingham from UCL and Oxford showed that this working memory for spatial positions caused extra activation in the prefrontal cortex. This is an area that is prone to decline in old age and so things that working memory are important for such as remembering why you walked into a room or keeping your train of thought on the tracks during a conversation sometimes suffer. Areas of the basal ganglia have also been shown to be important in acting as an irrelevance filter, which is important for good memory and determines what it is you remember, and what you forget. It could explain why some people are good at remembering things and why some are not. Torkel Klingberg and Fiona McNab from the Karolinska Institute in Sweden used fMRI to show that when the globus palladus is more active, less information is stored in the cortex. (Remember the inhibitory effect the basal ganglia have in movement?) It may be that problems with this region can lead to the inability to focus, and interruption by irrelevant distractions, an issue commonly associated with attention deficit hyperactivity disorder.

One of the main reasons that we know short-term or working memory uses different parts of the brain to long-term memory comes from patients who have severely impaired long-term memories but their short-term memory is fine. One such patient is Henry Molaison, immortalized as patient HM, certainly the most famous case study related to memory. HM was epileptic and suffered up to ten seizures a day. These were as a result of some brain damage HM had incurred at the age of nine when he got knocked off his bike. By 1953, his neurologist William Scoville had determined that the medial temporal lobes were where the seizure activity was originating (seizures are a common consequence of brain damage). Under a local anaesthetic, Scoville bored two holes into HM's forehead, pushed the frontal lobes up and out of the way with a spatula and pushed on through to the medial temporal cortex. He then proceeded to insert a knife and a suction pump and cut a tennis ball-sized lump of brain out of each hemisphere and sucked it out. Most of the hippocampus was removed along with the amygdalae and some of the surrounding cortex.

You might think that sounds barbaric, but surgeries like this had been performed before and as we will see later (Chapter 13), even the main connection between the left and right hemispheres, the corpus callosum, could be cut to treat epilepsy by stopping the seizure from spreading across the brain with few noticeable effects. HM was different however; more tissue than ever before had to be excised to get rid of the bits of his brain that were causing the epileptic fits and this was a step too far. It became apparent very quickly that HM was frozen in time, he had no capability of remembering anything of significance after his surgery and right up until his death in 2008, he still believed he was the young man he was at the time he had his surgery. Notwithstanding all of these significant downsides, HM's epilepsy was cured.

The exact problems that HM had could therefore be mapped onto the exact damage he had. Although his short-term memory was okay, if he got distracted or anything, the information was forgotten. In general however, he could follow a conversation well and remember short trains of up to eight numbers or letters. Another task that HM had no problem learning was a pursuit motor task that he could learn and remember forever (using long-term memory). This is a task in which you have to keep a stylus in contact with a metal disc that is moving in a circular pattern on a turntable. It's a bit tricky but most people (including HM) show improvement after a brief training session. Not only did HM show this improvement but he was also able to retain his skill between testing sessions (even though he couldn't remember ever learning it!). HM therefore showed evidence of procedural learning, in which memory for carrying out a procedure is picked up implicitly. Another example of a procedure that HM was able to learn was mirror drawing. He had to trace around a complicated shape but he could see only the mirror image of his hand and the shape. To cope with the fact that every movement creates the opposite effect to what you think it should takes a bit of practice to learn to deal with it, but HM was able to achieve a proficient level of performance in this assignment.

So, HM's procedural memory was still intact and was robust over long periods of time, but his long-term declarative memory and episodic memory was impaired in two ways. He had almost complete anterograde amnesia in that he could not remember anything that had happened after the surgery; he could not lay down new long-term memories. He also had an aspect of retrograde amnesia in that he could not remember anything that happened in the 11 years prior to the surgery, his memories before the age of 16 being mostly intact. This has lead some researchers to think that long-term memories may take many years to become permanently encoded in our brain.

Given HM's problems with memory and the damage that was centred on his hippocampus, many researchers focused their efforts on investigating this area's role in declarative memory. Much of the early work done with animal neurophysiology proved that the hippocampus was capable of something that Donald Hebb had predicted in the 1940s. Hebb believed that memories are formed when cells fire together and form stable synapses and that the increase in neural activity could be stable for a long time and this indicates learning. Such plasticity and stability of activity has been demonstrated in hippocampal neurons and is called long-term potentiation. In normal functioning humans, Endel Tulving used neuroimaging in the early 1990s to show the involvement of the hippocampus when new pictures are shown to subjects as opposed to pictures they have seen before, evidence that the memory is being encoded using the hippocampus. Not only that, but this area has also been shown to be involved in the retrieval of memory. Since then however, much more precise methods of scanning and experimentation have established that it's not just the hippocampus that is important, but a network of medial temporal areas (also damaged in HM) including the entorhinal cortex, the parahippocampal cortex, the perirhinal cortex, leading to higher level cortical areas such as cingulate cortex and frontal, temporal, parietal and occipital regions.

It would seem that input from the sensory cortex (for example the shape of an apple, a visual input from the occipital cortex) is fed through the perirhinal regions and on through the entorhinal cortex to the hippocampus (see Figure 12.2). The parahippocampal regions take their input from the parietal areas and so are important for visuospatial memory. This information is then fed back through the medial temporal regions to the sensory cortex so that the long-term memory can be stored in an area relevant to the item to be remembered. Therefore, the memory of an apple is stored in the object identification regions of the brain. The medial temporal structures are required for the storage and retrieval of those memories through these reciprocal connections and the integration of memory seems to happen at the level of the entorhinal cortex as it takes its input from both the parahippocampal and

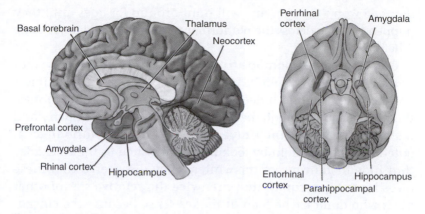

**Figure 12.2** Medial and subcortical brain regions involved in memory from a sagittal and ventral view. From *An Introduction to Brain and Behavior*, Third Edition by Bryan Kolb and Ian Q. Whishaw © 2011 by Worth Publishers. Used with permission.

perirhinal cortex, so you can remember the shape of the apple and where you saw it. Indeed, this is the part of the brain most at risk from the ravages of Alzheimer's disease which results in profound memory loss.

So, where does this leave the hippocampus? Sure, it's linked in with the other medial temporal cortex structures, but couldn't we get by just fine with only the entorhinal cortex and the others? Well, no. (Hadn't you guessed? The chapter isn't over yet after all ...) The hippocampus is specialized for another form of memory and one that is very important in our everyday lives and that is spatial memory. Lesion studies which selectively damage the hippocampus in monkeys has the effect of impairing their ability to learn the location of objects, i.e. their visuospatial learning is adversely affected. Rats with hippocampal damage can't remember where a platform is in a water maze. A water maze is a bath of milky water that you put the rat into and was first devised by Richard Morris at the University of St. Andrews over 30 years ago who built one out of hardboard and yacht resin over a weekend. Rats hate swimming, so they try to find a hidden platform (that isn't obvious because of the murky water) to get them out of the water. They'll usually find it after a bit of searching and then when they are placed in the bath again, from any position around the bath, they will go straight to the platform. Rats with hippocampal damage won't though, and will hunt around for ages until they happen to come across the platform, just as if they had never done it before.

Given the effect damage to the hippocampus has on visuo-spatial learning, it might be reasonable to assume that if animals and people need and indeed have good visuospatial memories, their hippocampus might be bigger than usual. David Sherry and his colleagues from the University of Western Ontario investigated just that thought by looking at birds such as the chickadee that hide food away for the winter. They discovered that these birds have hippocampi that are twice the relative size of other birds who don't cache food. It makes sense because the chickadee has to remember the exact positions in the whole wide world where they left their food and remembering where to go and finding it may be a matter of life or death. Bigger hippocampi can also be found in some species of kangaroo rats who store food in various places around their territory. What is really neat is that these rodents can be compared with the smaller hippocampi of other species of kangaroo rat who simply store their food in their burrows. It is the varied number of places that the food can be stored in that determines the size of the hippocampus. Of course, this reasoning works another way; the presence of a larger hippocampus in the first place may allow them to store food in more places.

Humans don't tend to store food in many different places but we do have a lot of stuff that we put in lots of different places that we have to remember so we use our hippocampus a lot. (Where are your keys right now?) But given the role of the hippocampus in visuo-spatial memory, another function that may be screaming out at you is navigation. For example, if I am at Buckingham Palace in London,  how do I get to the Houses of Parliament? Actually, the trick would be not to ask me; I get lost so often I am beginning to think my hippocampus must be the size of a pea. A very small pea. A mini pea. That's why I rely on London taxi drivers. They are trained to know every street in London and how to get from anywhere to anywhere else. It turns out that when Eleanor Maguire, Chris Frith, Richard Frackowiak and colleagues at UCL put them into an MRI scanner, they found that London taxi drivers have a much bigger hippocampus than others who don't require such high levels of visuospatial memory.

HM had spared procedural memory so it is a fair bet that the neural basis of this implicit memory does not require the areas that were damaged in his surgery. In the 1980s, Mort Mishkin and his colleagues at the National Institute for Mental Health in the USA hypothesized that the basal ganglia were very important in procedural memory. Remember in Chapter 6 we discovered that the basal ganglia is very important in gauging movement force? Well, it turns out that the proper functioning of the basal ganglia is also required in the implicit learning of tasks and remembering how to carry out tasks learned before the damage. Evidence comes from patients with Parkinson's disease who have basal ganglia that don't function well and have consequent trouble learning new tasks like the pursuit rotor task HM could do.

Mishkin determined that the basal ganglia get their input from the entire cerebral cortex as well as the dopamine-producing cells from the substantia nigra (the ones that are damaged in Parkinson's disease) and in turn send projections to the ventral thalamus and then the premotor cortex. This information flows only in one direction, unlike the feedforward and feedback connections between the medial temporal areas and the entire cerebral cortex. This may explain why procedural learning is unconscious; for memories to be conscious, the cerebral cortex regions must receive feedback.

The happenstance that a response can be linked to a stimulus is the basis of procedural memory, which includes any skills or habits that we have learned but which are retrieved automatically. Classical conditioning is a learning procedure by which this happens and was first demonstrated by Ivan Pavlov, a Russian physiologist. Pavlov was actually interested in the functioning of the digestive system and in 1904 won the Nobel Prize for Physiology and Medicine for his work in this field. In the late 1800s however, Pavlov began to investigate conditioned reflexes with his colleague

Ivan Tolochinov. In this case, Pavlov and Tolochinov rang a bell and this was the conditioned stimulus that normally would have no effect. But over a period of time, every time they rang the bell, they presented their dogs with food (an unconditioned stimulus). The food made the dogs salivate and over time, the linking of the bell with the food made the dogs salivate when they heard the bell ringing, even if it was rung without food. Thus, the bell, which shouldn't usually elicit salivation, is associated with the food and so makes the dog salivate. This is a really robust effect. You can teach it to your own dogs.

In humans, this has been investigated using an infinitely less fun paradigm involving eye blinks. In this case a neutral (conditioned) stimulus such as a tone comes to elicit a response because of its repeated pairing with another (unconditioned) stimulus such as a puff of air in the eye. The tone wouldn't usually cause an eye blink, but after linking the tone with the puff of air, the tone becomes associated with the puff and an eye blink occurs when the tone is heard. The brain region important for these kinds of associations is the cerebellum. It has circuits designed to pair various motor responses to environmental events and as we saw in Chapter 6, it is very important in practice of skills, be it playing the piano or hitting a tennis ball correctly etc. Next time you have to practice your trumpet playing and your housemates are complaining about the noise you are making, simply inform them that your cerebellum demands it. That should shut them up. It's not just your cerebellum that gets better when you practice a musical instrument however. The sensitivity of your somatosensory cortex improves too. This is particularly true of string instrument players whose finger position is of the utmost importance and indeed the area devoted to their fingers in the somatosensory strip is bigger as a result. In 2003, Lauren Stewart at the Institute of Cognitive Neuroscience in University College London undertook a Herculean effort to investigate the changes that happen in the brain when you learn how to play the piano. She recruited 12 people who had no musical knowledge at all and showed them musical notation and asked them to bang on the appropriate keys of a piano to produce the music. They looked at her like she was mad, but undeterred, she scanned their brain activity using fMRI whilst they undertook this task. Then she proceeded to train them to Piano Grade 1 standard over the next 15 weeks and scanned their brain activity again. Following the training, their brains were showing activity in the superior parietal cortex when the subjects read musical notation in the scanner which fits with the idea that music reading requires a sensorimotor translation in which the spatial characteristics of musical notation are used to automatically command a particular action, in this case a press on a specific key (remember, the parietal cortex is very important in perception for action; see Chapter 4). So this is further evidence that the function-specific memory is stored in the most sensible place in the cortex, in this case, the parietal cortex for visuomotor transformations.

You might have guessed by now (and from Chapter 11) that any learning or memory involving emotion requires another area of involvement. The main area of involvement is the amygdala, and it is this area that is involved in fear conditioning. This is emotional procedural memory and is shown by a conditioned learning experiment. A particular musical tone is played at the same time a mild electric shock is given. After a while, the animal shows fear when the tone is played even if there is no accompanying shock. Because the conditioning response is emotional, circuits of the amygdala, not the cerebellum, mediate fear conditioning. The limbic system emotional circuits are also involved in emotional declarative memories and because of the limbic systems connection with the autonomic nervous system, they can induce a bodily emotional effect. An extreme version of this occurs in post-traumatic stress disorder sufferers. Whether triggered by a terrorist attack or a natural disaster, a violent crime or a car crash, people with PTSD can be plagued by terrifying flashbacks and suffer crippling non-commensurate fear in reaction to reminders of their trauma. As we found out in Chapter 11 the fear response is mediated by the physiological fight or flight response. Margaret Altemus and colleagues at Cornell University have been using beta blockers to interfere with the physiological response by blocking the action of adrenalin and other stress hormones shortly after the trauma. This seems to result in a reduced response to the memory of the event. Therefore, the laying down of emotional memories may have a physiological as well as psychological component. The hippocampus has been shown to be smaller in sufferers of PTSD and Gilbertson and colleagues from Harvard Medical School believe that this is a necessary precursor to the occurrence of PTSD. Connected to the hypothalamus via the cingulate cortex and the thalamus, the hippocampus may therefore have an integrative or modulatory role between emotional affect and declarative memories and less hippocampal volume impairs this relationship.

Episodic memory is another psychological subset of memory that we know HM had trouble with. Endel Tulving also calls this autobiographical memory saying, in 2002, that it transforms the brain into a time machine that allows us to dwell on the past and make plans for the future. In essence it allows you to remember events that included you personally. HM couldn't describe anything that had happened to him since 11 years before his surgery; he could however describe some facts he had learned before the operation and so it is clear that the brain treats personal episodic memories differently from other forms of declarative memory. As Tulving predicted, people with retrograde amnesia have trouble planning for the future due to the lack of memory of the past. Indeed, studies using fMRI show that describing past events and imagining future events activate mostly the same areas including the hippocampus and the prefrontal cortex. Therefore, the role of the hippocampus is not just for spatial memory but personal memory too.

It's an old, but true, joke that if you go out on the town and get blotto (i.e. drunk) after having a few too many jars (i.e. alcoholic drinks) and you end up in such a state the next morning that you can't remember how you got home, you have killed off all the neurons related to that memory. A pretty crude way of describing it, but somewhat accurate nonetheless. You'll probably have a banging headache due to the fact that your brain has shrunk from dehydration and is tugging on your meninges (next stop, pain), and so your lack of memory may be the least of your worries. But long-term misuse of alcohol can have extremely lasting effects on your brain. Prolonged intake of large quantities of alcohol results in a Thiamine or Vitamin B1 deficiency because believe it or not, there are not huge quantities of the nutrients we need for life in a diet dominated by alcohol. The brain needs thiamine as it uses it to metabolize glucose, the only fuel it can use, so if you don't have thiamine you end up with a brain running on empty. This can cause massive cortical atrophy, and is generally irreversible. Sure, you can treat it by administering thiamine, but once the damage is done you will be left with severe retrograde and anterograde amnesia for declarative memory and will also suffer from apathy and confusion. This is called Korsakoff's syndrome and patients have trouble using reason with respect to their memories, which is a symptom of frontal lobe damage. For example, say you can't explicitly remember which you could do first, ride a bike or read. You might reason that since you learned how to ride a bike by reading a manual, you must have known how to read first. People with Korsakoff's syndrome and frontal damage have trouble with this kind of explanation.

Confabulation is a common occurrence with Korsakoff's but also in people with frontal lobe damage, children (remember, their frontal lobes aren't myelinated yet so they don't function as well) and healthy people under hypnosis! It occurs when we believe a fictitious story or memory and is often a somewhat sensible exten-sion of what we *can* remember and we confabulate to paper over the gaps. So, confabulation happens only on questions in which you would be expected to know the answer. Stroke victims with paralysis sometimes do this by explaining that their paralysed arm doesn't move because it doesn't belong to them. In fact, it is a hall-mark of confabulation that most of the confabulated answers are more pleasant than (or put a nicer spin on) the true answer. The problem would seem not to be that new memories are not made; it's that there is confusion between memory and present reality. There is an inability to recognize whether memories are relevant, real or current.

Therefore, there would seem to be a bit off cross-talk between what we think we know, and what we know we know. Do you think that a bit of prompting might influence what we think we know we know? Turns out (if you are still with me), yes, you can. Prompting and priming can change your memory of events. If I were to ask you "how fast do you think the car was going when it smashed into the wall?", you are sure to estimate a higher speed than if I asked "how fast do you think the car was going when it bumped into the wall?" This kind of top–down influence shows just how fallible your memory is and how vulnerable it is to interpretation based on the situation in which the question is framed. It has huge ramifications for eye-witness testimony for example, and remember, this can be easily demonstrated in any normal functioning human being!

One thing's for sure: our memory gets worse with age. Have I said that before? Almost any form of stress or emotional pressure can cause memory problems and that makes sense given the links between the declarative memory systems and the hypothalamus. Generally, a varied diet and lots of fluids (non-alcoholic) can improve memory. However, there is a clear decline of memory performance after the age of 30, and as we discovered in Chapter 7, our brains are most amenable to learning before this stage. But then, if we didn't forget some things, our brains would have to store a huge amount of useless information. The ability to forget unimportant information may be just as critical for normal brain function as retaining information that is significant. Dementia is a syndrome characterized by a failure of recent memory and other intellectual functions. Alzheimer's disease is the most common dementia and is characterized by the death of acetylcholine cells in all parts of the brain with particular damage occurring in the entorhinal cortex (important in declarative memory). Often forgetfulness in old people is merely attributed to old age and dementia but the milder forms of memory problems are just as likely to be reversible as they are due to poor diet, dehydration, loneliness and depression. But as with any cognitive ability, the old adage of "use it or lose it" applies and thanks to Donald Hebb, we know why. That and the brain's need for stimulation we talked about in Chapter 8 surely explain Countdown's enduring appeal.

## Feeling curious?

*Mind Sculpture: Your Brain's Untapped Potential* by Ian Robertson. 2000; Bantam Books. *A great read with some surprising theories on learning in both the normal and broken brain.*

*Your Memory: A User's Guide* by Alan D. Baddeley. 2006; Prion Books. *An accessible text in which memory systems in the brain and how you can make them work for you is discussed by a giant in the field.*

*Memory* by Alan Baddeley, Michael W. Eysenck, Michael C. Anderson. 2009; Psychology Press. *A more in-depth view of memory systems and pathologies relating to memory in the brain.*

Lauren Stewart (2005) "A Neurocognitive Approach to Music Reading. Annals of the New York" Academy of Sciences, *Volume 1060*, The Neurosciences and Music II: From Perception to Performance, pp. 377–86. *A lovely review of studies investigating the changes that happen in the brain when we learn to read music.*

Kevin S LaBar & Roberto Cabeza (2006) "Cognitive Neuroscience of Emotional Memory". *Nature Reviews Neuroscience* 7, 54–64 doi:10.1038/nrn1825. *The specialized mechanisms involved in emotional memory.*

Daniel L. Schacter, Donna Rose Addis & Randy L. Buckner (2007) "Remembering the Past to Imagine the Future: the Prospective Brain" *Nature Reviews Neuroscience* 8, 657–661 doi:10.1038/nrn2213. *This article discusses the importance of memory mechanisms in thoughts about the future.*

Philosophers over the years have bent over backwards trying to explain consciousness, and thinking about thinking. It was sometimes not a pretty sight. In the past 10 or 15 years or so, things have become a lot more sensible with people like psychologists and neuroscientists attacking the problem from the brain's point of view. Surely by now you will agree with me that this is the best way of looking at behaviour. If not, shame on you, go back to page 1, do not pass GO and do not collect 200 units of whatever currency you use. But what is the problem? Why do we find this aspect of our behaviour so hard to define?

Part of the problem is that thinking and consciousness have always been subjective things. Who is to say that the "white" colour of this page that I am looking at is the same as the "white" you are conscious of? This is an aspect called qualia or the phenomenological nature of consciousness and leads directly into the second problem which is that there is nothing physical in question here. Consciousness is something that happens outside of the body, more in the realm of the "mind" and as we saw in Chapter 1, this has been a problem for yonks. This is why it is much easier to think about neuronal processing underlying conscious behaviour. As Francis Crick (one of the discoverers of the structure of DNA) believed before his death in 2004, all of our hopes, dreams, fears, plans for the future, can be attributed to the activity of a bunch of neurons in our brains. So consciousness is created by our brain and doesn't exist outside of our brain.

This means that a non-fully-functioning brain would lead to a lack of consciousness. This is indeed true; there are examples from neuropsychology that we'll talk about in a bit. But this and the idea that consciousness is not a physical thing, pretty much nixes the idea that there is something, a spirit or a soul that lives on when we die. But is there any proof that the soul can be measured as if it were a physical thing? In 1907, an article entitled "Hypothesis Concerning Soul Substance Together with Experimental Evidence of The Existence of Such Substance" by an MD in Haverhill, Massachusetts, Duncan MacDougall, was published in *American Medicine*. It also made the headlines of the *New*

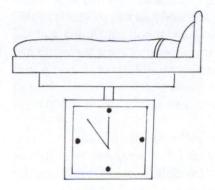

*York Times* due to its sensational nature. MacDougall postulated that if there was a soul then it must occupy space and if death represented the point at which the soul left the body, then he should be able to measure the substance of the soul. So he built a big bed weighing scales based on a large industrial silk weighing beam scale and placed dying men on it. One of his colleagues would watch for the point of death whilst he watched the scales. At the point of death, the bodies lost, on average ¾ of an ounce, or a little over 21 grams (hence the Hollywood movie of the same name). There were all kinds of fundamental problems with this experiment though such as the experimenters didn't quite know when the point of death occurred; remember, they couldn't touch the patient.

MacDougall actually tested six patients but only the first one was a good indicator of the phenomenon, a man dying of tuberculosis so chosen due to the stillness of the patient in their final hours. The second patient, MacDougall reported, had ceased to breathe for 15 minutes but the face was still showing contortions (something often seen in a dead head separated from the body by guillotine in Tudor times). MacDougall trusted the third tuberculosis case, he lost half an ounce (14 g) but there was a problem with the scales in the fourth subject, a woman in a diabetic coma. The fifth subject showed very strange fluctuations whilst the sixth died before MacDougall had a chance to adjust the beam. MacDougall repeated the experiment on 15 dogs and showed uniformly negative results, contingent with the prevailing view that animals have no soul. Only non-dog own-ers would attempt to postulate that dogs were not capable of consciousness.

Now, one could say that these 21 g were lost through the release of the residual air in the lungs (a point refuted by MacDougall as he himself lay on the scales and measured the weight of a deep exhalation, and this did not match that seen at the point of death). He also refuted the weight loss was coincident with any usual post-death defecation or excretion by the body as the products of this would remain on the bed. And so, MacDougall concluded that the soul had substance and was not immaterial. Given the wild vari-ability amongst the subjects, this study would never stand up in a statistical court of today; however it was widely enthused about in society of the day as people looked for proof that there was "some-thing" after death.

But let's say we give MacDougall's results an ounce of cre-dence. What else could explain this loss of weight? Well first of all, MacDougall's measurement of weight is compounded by the fact that weight doesn't just measure how much stuff was on the scales. Weight also takes into account the pull of the earth's grav-ity. Mass is actually, as Isaac Newton put it, the quantity of mat-ter, the amount of stuff in the body. Weight is mass multiplied by gravity. (The speed of something falling to Earth from a height is $9.81 \text{m/s}^2$.) In terms of force, Earthlings experience 1 g (as in one unit of gravity force) and so weighing scales are calibrated at this level. If I were to weigh myself in space where there is no gravity, I would be weightless as $50\text{kg} \times 0 \text{ m/s}^2$ is 0. Therefore all Weight Watchers meetings should be held in outer space; members will feel much better about themselves. But that doesn't mean they have no mass. The point here is that the decrease in weight is not a pure measure of what was lost from the body; this cannot be done until you take gravity out of the equation.

Say death, as indicated by the shutdown of the nervous system, causes an the efflux of neurotransmitter gases such as Nitric Oxide (NO: molecule of the year in 1992 you know) and NO has a molar mass of 30.006 grams per mole (where a mole is $6.022 \times 10^{23}$ mol-ecules). Could this account for the loss of mass? We'll never know until this experiment is repeated in a bubble in which the compo-sition of the air external to the body can be analysed before and after death. Another widely postulated reason is that the loss represents the "energy of the soul" leaving the body. Can energy have mass? Yes it can. In 1905, Einstein published his paper unveiling the famous $E = mc^2$ formula, which tells us that there is an equivalency between mass and the amount of energy it can produce and vice versa. Energy is some form of electromagnetic radiation which could be heat, sound, light etc. Certainly light comes in the form of electromagnetic waves as well as photons, little packets or quanta of light and these have a mass. In a related point, one of the central tenets of noetic science is that thoughts have mass. Noetic comes from the Greek word *noētikos* meaning mental, and has its roots in metaphysical philosophy. The movement was founded by the moon-walking Apollo 14 astronaut Edgar Mitchell in 1973. Immortalized in faction by Dan Brown's "The Lost Symbol" it seeks to address issues related to consciousness and intention and their impact on the physical world. However, MacDougall's experiments have never been replicated in any scientific rigorous manner despite spurious claims to the contrary involving an East German group in 1988.

Let's think about the living for a change. What is consciousness? Well, one way to examine this question is from an evolutionary perspective, something that Daniel Dennett from Tufts University in the USA is adept at doing and he is one of the most respected thinkers in the field. He frames the answer thus: life has existed on this planet over billions of years but for much of that there was no free will. The physics of the world has not changed and so determinism cannot explain the onset of consciousness. What has changed is biology and this has happened through evolution and the development of the brain, allowing us a competency to represent our reasons for behaviour. This is the key to consciousness; we can respond to challenges to our reasons for doing things; we can respond to situations and act accordingly. In fact, this is the root of the word responsibility; those actions are under our conscious control. We can think ahead, anticipate the consequences of our actions, share what we know with others. And this advanced competency is what makes us different from a meerkat or sea-lion or puffin.

But what is it about our evolved brain that allows us to achieve this higher conscious state with advanced thinking skills? Dennett believes that our brain has a "bunch of tricks" by which it brings about consciousness. Others, such as Crick and Steven Pinker from Harvard University, take a much more reductionist and mechanistic view. Pinker believes that the mechanisms of the brain create our behaviour, but with 100 million neurons and 100 trillion synapses this creates so much complexity and variability, a number of outcomes (that we mistakenly call choices) will result and will not be predictable in any simple way. We mistake this for free will but really, in his view, free will doesn't exist at all. Our thinking can take into account what has come before, what we have learned, how our genetics have made our brains and provide an outcome, or a number of outcomes as the case may be. In fact, our brain knows what we are going to do before we do. In 1985 Benjamin Libet discovered "preparatory potentials" or brain activity that happened hundreds of milliseconds (an age in brain processing terms) before a conscious decision was arrived at. He interpreted this finding as proof that free will is an illusion. This was followed up in 2002 but Chun Siong Soon from the Max Plank Institute in Germany who used fMRI to show that the brain knew which button was going to be pressed before the subjects were aware of it.

Consciousness may not even be necessary for functioning, reactively at least. As we know from Chapter 8 most things in our body are done without our knowledge; food is digested, blood pressure is regulated, water levels are monitored etc. We can walk without thinking about putting one foot in front of the other. Learning may be a conscious event but once learned other brain systems take over in order to make this automatic. Astronautical training is such that procedures are entirely automatic and taken out of the astronaut's control; they hear an alarm, they respond accordingly, they don't even think about it. Does this sound like eye blink conditioning to you? Thought it might.

Such evidence therefore not only questions whether we have free will but also why consciousness is necessary. With respect to eating, signals are sent from our digestive system to our brain telling us to eat, telling us when we are full, also keeping track of nutrients the lack of which can set up cravings. This is called pica, the urge to eat unusual things like gherkins with ice-cream (a personal favourite of mine) or soap (not so much) or even coal (never) and is particularly powerful in pregnant women. Do we really have free will, or are all of our actions determined by signals from our internal milieu (the determinism side of the story)? Well, I suppose we could say that we can overcome the signal coming from our body. We can choose not to eat or to over-ride the stop eating signals or choose a salad over that lovely juicy hamburger all your mates are eating. Even though you really want one. So the "will" or motivation may be determinist or even mechanistic in nature but you still have freedom to act upon it at least with respect to eating behaviours.

So perhaps we could separate our behaviours into reactive behaviour such as responding to nutrient levels and proactive behaviours over which we have more conscious control such as the question "what shall I have for dinner tonight?" (to which the best answer is chips with chocolate for dessert). This is the kind of processing Dennett refers to and is what distinguishes us from animals; the ability to assimilate information, share information, evaluate consequences and choose a course of action. But what is really interesting is that this almost philosophical view of consciousness is not incompatible with Pinker's neuroscientific view. For example, it's now well known that our frontal cortex is an area integral to our thinking behaviours and decision making and consciousness could merely be the natural result of coordinated activity in this and other regions of the cortex. The debate rages on and leads to lively arguments between people with quite entrenched views from many camps. Although everybody would love an answer, it will be a while coming because although we know what different parts of the brain generally do, we are only now getting to understand how these parts talk to each other to produce behaviour and this may be the key to unlocking "consciousness". Consciousness is just one of many behaviours in which the brain creates something many people perceive to be more than the sum of its parts.

Since this is a book about the brain, why don't we stop blathering on about the phenomenology (or lack thereof) of consciousness and talk about what the brain is doing during conscious tasks. People like Cristof Koch from CalTech, who used to work with Francis Crick, have devoted many experiments to finding out what the neural correlates of attention are, in other words, the bits of the brain that are active when somebody is doing something conscious, such as thinking. It's widely accepted that activity in these regions may not *cause* consciousness but they are active during it nonetheless. I have mentioned that the frontal cortex is generally accepted to be a region involved in thinking and decision making and being able to look to the future and evaluate consequences. But how do we know this? Well, there are two ways. The first is from neuropsychology. Remember Phineas Gage? He had a metal rod pass through his frontal lobes and his behaviour was forever changed. As did Agnes', whose husband had a surgeon perform a psychosurgical frontal lobectomy on her. When there is damage to the frontal cortex, not only does the control and interpretation of emotions suffer (Chapter 11) or the storage and retrieval of episodic memory (Chapter 12), the patient's ability to think coherently, solve problems or use information to predict consequences also suffer greatly. In short, damage to this area really impairs people's ability to think cogently. Evidence also comes from neurodevelopmental psychology. As we discovered in Chapter 7, the frontal lobes are the last part of the brain to be mylinated in children, and may not be fully completed until the age of 23 (hence all of those bad decisions you made as a teenager you can't reasonably explain). Children are particularly bad at seeing the consequences of their actions and this is compounded by kids having a poorly developed "theory of mind".

Theory of mind is a psychological term which is used to describe a person's ability to understand the emotions and emotional affect of another and is another tool used when thinking about consequences. Babies have to learn the effect walloping Mommy on the head with the wooden hammer has to take the response (an upset or even angry reaction) into account when deciding whether or not to ever do that again.

It is not just damage to the frontal lobe that can affect consciousness. Damage to other regions of the cortex can reduce or even abolish patients' awareness and there are a number of neurological conditions in which a person lacks conscious awareness about some information even though they are able to process it sub-consciously. In spatial neglect, a syndrome of symptoms resulting from damage to the right parietal and sometimes temporal lobe, patients often ignore the left half of their world. People with neglect do not think: "I cannot see to my left"; rather the left simply doesn't exist at all; it is neglected by the viewer. But that is not to say that information that the patient is not aware of cannot be used in later decisions. For example, show a patient suffering from neglect two pictures of houses that are identical on the right halves but different on their left in the respect that there is a raging fire happening in the left side of one of the houses. Then ask the patient which one they would prefer to live in. They will look at you quizzically as they believe they are both the same but they will always choose the house that is not on fire.

Blindsight is another such phenomenon and is caused by damage to the primary visual cortex of the occipital lobe (V1). The term was first coined in 1974 by Larry Weiskrantz from Oxford University (who loves a play on words) and is particularly apt as damage to this region will cause a blind area in the visual field (as the visual information from that area cannot be processed by the damaged cortex responsible for that region). However, some patients with this damage can, when forced to, respond as to whether or not a stimulus appeared in their blind field. They are not aware of it, but they can still "see" it. Others prefer the term "perception without awareness" but that's less catchy. The experiment would go something like this: first of all you would map the precise area that the patient could not see. Then in half of a block of trials you would present a stimulus, such as a flash of light, in their blind field. In the other half of the trials you would not present a flash. At the sound of a tone, you would then ask the patient whether or not they saw a flash and whether they were aware of it. This is called a two-alternative force choice test, i.e. did you see it or not, and if you don't know, guess. Patients say they can't do the task but in every case their performance is well above chance, meaning they are subconsciously processing the information. This behaviour is thought to result from an evolutionarily old visual pathway (remember the tecto pulvinar system from Chapter 4?) from the subcortical areas of the brain which is involved in eye-movements but with little or no image-forming capabilities. The most famous blindsight patient in the world is patient GY, who had a road accident when aged eight. He can see to his left but he is blind to everything on the right in both eyes and so has a very large blind field. Just after the accident he was always running into lamp posts and to this day he cannot recognize anything in his right field. GY has participated in many experiments for scientists all over the world to establish the limits of the blindsight effect. We now know that GY can determine direction of movement even though he can't consciously see it; he can detect things, but he is not aware of them. And recently, another eminent Oxford scientist Alan Cowey has determined that blindsight, at least in GY, is colour blind i.e. GY cannot detect differences based on colour. Therefore we know that vision is not entirely seeing; we can separate responding to visual information from the actual act of being visually aware. When GY is aware of a stimulus in his blind field, Alan and colleagues have noticed a coincident change in gamma wave activity. And so consciousness may be better thought of with respect to the pattern of activity seen in the brain denoting synchronisation of goings on between regions.

There is also evidence for unconscious processing in touch (numbtouch) and audition (deaf hearing) and there is also evidence of it in olfaction (anosmic smell) although this is harder to define. Crucially, blindsight shows that V1 is necessary for normal visual perception but it doesn't tell us whether or not it is activity in V1 that gives rise to conscious experience or whether processing in other regions is necessary. As V1 is the first stop on the visual processing loop, and these other areas will not get good information to work with if V1 is damaged, it is hard to tease apart. But from what we see in neglect, we would postulate that no, V1 on its own cannot directly produce consciousness as it is still intact in sufferers of neglect and they are still not aware of the left side of their space.

What if other extra-striate areas are selectively damaged? In these syndromes, the entire visual field can be seen; however patients have problems consciously perceiving aspects of it. Instead, damage to cortical areas with neurons attuned to certain stimuli leads to a corresponding deficit in consciousness of those features. For example, in visual form agnosia, patients are unable to recognise objects. Patient DF suffered carbon monoxide poisoning that resulted in extensive damage to the temporal lobe and she has been as obliging as GY in visiting neuroscientific labs so that we can examine the extent of her deficit and learn about the nature of conscious awareness. Despite her inability to identify objects however, her ability to grasp and reach for objects was unaffected. For example, say the object was a toothbrush. DF could not identify it but could pick it up and show you what it is used for by pantomiming the brushing teeth action. These findings suggest that the brain has different systems for visual object recognition and visual guidance of movement and have been central to David Milner and Mel Goodale's two-stream hypothesis we came across in Chapter 4. Moreover, it shows that you can process visual information that allows you to grasp an object correctly without being consciously aware of what it is. However, when DF uses an item she cannot recognise, she can then use this information to identify it.

Prosopagnosia is a specialised form of this condition in which people with damage to areas such as the fusiform face area in the occipital cortex have problems consciously perceiving the difference between faces, whilst leaving the ability to recognise other objects relatively intact. However, people familiar to us seem to get another form of processing in the brain. Cristof Koch has found evidence of activity in the hippocampus related to people familiar to us. Using listening electrodes he has found a cell that responds to all things related to Halle Berry. The cell responds to pictures of her dressed as a regular human as well as Catwoman and even her their name in print. Cristof has dubbed these "concept cells" and may be evidence that thinking about different aspects of a concept may be coordinated by a node in the brain.

Meanwhile, motion agnosia (or akinetopsia) robs sufferers of their ability to consciously perceive movement and results from lesions to the area of the occipital cortex that processes movement, V5. For example, LM, whom Josep Zihl tested at the Max Plank Institute in Germany in 1983, saw the world in strobe, she would see moving objects appear in one position and then another. She would fail to see the level of tea she was pouring into a cup rise and would be surprised when it overflowed. LM's case was particularly bad as she had bilateral lesions to V5.

Achromatopsia, or cortical colour blindness, comes about from damage to area V4, the main colour processing area of the occipital cortex. The idea that this area is involved in our conscious perception of colour is supported by patients with lesions to V4 who are unable to distinguish between different colours or hues. They often report that colours become bland reflecting dirty shades of grey. CB was a 28-year-old, highly educated civil servant who was examined by Alan Cowey. CB had diffuse damage in his brain following a road traffic accident which seemed to resolve over the ensuing four weeks; however, his visual function was impaired to the degree that he could read only if the print were enlarged. Most interestingly though, he could not recognise the difference between colours. A yellowish green looked the same as a deep orange to him; that's a ten-point difference on a scale in which normal functioning people can see a one-point difference! He just was not aware of the difference.

Each of these cases prove at the very least that the area in question is required for normal perception and this is required to evoke consciousness of the attribute processed in that area. It's not entirely clear however. Using fMRI we can see that presenting an object in the blind field of somebody with damage to V1 (which can result in blindsight) can activate extrastriate regions, through the tectopulvinar pathway. But these subjects don't consciously see the stimulus; all they can do is guess correctly. So extrastriate activation on its own is not enough for conscious perception. This has led to the view that perhaps activity in one region on its own is not enough for consciousness; areas have to talk to each other in feedforward (in vision: V1 to extrastriate regions) and feedback (extrastriate to V1) ways to tailor our conscious perception. This has been confirmed recently using a variety of neuroscientific techniques. As Cristof Koch puts it, a single molecule of water does not give rise to wetness; there is no reason to assume the brain is any different with respect to one area creating a conscious experience. For consciousness in vision at least, we need a functioning area specific to the processing of the stimulus as well as a functioning V1.

Things that bypass awareness can influence behaviour not only in brain-damaged patients (as we saw in neglect and blindsight) but this occurrence can also happen in normal functioning people. What are the limits of our subconscious? Well, we have talked about how learning makes many tasks automatic. You have to concentrate on learning the fingering on a violin for example, but with time this becomes automatic, subconscious and you don't have to think about it. David Beckham spent years kicking a ball

against the shed, learning the probable outcome of kicking the ball a certain way. He became a master of the free kick in soccer, an automatic process for him that he doesn't even have to think about while he's doing it. In visual processing, we can quantify the effect of unconscious processing on behaviour and in the brain quite easily. Psychologists have used experimental paradigms such as masking to study subconscious processing in the brain. For example: a subject is shown one of two pictures of a boy, he could either be about to throw a cake looking mean, or he could be merely holding a cake, looking angelic. The image is shown for a split second; people are not even aware they saw it. Then, a picture of the boy looking neutral is presented and subjects are asked to judge the personality of the boy. Subjects who were presented the throwing picture rate him as being mean whereas those who saw him simply holding the cake have much more favourable impressions.

So although we are not consciously aware of the masked stimulus, we can still use its information in later processing. In fact, this is the basis of the act of many a mind-reader, who will place subliminal cues in your path to make you act in a certain way on stage. It has been banned in advertising due to its ability to make us act on these subconscious cues. Stanislas Dehaene and colleagues from INSERM in France used fMRI to quantify the difference in neural processing when a stimulus was masked or seen. Although a masked word does evoke activity in the brain, Dehaene discovered ten times less activation in extrastriate visual regions if the subject didn't see the masked word than if they did. Perhaps processing in the brain needs to reach a threshold of some kind in order to reach consciousness. Such thresholds can be easily examined in the most common subconscious state: sleep. We know from Chapter 9 that the thalamus regulates and synchronises the activity of the brain to a slower rhythm and that this is coincident with a decrease in our levels of consciousness. How does the brain react to stimuli in this state? Could this be the key to our understanding of consciousness?

Marcello Massimini from the University of Wisconsin, Madison has been investigating this issue. He uses EEG to examine the neural activity whilst his subjects are awake and asleep but one crucial difference is that he applied a TMS pulse to examine the effect this has on the activity of the brain and records the outcome. When you apply the TMS pulse in the awake brain we see activity in the brain under the coil but also secondary activity in areas connected to the stimulated region wither functionally or anatomically and this can be quite far away in a complex pattern. Areas talk to other areas and interact with each other in a network. When the same stimulation is applied when the subject is asleep, Massimo sees activation at the place in the brain where the pulse is delivered but the activity remains local. The network of communication of the pulse when you are awake is broken down when you are asleep. Therefore we can take this as further evidence that we need many areas to be involved in a processing network in order to achieve consciousness.

Normally, one of the main communication channels in the brain is that between the hemispheres. The corpus callosum is a huge tract of nerve fibres connecting the left and right hemispheres all along the brain's length. However, for patients with epilepsy it is sometimes necessary to cut the corpus callosum to prevent the spread of seizures from one hemisphere to the other. The postoperative "split-brain" patient's function remains remarkably unscathed. According to one patient Joe, although his left and right hemispheres are working independently from each other, the effect is easy to adapt to and life feels no different from how it was before. However, neuropsychological testing can reveal some really interesting findings that have remarkable insights into conscious perception. The key here is that language in most people is lateralised to the left hemisphere, meaning that in order for something processed in the right hemisphere to be talked about, the information needs to travel, via the corpus callosum, to the speech areas in the left hemisphere. This isn't possible in the split-brain patient. Michael Gazzaniga from the University of California, Santa Barbara has tested Joe extensively. The early experiments in the 1980s went something like this. Michael got Joe to sit in front of a screen and look at the central fixation cross. This meant that anything presented to the left of the screen would be processed by the right hemisphere and everything on the left would be processed by the left hemisphere of the brain. Joe could only verbally report a word or a picture that was presented on the right side of the screen and processed by the left hemisphere, which is capable of language. If the picture or word was presented on the left side of the screen, Joe would report that he didn't see anything. Michael would then ask Joe to take a pen in his left hand, close his eyes and let his left hand draw what was on the screen, which Joe could do to great effect even though he couldn't name it initially. His recognition was not affected as he could name the object based on his drawing of the object. Michael then made the task more complex. He presented a hammer to the right of the fixation point and a handsaw to the left and asked Joe to close his eyes and draw the object. Joe drew a handsaw, which he then identified, but when asked what he saw on the screen he said "a hammer". Michael asked, "what did you draw that for then?" Joe replied, "I don't know".

Michael presented a snow scene to the left and a chicken claw to the right to another split-brain patient called PS. PS had to point to a number of pictures presented below that were associated with the pictures he's already been shown, things such as a lawnmower, rake, shovel and pickaxe on the left with a cow, chicken, ram and apple on the right. PS used his right hand to pick the chicken (to go with the claw) and a shovel with his left hand (to go with the snow scene). When asked why he chose the shovel (remember, the snow scene was processed by his non-verbal right hemisphere), he explained that the shovel could be used to clean the chicken shed! The brain will always look for a reason to explain behaviour and as we found out in Chapter 12 this is the basis of confabulation and may happen not just when there is a break between memory and reality but consciousness and reality. This is even more evident when a patient was presented the word "laugh" on the left side of the screen prompting laughter from the patient. When asked why they were laughing they said, "You guys come up and test us every month. What a way to make a living!" If the command "Walk" is presented to the left side of the fixation cross, the patient got up and left the testing area. When asked why, she said, "I'm going into the house to get a Coke."

One way of interpreting these findings is that if we can't use our verbal left hemisphere then we are not conscious of our actions and that consciousness is intimately tied with language. This is an intuitive theory; when we think about a problem, many of us use words in our heads. However, Michael Gazzaniga and his colleague Joseph Ledoux arrived at a more general theory. They believe that the human brain has a specialised system in our left hemisphere to interpret our world and that language is simply a part of that. The interpreter is a system which seeks to explain internal and external events so that an appropriate response can be made. Our left frontal lobe is important in issues of order, and this is very important in seeing how events relate to one another and can work under our conscious awareness or outside it. How many times have you not been able to come up with a solution to a problem but if you take a break, walk away or play solitare instead the answer just hits you? This is because your subconscious thought processes have been working on it without your knowledge. In fact, there is evidence from an fMRI study investigating how we asses risk in gambling that a decision based on your subconscious gut feeling is sometimes more advantageous than a conscious one as they take emotional cues such as the blackjack dealer's expression into account whereas thinking can rationalise these emotions and discount them. A healthy mix of both signals seems to get us by.

Language is just one, yet important part of expressing our consciousness. Other mechanisms include gestures, eye movements and facial expression. In locked-in syndrome, a term coined in the 1960s by Jerome Posner and Fred Plum, all of these methods of communication of consciousness are damaged due to a complete paralysis of nearly all voluntary muscles in the body (including the eyes in extreme forms) because of a lesion in the brainstem in which the pons is damaged. It is therefore a condition in which the patient is aware and awake but cannot move or communicate verbally or non-verbally, which is understandably pretty harrowing for sufferers particularly if their loved ones do not know they are aware of what is going on. Life support may be necessary for patients such as this as the brainstem, which controls breathing, is damaged. Apparent inactivity of either the whole brain or brainstem is the legal indicator of death in many countries and so you can see why life support could be switched off in locked-in patients. Thankfully we now have clear guidelines and reliable methods for gathering evidence of brain activity and interpreting it correctly to ascertain the conscious state of the brain and the possible retrievability of some quality of life.

Various examples of coma patients have made the investigation into consciousness of paramount importance in recent years. For example, Terry Wallis was a 19-year-old man when he fell into a coma after a car accident which later stabilised into a minimally conscious state. However, after nearly 20 years, he woke up in 2003 regaining many, but not all functions. Diffusion Tensor Imaging, which defines the connections in the brain, showed that Terry's brain had re-wired itself to allow him to come out of a state in which he was sleeping, waking and breathing unaided, was aware but uncommunicative and unresponsive with irregular movements. The next stage down the consciousness ladder is the vegetative state in which there is sleeping and waking but no awareness. Again, breathing is unaided and movements are not purposeful and reflexes are intact. If this status persists for more than four weeks it becomes a persistent vegetative state and after one year is termed a permanent vegetative state. This condition is not classified as death in any judicial system but there is controversy as to whether or not such patients should be allowed to die as patients are "highly unlikely" to achieve higher brain function. These issues were fully debated in the high profile court case of Teresa Schiavo who finally had her feeding tube removed and died in Florida in 2005, 15 years after hypoxic brain injury caused by a heart attack. Recovery after one year is highly unlikely.

The amount of consciousness vegetative patients have has recently been scrutinised by Adrian Owen and colleagues from Cambridge University. The diagnosis of vegetative state relies on there being no reproducible evidence of purposeful behaviour in response to external stimuli. But what Adrian and his colleagues wanted to examine was whether there was an internal consciousness, one that could not produce any external indication of consciousness. The findings were clear. When they asked a patient who was behaviourally vegetative to imagine playing tennis, the region of the brain which is involved in planning movements etc. becomes active. The same thing happens in normal brains when people are given such mental imagery tasks to use. Even thinking about the movement makes the movement areas active even though no movement is made. In the case of the vegetative patients it means they can voluntarily follow instructions and that by taking the body out of the consciousness equation we can see that many of these patients have more awareness than previously thought just as now we know happens with respect to locked-in syndrome.

Many of us have experienced the next stage on the consciousness ladder as it happens when we are under general anaesthetic; our eyes are closed, we are completely unconscious to stimuli (a great thing if you are having an operation) and we breathe normally. As anaesthetic drugs work by increasing the amount of GABA (the main inhibitory neurotransmitter in the brain) in the thalamus so that the proper awake signal is not sent to the cortex, the effects are quickly reversed as soon as the anaesthetic wears off. Therefore we know that as important as the cortical regions we have talked about thus far are to consciousness, without the thalamus, awareness would be impossible. However the next stage, coma, represents a state in which the eyes are closed, patients are unconscious without awareness of external stimuli and there is no waking. There is reduced brain activity and patients may need artificial life support. It is possible to come out of coma and climb the ladder back to full consciousness; however, as can be seen with these pathologies, we must be very careful in making sweeping statements about the patient's conscious abilities. Just because we cannot see the normal fruits of their awareness such as responses, interaction, language or purposeful movement or motivation, does not mean they are not conscious. Therefore, in the face of the debate as to what consciousness is, it seems the cleanest way is to stop bickering and just look at what the brain is doing. But that's my motto for everything.

## Feeling curious?

Michael S. Gazzaniga (2005) "Forty-Five Years of Split-Brain Research and Still Going Strong" *Nature Reviews Neuroscience* 6, 653–659 doi:10.1038/nrn1723. *A great review of the field over nearly half a century by this prolific split-brain researcher.*

*Consciousness Explained* by Daniel C. Dennett. 1993; Penguin. *A discussion of what consciousness is not and how it might be explained with reference to neuroscience, psychology and artificial intelligence.*

Steven Pinker (2007) "The Brain: The Mystery of Consciousness". *Time* Magazine. 29 January Read more: http://www.time.com /time/magazine/article/0,9171,1580394,00.html#ixzz1jFeXcDYE *Pinker's thoughts on what consciousness is and how it comes about.*

"Consciousness Lost and Found: A Neuropsychological Exploration" by Lawrence Weiskrantz. 1997; Oxford University Press. *A discussion of consciousness from the neuropsychological point of view including the limits of our performance when we have no conscious awareness.*

Adrian M. Owen & Martin R. Coleman (2008) "Functional Neuroimaging of the Vegetative State". *Nature Reviews Neuroscience* 9, 235–243 doi:10.1038/nrn2330 *A review of the work that has been done to define awareness in the vegetative state.*

*The Astonishing Hypothesis: The Scientific Search for the Soul* by Francis Crick. 1995; Simon & Schuster. *Although much of the discourse relates to the visual system, the thoughts of one of the discoverers of DNA on consciousness are much valued and revolutionary in their day.*

R. Quian Quiroga, L. Reddy, G. Kreiman, C. Koch & I. Fried (2005) "Invariant Visual Representation by Single Neurons in the Human Brain". *Nature* 435, 1102–1107 doi:10.1038/nature03687. *This is Christoph Koch's Halle Berry cell experiment!*

CHAPTER **14** **Put it all together ...**

We've pretty much covered the basics of what we know about how our brains bring about all of our functions, our emotions and our realities. It seems like we know an awful lot doesn't it, and then you can go ahead and scratch the surface to reveal a myriad of new complexities that underlie these basics. Understanding the brain and how it influences behaviour is incredibly interesting on its own, but most people have a vested interest. People want to know the answer to problems such as Parkinson's Disease, Alzheimer's Disease, stroke, the effects of brain injury and any number of mental illnesses that exist in medical dictionaries. It's true, there is a gulf between knowing what you now know from the previous chapters and being able to help people with disorders of the brain but that is not unique to you. There is a wide gap between science and medical practice that is more informed by what we don't know than what we do. In 2000 I attended a Society for Neuroscience conference in New Orleans at which Christopher Reeve was the plenary speaker. To a packed room of active neuro-scientists, the former Superman but sadly then quadriplegic due to a riding accident made the case that the gap was too wide because of fear that our actions, well intentioned and meant to help, would actually make the patient worse because of some unforeseen circumstance. He understood that we don't know everything. It will be an incredibly long time until we do, but Chris's point was that that shouldn't stop us from trying to help people such as him with novel approaches. In fact, he rather presciently said that people in his position can't wait very long for advancements to come along and within four years of the speech I attended, he died.

Medicine always seems to the patient to be quite unchanging and slow to bring out new treatments but there is a whole scientific community at its back paddling like crazy to get ahead of whatever disorder is in question. First we need to understand how the normal brain works, then we need to know how it's working in the abnormal brain and then we need to work out what we can do about that. Most problems are surmountable, problems such as funding, technological, ethical and other issues; but these matters add up to impede on a process that is by its very nature time consuming in order for good science to be done. In the past couple of decades however, there have been a few leaps and bounds that stand out that have ramifications not just for single disorders that affect the brain, but many disorders and that's what makes them really exciting. One such sea change can be attributed to the concept of Thalamocortical Dysrhythmia or TCD for short.

You'll remember from previous chapters that the thalamus is the grand relay station of the brain, everything comes into the thalamus and is sent back out into the cortex again in thalamo-cortical loops. Part of the diencephalon, the thalamus is a two-lobed structure that sits in the very middle of the brain and each of its anatomical regions can be subdivided according to function including memory, motor control, vision, audition, sensation and many others. In 1999, Rodolfo Llinás from the New York University School of Medicine and colleagues including Daniel Jeanmonod from the University Hospital in Zurich used magnetoencephalopgraphy (MEG) to show that the pattern of firing in the thalamo-cortical loops is important for normal functioning, and misfiring or abnormal patterns can be directly linked to functionally specific changes in behaviour. MEG detects the magnetic fields that result from the electrical activity of the brain and so are a direct measure of activity as opposed to an indirect measure such as that seen in fMRI where we infer activity based on blood flow changes. Therefore, it was the perfect technique for Llinás to use to investigate the electrical activity in the thalamus and elsewhere in the entire cortex.

Llinás had been working on the issue much earlier than 1999 however. Remember the preoptic region in the hypothalamus that promotes sleep-like patterns of firing in neurons in the brain? It does this through the thalamus, which relays the signals out to the cortex through its thalamocortical loops. Well, in 1982, Llinás first detected an abnormal switch from waking to sleeping rhythms in individual neurons in the thalamus. If the thalamus is sending slow patterns of neural firing, the connecting neurons in the cortex fire at a slower rate also. Llinás determined that Parkinsonian twitches happen at a theta rhythm of 3–6 twitches per second. Using MEG he found the same rhythmic activity in the motor-related cortex originating from the related area of thalamus. In theory, abnormal rhythms may occur in any of the thalamocortical loops and affect any function and in fact, TCD can be found as a symptom, not a cause mind, in many neurological disorders like Parkinson's, dystonia, migraine headache, chronic pain, obsessive compulsive disorder and tinnitus amongst others. It depends on where the slower rhythms are being sent, be it motor cortex in the case of Parkinson's and dystonia or it could be auditory cortex in the case of tinnitus or visual cortex for migraine.

Knowing this, Daniel Jeanmonod routinely destroyed small parts of the thalamus to treat Parkinsonian tremor, as it would be better to have no signals than screwy signals. But side effects, such as defects in language and analytical thinking to paralysis were common. And so, to target ablation better, he used electrodes to "listen" to the neural activity to pinpoint the abnormal region. But nowadays, instead of killing off the neurons that are sending the wrong signals, neurosurgeons all over the world implant electrodes hooked up to a pacemaker battery pack located just below the collar bone, to regulate the firing of the neurons. How cool is that? Such operations are difficult but becoming easier due to technological advances and are done with an awake patient so that they know immediately when the electrode is in the right place as their behavioural symptoms disappear. In some cases where the thalamus is being fed bad signals from elsewhere, it is possible to change the signal input to the thalamus to lessen symptoms. A good example of this is Parkinson's disease. In the normal brain, dopamine inhibits the globus pallidus, which in turn normally inhibits the thalamus. In Parkinson's disease a lack of dopamine means that the globus pallidus becomes overactive and over-inhibits the thalamus. Frequencies of electricity of 100–130Hz inhibits cell firing, so injection of such a current to the globus pallidus would restore its normal inhibitory activity. This is the principle of Deep Brain Stimulation, and although not without its risks for the patient, it shows enormous promise in a range of neurological problems when medication just doesn't help.

Another great hope in the field of medical neurology is the use of stem cells to re-grow damaged tissue. As you know from Chapter 7, stem cells are the precursors of all cells in the body and have the potential to turn into any tissue that the body needs. They can self-renew and divide until the end of time. Stem cells can be cultured in the lab as an unlimited source of repair tissue for many ailments whilst those with genetic defects can be used to understand how diseases such as Parkinson's disease develop. However, stem cells can also be transplanted into damaged areas of the brain to repair the surrounding tissue. In 2010, Keith Muir and colleagues from Glasgow University began a trial in which stem cells were injected into the brain of a stroke patient and improved his function as a result. The study drew criticism in that foetal stem cells gave rise to the therapeutic cell's creation, but in the future, the necessity for this will lessen. Personalised tissue therapy involves taking any kind of cell from the patient, say a skin cell for example, and dialling it back in its evolutionary life so that it expresses all of its genes and not just the ones that make it a skin cell. That means it can in turn become anything we want it to be. It circumvents the ethical argument as it engineers cells without recourse to an embryo and as each subject's own tissue is used, there are no rejection issues. If stem cells from an embryo are used, the body sees these as foreign in the same ways as it does following an organ transplant and so the patient has to be put on immune blockers to stop their rejection. The obvious flaw with this is that this is a pointless therapy for something like Parkinson's disease or Huntington's, as the harvested and de-differentiated cells will have the capacity to develop Parkinson's or Huntington's again. But for stroke or spinal cord damage, this could be a fruitful way forward. Stem cell approaches are still in their infancy and the reconstruction of neural circuitry that will bring about normal function has not yet been shown. It might not just be the neurons that are damaged in Parkinson's or Huntington's or spinal cord damage that are important. Equally essential are the glioblasts that differentiate into support cells which mop up toxins, reduce inflammation and remyelinate the neurons that are spared to improve function. The treatment is improving; stem cells are now injected into damaged regions in a cocktail of growth hormone (to help cell proliferation) and anti-inflammatories which help the transplanted cells survive.

In spinal cord injury however it would seem that time is of the essence and that the optimal time of treatment in rats is 2–3 weeks post-damage. There are risks however, as it is important to control stem cell differentiation after transplantation.

Another neurodegenerative disease which could also, in theory, benefit from stem cell transplantation is Alzheimer's disease. This is one form of dementia which comes from the latin for "without (de-) mind (mens)". We all know that as we get older our cognitive processing gets a bit rusty; we forget things; we have to concentrate more to work sums out perhaps. This is associated with the normal age-related brain shrinkage which, incidentally, is a uniquely human event, and by age 80, our brains will have lost 15% of their mass. Dementia is a non-specific term that denotes a problem in memory, attention, language and/or problem solving beyond what might be expected from normal aging. Alzheimer's disease can strike much earlier than old age (generally defined as over 65 years of age) however, and given the widespread damage, it is unlikely that neural stem cells would receive the correct direction to divide and differentiate properly. Alzheimer's disease is characterised by neuronal and synaptic loss throughout the brain, involving the amygdala (emotion), hippocampus (memory) and other cortical areas including the basal forebrain cholinergic system (reasoning). Because of this latter effect of the disease, it was thought that Alzheimer's was caused by a lack of the neurotransmitter acetylcholine in the brain. Therefore, drugs that stop the breakdown of acetylcholine in the synaptic cleft thus increasing the amount of acetylcholine in the system should help. However, such acetylecholinesterase inhibitors give only temporary relief. Basal forebrain grafts of non-neural stem cells that release nerve growth factors can counteract the cholinergic cell death stimulating cell function and improving memory in humans. In fact, even the injection of anti-inflammatories on their own seem to cause a functional improvement even in advanced patients exhibiting severe memory loss.

In 2008, Edward Tobinick from UCLA demonstrated "miracle awakenings" in patients two hours after receipt of an injection of an anti-inflammatory drug called etanercept, normally used in the treatment of rheumatoid arthritis. The underlying reason as to why this works is based on the other theory of Alzheimer's disease, that the functional effects are caused by the formation of beta-amyloid plaques, clumps of protein in the brain that tangle up neurons, cause inflammation and eventually destroy the neurons. The formation of the plaques may or may not be a cause or effect of the acetylcholine depletion; however there is a genetic link to chromosome 21 and the expression of the amyloid precursor protein gene. As with TCD however, if we can interfere with the symptom, i.e. inflammation caused by plaques, we can ameliorate the effects right? Well, Tobinick courted controversy by publishing the results of his "clinical trial" without using a group which was given a placebo drug and so it was a non-controlled study. The reason why he carried it out this way was because randomised controlled trials are very laborious and expensive to carry out and due to lack of interest from the academic community and drug companies, he wasn't in a position carry out such an experiment. As a consequence, the study was viewed with suspicion amongst the scientific community. Other options include drugs to break-up the plaques and there has been limited reported success in that function improved in patients over time. Many brains of elderly people when examined post-mortem have as many plaques as Alzheimer's sufferers but they are not symptomatic. Tobinick believes that the plaques are in fact a red-herring and that it is the inflammation they cause in certain people, who perhaps have damage in inopportune places such as the locus corerulus that normally releases endogenous anti-inflammatories, that creates all the problems. The treatment is not without its difficulties; people who are taking etanercept for rheumatoid arthritis aren't insulated against the effects of Alzheimer's and that's because it ordinarily wouldn't cross the blood brain barrier. What Tobinick has been doing was injecting it into the neck where there are hundreds of tiny veins surrounding the spinal cord. Then he tilts the patient's head downwards at an angle of about 30 degrees for 5 minutes to maximise blood brain transfer. So, it's not the most straightforward of deliveries and may entail its own risks. Well, as of 2011, this treatment is finally undergoing clinical trials at the University of Southampton for full evaluation. Fingers crossed.

This is not the only instance in which a non-intuitive treatment seems to work for a disease or disorder. Multiple Sclerosis (MS) is a disease for which people are thought to have a genetic disposition which can be triggered by a virus; however the jury is still out as to the cause. It leads to an inflammatory auto-immune response in which the body's immune system attacks and damages the myelin sheath of neurons in the brain and spinal cord. As a result, neurons can't communicate with each other as effectively as they used to, slowing down signals and leading to all sorts of problems affecting every system of the brain and body. There is no cure, and management of the disease mainly takes an anti-inflammatory approach to try to slow the progression of the disease. Clinical trials in the use of stem cells in treatment have just begun. Also recently, some surgeons have been offering a surgery to insert a stent to open up the vascular system below the cerebellum. This is because of the observation made by Paolo Zamboni, a vascular surgeon from the University of Ferrara in Italy, that MS is coincident with a chronic cerebro-spinal venous insufficiency (CCSVI). It was found due to an observed increased iron content in the thalamus and basal ganglia (which indicates impaired venous draining). This could in itself set up many of the symptoms of MS and could trigger the autoimmunity and the degradation of the myelin sheath leading Zamboni to think that CCSVI causes MS in at least 90% of cases. It's also possible that the CCSVI is correlative with MS and not causative but again, it doesn't really matter as it would seem that if a stent is put into the vascular system below the cerebellum to improve flow the progression of MS is arrested. Although surgery such as this has inherent risks and further research is required to confirm its efficacy in bigger patient groups; the insertion of a stent soon after diagnosis would be preferable as symptoms would be arrested at an early stage.

It's been reported that over 20 million people per year worldwide experience a stroke and it is categorised as being the third biggest cause of death. The effects of a stroke can be extremely varied in nature depending on what kind of stroke it was, where the damage occurred, how big an area of the brain was damaged etc. Stroke is such a funny word to use to describe the brain attack that is caused either by bleeding in the brain (haemorrhagic stroke) or starving the tissue of oxygen because of a blood clot getting stuck in a blood vessel (ischemic stroke); 70% of strokes occur this way. In this way, it is quite analogous to a heart attack. Hippocrates called it "apoplexy", which means sudden, which is a fair description as there is generally little warning of the onset of a stroke. Other descriptions include cerebro-vascular accident, again, much more descriptive and intuitive than the term "stroke". In 1599, the term stroke was first used in English to extol the virtues of cinnamon water in the treatment of the "stroke of God's hand"; stroke has somehow stuck as a lay man's term for apoplexy. I suppose it fits with a conceptual view of the brain being struck down by a neurological problem. Either way, a stroke can be recognised in a patient who loses muscle tone, most obviously in the face and arms. Their speech may be affected (if the damage is happening in the left side of the brain). Given the fact that almost two million brain cells are affected for every minute a stroke goes untreated, it is really important to get medical help promptly to limit the effects of this invasive neurological insult.

Seventy per cent of strokes are caused by blockages in the blood vessels of the brain and so the administration of thrombolytic drugs which break down the blood clots can really effect a better outcome for patients but they must be given within three hours of the stroke. That's difficult because many strokes onset during sleep and another problem is that if you give thrombolytic drugs to somebody who is suffering from a haemorrhagic stroke, the effects could be disastrous. Haemorrhagic stroke has a set of symptoms that is unique however, such as the onset of seizure, the level of thinners in the blood as well as indications from the patient's history, and this, coupled with the results of a CT or MRI scan means doctors can make an educated decision as to what kind of stroke was experienced. Some patients present with transient ischemic attacks (TIAs) in which they experience weakening or perhaps disturbed speech that recovers over a relatively short period of time. This indicates recoverable neural damage but not death, but is indicative also of this patient being at risk of a stroke. The patient may be given blood thinners such as aspirin to reduce the likelihood that clots will form. Since the treatment is so mild, it would seem that it doesn't increase the likelihood of the bleeding type of stroke. More aggressive treatments may be given to people with forms of heart disease that are prone to producing clots that can travel to the brain and gum up the works. These include warfarin, which you may have heard of from its other guise of rat poison, but when given in small amounts to such patients can reduce the likelihood of stroke by 75% as it has a stronger blood thinning effect. An even more invasive treatment is to open up the carotid artery which feeds the brain with oxygenated blood in order to clear out any gunk that may have collected there impeding the flow of blood to the brain.

It sounds like prevention is better than cure and yes that is true. Stroke can cause all sorts of effects, some that we as concerned onlookers can see, be it muscle weakness because of damage to the motor areas or slurred speech because of damage to the speech areas in the left hemisphere. These can sometimes be treated by physiotherapy in order to regain functions like speaking or moving. However, some non-obvious effects can occur. Stroke comes as a huge shock to patients; it's rarely expected and its effect on our ability to function can be utterly devastating. But the neurological status of a patient doesn't always relate to the patient's quality of life, which can sometimes be much worse than should be predicted based on the brain damage incurred. Adam Noble and Thomas Schenk, then from Durham University, were curious about this and have been finding since 2008 that stroke victims suffer from fatigue that is even worse than patients undergoing aggressive chemotherapy for cancer, which is notoriously high anyway. On further investigation, they found that one-third of stroke patients suffer from post-traumatic stress, fearing reoccurrence of another stroke and decreasing the likelihood that standard rehabilitation treatments will work for them. However, if the PTSD is treated through psychological behavioural therapies, the sense of pessimism lifts promoting a better outcome from rehab. Interestingly, but perhaps intuitively, Noble and Schenk also found that 26% of significant others suffer from PTSD, three times more than the rate of PTSD in the general population, and predict that providing support to family members in order to teach them better coping strategies may prevent PTSD or other psychosocial disabilities from developing.

Another non-obvious effect is the ability of patients to see and explore the world around them visually. Vision can be affected in that patients can't see part of their visual field due to damage to the occipital cortex or the optic radiation from the LGN. If the left side of the occipital regions are damaged then patients will be unable to see anything on the right side of wherever their eyes are. This is called hemianopia, and usually affects both eyes; the patient is blind to the right side of the visual world coming into each eye, a happenstance that necessitates the more specific term of homonymous hemianopia. It's not always half the visual field, it can be a quadrant (quadrantanopia) or just a spot in the visual field that the patient can't see, called a scotoma. A more curious effect is called neglect, which is usually hemi-spatial. In this case, the patient can see perfectly well; however due to damage to the parietal cortex or the superior temporal cortex, patients have trouble orienting their attention to stimuli in the visual field. There is a memory component also as if you ask a patient to describe a visual image from their memory, they will describe only one half (usually the right side as neglect most often occurs following right hemisphere damage meaning the left side of space is "neglected"). It leads to functional effects of people eating only what is on the right side of their plate however, both hemianopia and neglect can have more life-threatening ramifications. Imagine how hard it would be to cross a road for example.

So, what can we do? Well, the obvious way around not being able to see or attend to part of your visual field is to use your eye movements more to fill in the gaps. But because of their damage, patients are not inclined to make eye movements into their blind or unattended fields. Therefore, one way of tackling the problem is to train patients how to explore their world visually and/or retrain their attentional mechanisms to compensate for their deficits in function. However, no such paradigms are currently routinely offered by public health services despite the fact that they can have life-changing effects meaning that patients can re-enter the workforce thus providing socio-economic benefits and have a more fulfilling life than they might have previously expected. Improvements in function following stroke may result from neural restitution in which the neurons that were damaged (as opposed to killed) recover their function and this can actually happen all by itself. The other way function can be restored is through the brain compensating for the lack of certain parts working optimally and finding some other way to produce function. Both of these issues can occur independent of any neurorehabilitation training; in fact the brain is very good at finding a way of carrying on and is called neuroplasticity. However, training can improve visual performance over and above that seen in natural recovery.

More research is required to understand why some neurorehabilitation paradigms such as re-training work, and why some don't
and for patients with some types of damage over patients with
others. This would lead to more cost-effective treatments for the
damage caused to the visual system by stroke.

Of course, if we could interact with the damaged brain tissue
directly, we may be able to change function directly. For example,
one theory of why people with neglect act the way the do is that
over time, the undamaged left hemisphere over-inhibits the right
hemisphere which is recovering after damage. The right hemisphere is responsible for orientating our attention to both the left
and right visual fields so damage here leaves you with only the
left hemisphere which can orient your attention only to the right
hemisphere. Initially, the left hemisphere inhibiting the output of
the right hemisphere makes sense as the output from the damaged
right will be very warbled. But as it recovers, it becomes counterproductive. If we could find a way to disrupt the inhibition of
the left hemisphere over the right, could we improve patient's visual performance? Claus Hilgetag and Alvaro Pascual-Leone from
Harvard University investigated this in 2001 and it turns out, if we
use TMS to give the neurons in the left hemisphere something else
to do other than inhibit the right, patients' performance on tasks
used to diagnose neglect improves. However, the TMS machine is
quite bulky and you certainly can't walk around with one stuck to
your head and also the effects of TMS don't last very long, so such
experiments prove the principle but don't help us with respect to
treatment. Another technique that may be more amenable to our
aims is transcranial direct current stimulation (tDCS), which sends
a low-intensity current between two electrodes placed on the scalp.
It has the capacity to decrease the likelihood of action potentials
below the cathodal electrode and increase it below the anode and
so we can play with the relative excitability of the brain. If, for
example, we do as Gereon Fink, Roland Sparing and colleagues
from Cologne did in 2009 and we decrease the activity of the left
parietal cortex (which is having an inhibitory effect on the right,
so we decrease inhibition) and increase the activity of the right
parietal lobe, we should be able to ameliorate the symptoms of
neglect and lead to an improvement in the detection of targets
present in the left visual field which was previously neglected.

Although the effects of tDCS last longer than TMS, the effect on function in visual tasks does not last longer than 20 minutes. But current research being carried out by Alison Lane, Daniel Smith and I at Durham University is using the changes in excitability induced by tDCS to make the damaged brain more receptive to learning. If we apply tDCS whilst our patients are carrying out neurorehabilitative paradigms such as exploratory or attentional training, we should be able to make the changes in function come about quicker and stick for longer. Visual deficits following stroke are not the only problems tDCS can be used in the treatment of; it has also been used to help speech disorders such as aphasia, muscle weakness and pain as well as attempting to improve memory retrieval in Alzheimer's.

We've just talked about what we can do with some brain disorders but there are many more that we rarely hear about. This may be because they are uncommon and because not many people suffer from them; the money for research just isn't there either from the public or the drug companies. This is why neuroscience can be so exciting as a good understanding of the brain and how it works may lead to more widespread solutions by getting at the underlying mechanisms of the brain. Sure, TCD doesn't cause obsessive compulsive disorder, migraine, dystonia, Parkinson's, tinnitus amongst others but treating it can bring about real qualitative differences to patient's lives. Treatment involving tDCS may affect lots of different functions using the same underlying mechanism. Unfortunately, examples such as this are pretty isolated. Neuroscience, a discipline which encompasses physiologists, psychologists, neurologists, pharmacologists, even physicists, still needs to work hard in partnership with clinicians to lessen the gulf between what we know about the normal and the broken brain and how we can fix it when it goes wrong.

## Feeling curious?

Rodolfo R. Llinás, Urs Ribary, Daniel Jeanmonod, Eugene Kronberg and Partha P. Mitra. (1999) "Thalamocortical Dysrhythmia: A Neurological and Neuropsychiatric Syndrome Characterized by Magnetoencephalography". *Proceedings of the National Academy of Sciences*, 96, 15222–15227 doi: 10.1073/pnas.96.26.15222. *The original ground-breaking paper outlining the evidence and importance of TCD.*

*My Stroke of Insight* by Jill Bolte Taylor. 2009; Hodder. *A book which explains the effect of stroke in the brain and patient recovery from a very personal standpoint.*

*Intervening in the Brain: Changing Psyche and Society* by F. Wuetscher, Reinhard Merkel, G. Boer, J. Fegert, T. Galert, D. Hartmann, B. Nuttin, S. Rosahl 2010; Springer. *This book has a good section covering neurotransplantation and gene transfer.*

Olle Lindvall & Zaal Kokaia (2010) "Stem Cells in Human Neurodegenerative Disorders – Time for Clinical Translation?" *Journal of Clinical Investigation* 120, 29–40. *This review article evaluates the use of stem cells in a variety of neurological disorders.*

*Stem Cells For Dummies* by Lawrence S.B. Goldstein & Meg Schneider 2010; John Wiley & Sons. *A recent book that covers the controversies associated with stem cell use in medicine as well as explaining what stem cells are and what they can do.*

*The Biology of Psychological Disorders* by David Linden. 2012; Palgrave Macmillan. *A thorough book that lays the foundations for understanding and treating a variety of psychological disorders.*

# Index

**DATE DUE**

GAYLORD     #3522PI     Printed in USA